Multidisciplinary Functions of Blockchain Technology in AI and IoT Applications

Niaz Chowdhury
The Open University, Milton Keynes, UK

Ganesh Chandra Deka
Ministry of Skill Development and Entrepreneurship, New Delhi, India

A volume in the Advances in Data Mining and Database Management (ADMDM) Book Series

Published in the United States of America by
IGI Global
Engineering Science Reference (an imprint of IGI Global)
701 E. Chocolate Avenue
Hershey PA, USA 17033
Tel: 717-533-8845
Fax: 717-533-8661
E-mail: cust@igi-global.com
Web site: http://www.igi-global.com

Library of Congress Cataloging-in-Publication Data

Names: Chowdhury, Niaz, 1984- editor. | Deka, Ganesh Chandra, 1969- editor.

Title: Multidisciplinary functions of blockchain technology in AI and IoT
    applications / Niaz Chowdhury and Ganesh Chandra Deka, editors.
Description: Hershey, PA : Engineering Science Reference, an imprint of IGI
    Global, [2021] | Includes bibliographical references and index. |
    Summary: "This edited book deliberates upon prospects of blockchain
    technology for facilitating the analysis and acquisition of big data
    using AI and IoT devices in various application domains"-- Provided by
    publisher.
Identifiers: LCCN 2020026777 (print) | LCCN 2020026778 (ebook) | ISBN
    9781799858768 (hardcover) | ISBN 9781799858775 (ebook)
Subjects: LCSH: Blockchains (Databases)
Classification: LCC QA76.9.B56 H36 2021 (print) | LCC QA76.9.B56 (ebook)
    | DDC --dc23
LC record available at https://lccn.loc.gov/2020026777
LC ebook record available at https://lccn.loc.gov/2020026778

This book is published in the IGI Global book series Advances in Data Mining and Database Management (ADMDM) (ISSN: 2327-1981; eISSN: 2327-199X)

British Cataloguing in Publication Data
A Cataloguing in Publication record for this book is available from the British Library.

All work contributed to this book is new, previously-unpublished material.
The views expressed in this book are those of the authors, but not necessarily of the publisher.

For electronic access to this publication, please contact: eresources@igi-global.com.

Advances in Data Mining and Database Management (ADMDM) Book Series

ISSN:2327-1981
EISSN:2327-199X

Editor-in-Chief: David Taniar Monash University, Australia

MISSION

With the large amounts of information available to organizations in today's digital world, there is a need for continual research surrounding emerging methods and tools for collecting, analyzing, and storing data.

The **Advances in Data Mining & Database Management (ADMDM)** series aims to bring together research in information retrieval, data analysis, data warehousing, and related areas in order to become an ideal resource for those working and studying in these fields. IT professionals, software engineers, academicians and upper-level students will find titles within the ADMDM book series particularly useful for staying up-to-date on emerging research, theories, and applications in the fields of data mining and database management.

COVERAGE

- Database Testing
- Association Rule Learning
- Data Quality
- Cluster Analysis
- Web-based information systems
- Data Warehousing
- Sequence analysis
- Data Analysis
- Heterogeneous and Distributed Databases
- Factor Analysis

IGI Global is currently accepting manuscripts for publication within this series. To submit a proposal for a volume in this series, please contact our Acquisition Editors at Acquisitions@igi-global.com or visit: http://www.igi-global.com/publish/.

Titles in this Series

For a list of additional titles in this series, please visit:
http://www.igi-global.com/book-series/advances-data-mining-database-management/37146

Opportunities and Challenges for Blockchain Technology in Autonomous Vehicles
Amit Kumar Tyagi (Vellore Institute of Technolgy, Chennai, India) Gillala Rekha (K. L. University, India) and N. Sreenath (Pondicherry Engineering College, India)
Engineering Science Reference • © 2021 • 316pp • H/C (ISBN: 9781799832959) • US $245.00

Cross-Industry Use of Blockchain Technology and Opportunities for the Future
Idongesit Williams (Aalborg University, Denmark)
Engineering Science Reference • © 2020 • 228pp • H/C (ISBN: 9781799836322) • US $225.00

Applications and Developments in Semantic Process Mining
Kingsley Okoye (University of East London, UK)
Engineering Science Reference • © 2020 • 248pp • H/C (ISBN: 9781799826682) • US $195.00

Challenges and Applications of Data Analytics in Social Perspectives
V. Sathiyamoorthi (Sona College of Technology, India) and Atilla Elci (Aksaray University, Turkey)
Engineering Science Reference • © 2020 • 330pp • H/C (ISBN: 9781799825661) • US $245.00

Handling Priority Inversion in Time-Constrained Distributed Databases
Udai Shanker (Madan Mohan Malaviya University of Technology, India) and Sarvesh Pandey (Madan Mohan Malaviya University of Technology, India)
Engineering Science Reference • © 2020 • 338pp • H/C (ISBN: 9781799824916) • US $225.00

For an entire list of titles in this series, please visit:
http://www.igi-global.com/book-series/advances-data-mining-database-management/37146

701 East Chocolate Avenue, Hershey, PA 17033, USA
Tel: 717-533-8845 x100 • Fax: 717-533-8661
E-Mail: cust@igi-global.com • www.igi-global.com

Editorial Advisory Board

Table of Contents

Detailed Table of Contents

Chapter 1
Integrating Blockchain With AI 1
>   *Radha Madhu Seekar Vedula, Atal Bihari Vajpayee Indian Institute of*
>   *Information Technology and Management, Gwalior, India*
>   *Robin Singh Bhadoria, Machine Intelligence Research (MIR) Labs,*
>   *India*
>   *Manish Dixit, Madhav Institute of Technology and Science, India*

The advancement in AI and blockchain can fundamentally reshape our way of working, learning, and almost our way of living. Though the research in both areas helps us in advancing our knowledge, it is even more advantageous by converging concepts of blockchain and AI (i.e., developing the thinking through blockchain). Blockchain is decentralized, distributed, and often a public system. Thinking, fundamentally defined as rationally concluding something, with a few known premises, is the fundamental concept behind AI and implementing the AI to become as close to human intelligence as possible; therefore, improvements in thinking are always welcomed. Both being incomplete, AI suffers from issues with trustworthiness, explainability, and privacy, while blockchain suffers in case of security, scalability, and efficiency. Bringing these two together can complement each other and make the system efficient. The chapter deals with various uses of integrating blockchain with AI. It also gives a brief on the uses of blockchain for improving both human and machine thinking.

Chapter 2

The internet of things (IoT) refers to a network comprised of physical objects capable of gathering and sharing electronic information. Internet of things will be connected with physical objects that are accessible through the internet. In general, IoT is a collection of all things in the world and that should be connected over internet. But in any technology, there exist some risk factor which will diminish the performance of an organization. In IoT, security of information is always a challenging task. Security is an essential pillar of the internet, 'the' most significant challenge for the IoT. When the number of connected devices increases, the opportunity of risk factor in positive and negative side will work to implement the IoT. Risk analysis is the review of the risks associated with a particular event or action. In this chapter, challenges of security and analysis of risk have discussed to reduce the problems.

The agricultural supply chain consists of many participants like producer (generally farmer), consumer (people who buy the product and consume them), wholesalers, and retailers. This system consists of many levels of mediator parties as well which have different policies of the commission. Due to the difference in these policies, the producers do not get their fair share of price. Due to the varying prices, consumers also suffer as they do not get the right quality of the product for the right price. There are no central records maintained regarding the transactions between the participants which could lead to many serious problems. To tackle the above-mentioned issues, we need a holistic approach that can provide solutions to most of the above issues. Here, blockchain-based solution can be used to achieve traceability (we can trace the whereabouts of the product, the origin of the product, etc.), transparency (so that a sense of trust is achieved), fairness (by removing the intermediaries), assurance of food safety and pricing (so that nobody has to bear the loss).

Chapter 4

Nishu Sethi, Amity School of Engineering and Technology, Amity University, Gurugram, India

Shalini Bhaskar Bajaj, Amity School of Engineering and Technology, Amity University, Gurugram, India

Jitendra Kumar Verma, Amity School of Engineering and Technology, Amity University, Gurugram, India

Utpal Shrivastava, Amity School of Engineering and Technology, Amity University, Gurugram, India

Human beings tend to make predictions about future events irrespective of probability of occurrence. We are fascinated to solve puzzles and patterns. One such area which intrigues many, full of complexity and unpredicted behavior, is the stock market. For the last decade or so, we have been trying to find patterns and understand the behavior of the stock market with the help of robust computation systems and new approaches to extract and analyze the huge amount of data. In this chapter, the authors have tried to understand stock price movement using a long short-term memory (LSTM) network and predict future behavior of stock price.

Chapter 5

Muralidhar Kurni, Jawaharlal Nehru Technological University, Anantapuramu, India

Somasena Reddy K., Jawaharlal Nehru Technological University, Anantapuramu, India

Connected devices have access to every part of our lives with the increasing implementation of the internet of things (IoT), from home automation, health and fitness, automobile, logistics, to smart cities, and industrial IoT. Therefore, it is only natural that IoT, connected devices, and automation find their application in agriculture, and as such, greatly enhance almost every facet of it. In recent decades, farming has undergone a variety of technological changes, becoming more industrialized and powered by technology. Farmers have gained effective control and efficiency over the process of raising livestock and growing crops through the use of various smart farming devices. Within this chapter, the authors discuss and analyze the advantages of using IoT within agriculture. They present the IoT system architecture to allow smart farming. This chapter also covers the advantages of integrating the blockchain into the agricultural field. Case studies are included in the end for your reference.

Chapter 6

This chapter presents artificial and natural intelligence technologies. As part of the digital economy of the virtual world program, it is envisaged to increase the efficiency of electronic commerce and entrepreneurship; a similar task has been set by the leadership of the People's Republic of China. At present, thinking in the virtual world and China is radically transforming, along with methodological approaches to the development of trade policy and its tools in the digital economy. It is these circumstances that determine the relevance of the study, the results of which are presented in this chapter. Development of the fundamental foundations for improving the efficiency of electronic commerce and entrepreneurship in virtual world and China based on the virtual exchange of intellectual knowledge using blockchain technology and implementation multi-chain open source platform is the goal. An acceleration of scientific and technological progress in all areas of knowledge raises the task for ensuring the continuous growth of professional skills throughout the whole life.

Chapter 7

The last few months have produced a remarkable expansion in research and deep study in the field of machine learning. Machine learning is a technique in which the set of the methods are used by the computers to make prediction, improve prediction and behavior prediction based on dataset. The learning techniques can be classified as supervised and unsupervised learning. The focus is on supervised machine learning that covers all the predictions problem for which we had the dataset in which the outcome is already known. Some of the algorithm like naive bayes, linear regression, SVM, k-nearest neighbor, especially neural network have gain growth in this area. The classifiers of machine learning are completely unconstrained with the assumptions of statistical and for that they are adapted by complex data. The authors have demonstrated the application of machine learning techniques and its ethical issues.

Chapter 8

Ankit Khushal Barai, Department of CSE, Indian Institute of
Information Technology, Nagpur, India
Robin Singh Bhadoria, Department of Computer Science and
Engineering, Hindustan College of Science and Technology, India
Jyotshana Bagwari, Department of CSE, Uttarakhand Technical
University, India
Ivan Perl, ITMO University, Russia

Conventional machine learning (ML) needs centralized training data to be present on a given machine or datacenter. The healthcare, finance, and other institutions where data sharing is prohibited require an approach for training ML models in secured architecture. Recently, techniques such as federated learning (FL), MIT Media Lab's Split Neural networks, blockchain, aim to address privacy and regulation of data. However, there are difference between the design principles of FL and the requirements of Institutions like healthcare, finance, etc., which needs blockchain-orchestrated FL having the following features: clients with their local data can define access policies to their data and define how updated weights are to be encrypted between the workers and the aggregator using blockchain technology and also prepares audit trail logs undertaken within network and it keeps actual list of participants hidden. This is expected to remove barriers in a range of sectors including healthcare, finance, security, logistics, governance, operations, and manufacturing.

Chapter 9

Pushpa Singh, Delhi Technical Campus, Greater Noida, India
Narendra Singh, G. L. Bajaj Institute of Management and Research,
India
Ganesh Chandra Deka, Ministry of Skill Development and
Entrepreneurship, Guwahati, India

Presently, machine learning (ML) techniques have gained considerable attention, with growing interest in various areas and applications. Healthcare, agriculture, and bioinformatics are the most identified areas to study with the help of ML. This chapter introduces about the basic principle of ML such as data, model, basic mathematical details of ML, and types of learning. The important aspect of ML is "how to teach a machine." This chapter focuses on the types of learning: supervised, unsupervised, semi-supervised, and reinforcement learning. Some commonly used ML algorithms such as decision tree (DT), k-nearest neighbor (KNN), support vector machine

(SVM), naïve Bayes, k-mean, q-learning, etc. are briefly discussed for understanding. Finally, the author offers the application of ML with blockchain that is reforming the traditional healthcare and agricultural sector to a more reliable means.

Chapter 10
Using AI Technology to Support Speaking Skill Development for the
Teaching of Chinese as a Foreign Language 209
Goh Ying Yingsoon, Universiti Teknologi MARA, Malaysia

The teaching of Chinese as a foreign language can be supported by using AI technology. Traditionally, the non-native learners can only interact with the instructors and depend on them solely for speaking practices. However, with the advancement of AI technology, the learners can use AI technology for interactive speaking skill development. In this study, the learners were instructed to download an application at https://m.wandoujia.com/apps/6790950. The process on the preparation of this AI technology in supporting their speaking skill development can be accessed at https://sites.google.com/site/gohyi141/assignments/projectinteractivespeakingapp. By using this AI technology, the findings showed a tremendous affirmative responses pertaining to the use of this AI technology. Hence, AI technology should be encouraged in active utilization for the teaching of Chinese as a foreign language in particular and for all language speaking skill development in general.

Foreword

The joint market survey report by "Huawei" with "Oxford Economics" predicts that the Digital Economy is likely to comprise 24.3% of the world's GDP (Gross Domestic Product) by 2025 which will be around $23 trillion (Xu & Cooper, 2017). Similarly, the IDC White Paper "The Digitization of the World From Edge to Core" by David Reinsel, John Gantz and John Rydning published in November 2018 states that, "The global datasphere will grow to 175 ZB by 2025". "Each connected person will have at least one data interaction every 18 seconds and nearly 30% of the world's data will need real-time processing" (Reinsel, Gantz, & Rydning, 2018).

Machine Learning (ML) is one of the fastest developing research areas in computer science to form precise decisions from massive datasets. Machine learning techniques have the great ability to data analysis. Novel and advanced data models are utilizing the secured decentralized property of Blockchain technology. The use of machine learning with Blockchain technology can provide a robust distributed ML network to deal with lots of complex problems.

Explainable Artificial Intelligence (XAI) is a new trend of AI algorithms that provide explanations of AI decisions. Blockchain provides the key feature for an XAI system such as Transparency and visibility, Immutability, Traceability and Non-repudiation (Nassar, Salah, Ur Rehman, 2019). The convergence of AI, ML and Blockchain technology are likely to build robust, sustainable IT ecosystems.

This book titled *Multidisciplinary Functions of Blockchain Technology in AI and IoT Applications* in 10 chapters contributed by renowned researchers have very lucidly deliberated upon integrating blockchain with ai, internet of thing and ML in supply-chain management and federated learning (e-learning).

The topics coved are awesome. This is book is really a worth reading.

Malaya Dutta Borah
Department of Computer Science and Engineering, National Institute of Technology, Silchar, India

REFERENCES

Nassar, M., Salah, K., Ur Rehman, M. H., & Svetinovic, D. (2019). Blockchain for explainable and trustworthy artificial intelligence. *WIREs Data Mining and Knowledge Discovery*, *10*(1). Advance online publication. doi:10.1002/widm.1340

Reinsel, D., Gantz, J., & Rydning, J. (2018, November). *The Digitization of the World-From Edge to Core*. Seagate - Maximize data's potential | Seagate US. https://www.seagate.com/files/www-content/our-story/trends/files/idc-seagate-dataage-whitepaper.pdf

Xu, W., & Cooper, A. (2017). *Digital Spillover-Measuring the true impact of the digital economy*. Huawei - Building a Fully Connected, Intelligent World. https://www.huawei.com/minisite/gci/en/digital-spillover/files/gci_digital_spillover.pdf

Preface

Over the past two decades, almost all kinds of physical, mechanical, electrical, and electronic devices in our personal and professional environments has joined the mainstream computing. As such, Artificial Intelligence (AI), the Internet of Things (IoT) and Blockchain Technology have emerged as the most prominent enablers of this digital revolution.

IoT promises many applications that fit into our day-to-day activities, making life more comfortable, safe and smart. These devices generate a massive amount of real-time data enabling researchers and developers to dig down deep inside using AI techniques to offer benefits and solve problems that would not be obvious to detect otherwise.

Blockchain technology is defined as one of the best inventions after the Internet as presented in various literature. This technology allows value exchange without the need for a central authority and ensures trust powered by its decentralized architecture. As such, the growing use of the Internet of Things (IoT) and the rise of Artificial Intelligence are to be benefited immensely by this technology that can offer devices and applications with data security, decentralization, accountability, and reliable authentication.

The proposed edited book in 10 chapters will deliberate upon prospects of Blockchain Technology using AI and IoT devices in various application domains. The primary audiences of the book are Faculty members, IT industry professionals, final year undergraduate students & postgraduate students of computer science & software engineering undertaking courses/research in IoT.

The secondary audiences are:

- Research Scholars researching in Artificial Intelligence, Internet of Things (IoT), Blockchain Technology and AI Application
- Professionals working in the field of AI and IoT-based infrastructures and Blockchain Technology

The Blockchain is decentralized, distributed, and often a public system. AI suffers from issues with trustworthiness; explainability, and privacy, while Blockchain suffers in case of security, scalability, and efficiency. Bringing these two together can complement each other's weaknesses and make the system efficient. Chapter 1 titled "Integrating Blockchain With AI" deals with various uses of integrating Blockchain with AI. It also gives a brief on the uses of Blockchain for improving both human and machine thinking.

In IoT, the security of information is always a challenging task. Security is an essential pillar of the Internet 'the' most significant challenge for the IoT. As the number of connected devices increases, the risk factor in to implement the IoT increases accordingly. Chapter 2 titled "Study of Risk Analysis in the Internet of Things" is an analytical study of challenges of security associated with IoT.

The Agricultural supply chain consists of many participants like Producer (Farmer), Consumer (people who buy the product and consumption), Wholesalers and Retailers. This system consists of many levels of mediators which have different policies of the commission. Since there are no central records maintained regarding the transactions between the participants, this leads to too many serious problems. To deal with the issues mentioned above, a holistic approach is a must. Here, Blockchain-based solution can be used to achieve Traceability (to trace the whereabouts and origin of the product), Transparency (to achieve a sense of trust), Fairness (removing the intermediaries) and Assurance of food safety and pricing. Chapter 3 titled "Supply Chain Management for Agri Foods Using Blockchain Technology" deal about the Agricultural supply chain management.

We are fascinated to solve puzzles and patterns. One such area which intrigues complexity and full of unpredictability is the stock market. Chapter 4 titled "Google Stock Movement: A Time Series Study Using LSTM Network" deals with stock price movement using a Long Short-Term Memory (LSTM) network to forecast the stock market price.

Connected devices (Internet of Things (IoT)) have access to every part of our lives with the increasing implementation for Home Automation, Healthcare, Fitness, Automobile, Logistics, Smart Cities and Industrial automation. In recent decades farming has undergone a variety of technological changes. Farmers have sufficient control over the process of raising livestock and growing crops using various Smart Farming Devices. Chapter 5 titled "Internet of Things (IoT) in Agriculture" discusses the advantages of integrating the Blockchain into agriculture. Case studies are included in the end for the benefit of readers'.

Chapter 6 titled "The Internet of Things and Blockchain Technologies Adaptive Trade Systems in Virtual World: By Creating Virtual Accomplices' Worldwide" presents the idea of using the Artificial and Natural Intelligence Technologies to increase the efficiency of electronic commerce and entrepreneurship.

Machine Learning is a technique in which the set of methods are used by the computers to make a prediction, improve prediction and behaviour prediction based on the dataset. Chapter 7 titled "An Analytical Study on Machine Learning Techniques" deliberates upon the application of machine learning techniques and its ethical issues.

Chapter 8 titled "A Blockchain-Based Federated Learning: Concepts and Applications" discusses the techniques Federated Learning (FL) and MIT Media lab's Split Neural networks, and how the Blockchain can address privacy and regulation of data in a range of sectors including Healthcare, Finance, Security, Logistics, Governance and Manufacturing.

Chapter 9 titled "Prospects of Machine Learning With Blockchain in Healthcare and Agriculture" is an analytical study on types of learning, i.e. Supervised, Unsupervised, Semi-supervised and Reinforcement Learning. Some commonly used ML algorithms such as Decision tree (DT), K Nearest Neighbor (KNN), Support Vector Machine (SVM), Naïve Bayes, K-Mean, Q-Learning are briefly discussed for understanding. Finally, the application of ML with Blockchain in Healthcare and Agricultural sector is introduced.

Chapter 10, the concluding chapter, titled "Using AI Technology to Support Speaking Skill Development for the Teaching of Chinese as a Foreign Language" deals with how the teaching of Chinese as a foreign language can be supported by using AI technology. Traditionally the non-native learners can only interact with the instructors and depend on them solely for speaking practices. However, with the advancement of AI technology, learners can use AI technology for interactive speaking skill development. In this chapter, the learners were instructed to download an application at https://m.wandoujia.com/apps/6790950. The process of the preparation of this AI technology in supporting their speaking skill development can be accessed at https://sites.google.com/site/gohyi141/assignments/projectinteractivespeakingapp. By using this AI technology, the findings showed a tremendous affirmative response about the use of this AI technology. Hence, AI technology should be encouraged inactive utilization for the teaching of Chinese as a foreign language in particular and all language speaking skill development in general.

Hence this edited book is an excellent collection of chapters on ML, IoT and AI in areas of Security issues of IoT, Farming, Supply Chain Management (Agriculture), Predictive Analytics (Stock Market) and Natural Languages Processing (learning Chinese language). We hope the book will be useful for the intended readers.

Ganesh Chandra Deka
Ministry of Skill Development and Entrepreneurship, New Delhi, India

Niaz Chowdhury
The Open University, Milton Keynes, UK

Acknowledgment

Sincere thanks to all the Chapter Contributors and Reviewers for the excellent contribution.

Chapter 1
Integrating Blockchain With AI

Radha Madhu Seekar Vedula
Atal Bihari Vajpayee Indian Institute of Information Technology and Management, Gwalior, India

Robin Singh Bhadoria
 https://orcid.org/0000-0002-6314-4736
Machine Intelligence Research (MIR) Labs, India

Manish Dixit
Madhav Institute of Technology and Science, India

ABSTRACT

The advancement in AI and blockchain can fundamentally reshape our way of working, learning, and almost our way of living. Though the research in both areas helps us in advancing our knowledge, it is even more advantageous by converging concepts of blockchain and AI (i.e., developing the thinking through blockchain). Blockchain is decentralized, distributed, and often a public system. Thinking, fundamentally defined as rationally concluding something, with a few known premises, is the fundamental concept behind AI and implementing the AI to become as close to human intelligence as possible; therefore, improvements in thinking are always welcomed. Both being incomplete, AI suffers from issues with trustworthiness, explainability, and privacy, while blockchain suffers in case of security, scalability, and efficiency. Bringing these two together can complement each other and make the system efficient. The chapter deals with various uses of integrating blockchain with AI. It also gives a brief on the uses of blockchain for improving both human and machine thinking.

DOI: 10.4018/978-1-7998-5876-8.ch001

1. INTRODUCTION

Inventions of Blockchain and Artificial Intelligence brought many revelations in technology. While automation of payments in cryptocurrency was made possible by Blockchain (Morris, 2016), decision making and intelligence are given to machines using AI. Blockchain also made it possible for governing interactions by introducing smart contracts (Morris, 2014), with no longer a requirement of a trusted third party. Both these technologies are advancing at a wonderful pace along with helping innovations in other fields and bringing out more possibilities in every industry. We cannot deny that both technologies have a different amount of technological complexities. Also, the idea about blockchain being decentralized and under no one's control might be a bit of exaggeration as it still has to be *developed* by many *developers* and thus makes it prone to errors.

Analysis of data through various methods like Deep Learning and Machine learning led to the development of present-day AI. To this day, most of the methods and algorithms of deep learning and machine learning for AI follow a centralized model. In such centralized models, the machine is trained by a group of servers that validate and organize the data by training through different datasets. These datasets and chunks of data are managed by various organizations to make decisions. These third-party organizations might be the cause of a variety of problems. The centralized nature of AI leads the data to be tampered with or the parties getting hacked. Either of these can lead the decisions of AI to be highly erroneous.

This led to the research of a Decentralized AI. This is where the inclusion of Blockchain to AI started (Team N.A., 2018). A Blockchain though not perfectly, is a Decentralized system. A decentralized AI processes and performs decision making over data on the blockchain, which was previously transacted and stored on it, by digitally signing it and using secure sharing, and removing the requirement to use a Trusted Third Party or other intermediaries (Dinh & Thai, 2018). So, here what exactly is happening is that the AI, which can handle a lot of data and process, is using the data stored on a blockchain. The blockchain is eligible for this procedure due to the security of data on it. Use of smart contracts can further advance the usage as it can make the blockchain to be programmed in such a way that it can govern the data for decision making and also on generating and accessing the data among the participants (Wood, 2014). There a various researches going on how to improve blockchain and AI, but in an isolated manner. Recent studies show that the integration of blockchain and AI can lead to many revolutions and can also help to improve both the areas.

Another important and interesting application of integrating these two is blockchain thinking (Swan, 2015). This specifically deals with formulating thinking itself as a blockchain process. The researchers claim that this not only helps with AI but also helps in enhancing human thinking along with integrating both. Blockchain thinking is mostly used as a computational system with an I/O unit and a processing system. Blockchain thinking can give rise to self-mining ecologies and intelligence proof models. While the blockchain in normal applications is used for redistributing the cryptocurrency, blockchain thinking, can help in redistributing the brain currencies, such as ideas and potential. Blockchain thinking can help in both near and far futures to further the progress of human and machine intelligence and co-existence of both in a digital world.

2. BACKGROUND

An introduction to Blockchain and AI followed by a theoretical introduction for thinking are given in this section for a better understanding of the integration of Blockchain and AI.

2.1. Blockchain

A blockchain in practice is an open-source, immutable, distributed public-ledger among the network peers (Nakamoto, 2019). In theory, a fundamental blockchain is made from a chain of blocks, which in turn form the ledger as a whole. In simpler terms, a blockchain is an unalterable, distributed, digital ledger, for the networked users. It is a permanent record of data and transactions done between the users of the network(Salah, Alfalasi, & Alfalasi, 2019). It started with a cryptocurrency called Bitcoin, which potentially used in many industries now. To understand the working of a blockchain, let us see how the most important applications of it in cryptocurrency like Bitcoin and Ether work.

In both these currencies, the blockchain stores each and every detail of the transactions between the networked users in a chunk called as blocks. Both of them are considered to be proof-of-work (POW) blockchains. In POW, users, or technically called as miners, solve a computationally hard problem to create a new block. The reason why they are called Miners is because they mine the data. The one who was able to successfully mine will create the block and earn the transaction fee. The effort one keeps for creation of block is dependent on the reward, the cryptocurrency one would get. Due to this, the new blockchains are using a protocol called proof-of-stake (POS). In this, there is no consumption of energy like in POW. The creation of block by a certain user is dependent on the coins, the currency they have at their disposal for the stake.

In Bitcoin, every block has a maximum size of one Megabyte. Also, one major drawback is that the validation of digital currencies takes place in the Bitcoin system.

This issue was addressed by the introduction of the concept of Smart Contracts. A smart contract can handle the verification of a transaction about the enforcement of predefined T&C. In general, it is an automated program. These can normally be executed by the nodes that participate in blockchain mining. With this, instead of validating the cryptocurrency each and every time, the miners themselves will execute, verify, and finally store the data(Salah, Rehman, Nizamuddin, & Al-Fuqaha, 2019).

So, with a little bit of machine learning integration to the above systems, they can become autonomous and will be able to learn and adapt to changes in the future and make accurate and trustable decisions. Then those decisions can be verified by all of the miners present in the network. With the help of blockchain, and the inclusion of these smart contracts, the above decisions cannot be disproved and can be traced back. Later, all of the participants (or) users of the network can validate them.

The Ethereum system is an open-source platform that provides the facility of programming a required smart contract. Ether is the cryptocurrency used for transactions in the Ethereum. An EA (Ethereum Address) is given to each participant of the network and for every transaction; the smart contract consigns it to the respective EA and executes the transaction.

As mentioned before a Bitcoin has only 1MB per each of the blocks, which is not feasible to save huge data. Any theoretical and conventional blockchain suffers from the same. This limitation was addressed by storing the hashes of the data under smart contracts in blockchain nodes or storing in blockchain blocks and storing the actual data in a decentralized storage system. One such implemented and successful system is the Interplanetary File system (IPFS) (Banet, 2014). An IPFS is a connected file system across several nodes of computers connected with the same file system. It is a decentralized and distributed file system. IPFS is also considered to be content addressable. That means the contents of the system can be accessed using the respective address in the form of hash. Also having a list of nodes as the parts of the file system, this also became an indisputable file system not allowing data to be tampered. Even if one node gets disconnected, the files will still be open for access due to the decentralized nature.

2.2. Artificial Intelligence

Intelligence is defined as the capacity for logical thinking, understanding, learning, and the ability to acquire and apply knowledge and skills. Generally, it can be defined as the ability to perceive and/or infer information and store this as knowledge and when needed apply this in the future. The intelligence itself can be divided into group and individual intelligence. AI thus can be defined as the artificially induced or artificially made intelligence. AI is defined by the fathers of the field as any task or action of a machine or a program requiring intelligence(Dinh, & Thai, 2018).

Intelligence is a property of the brain, and biologically speaking the intelligence in the brain is due to the neurons, connected in neural networks. Artificially made neural networks hence help in making AI along with other elements such as support vector machines and fuzzy logic.

The research of the AI system is defined as the study of intelligent systems/ agents, which are the devices that can perceive the parameters it has and try to achieve a goal with the maximum success possible with the intelligence or more precisely the information previously given or processed. The AI though started as a revolution to make the systems to think on its own, it was constantly dragged onto the current AI systems, which use related databases to make their decisions, due to the complications and many unknown factors that impede intelligence of a biological brain. Researchers are still striving hard to make truly artificial intelligent systems that can make the proper decisions in some areas. It must be obvious by now that the AI systems are centralized. As one can see most of the process involved in the decision making procedure is dependent on the datasets. In case of unauthorized modifications or tampering with this data can bring out erroneous results in the decision making of the AI systems.

We need a system where we can store the records of data used by AI algorithms before, after, and even during the process of learning from data and making required decisions after the training. This can be implemented by using decentralized AI systems, made possible by the integration of AI and blockchain. This can give the system access to secure and shared platform of data, logs. The storage can even have knowledge and decisions made by the system (Panarello, Tapas, Merlino, Longo, & Puliafito, 2018).

3. THE INTEGRATION

Both the systems have their own level of complexity and integrating both can be a hard process, but with the technological advancements of the present day, it is not impossible. Blockchain though seemingly perfect has its own weaknesses such as scalability, efficiency, and security. Similarly, AI also suffers from weaknesses in trustworthiness, explainability, and privacy. It is fair to assume with the strengths and weaknesses of both the fields that integrating these two can make a perfect cup of coffee, as they seem to complement each other's weaknesses. AI can bring out security, scalability, and better governance and personalization to Blockchain by introducing machine learning principles. On the other hand, the blockchain can bring trustworthiness, explainability, and better privacy for AI systems.

3.1. AI Transformed by Blockchain

The application of blockchain can power AI systems with decentralized systems and coordinated platforms. Thus we can safely say that the blockchain can make the AI trustworthy, explainable, and transparent. The only issue with this is that AI here has to provide the users' security and privacy as, probably all or most of the data on the blockchain is available in public, which can be easily handled by the current AI systems.

The main vulnerability in AI comes from the less security of data through which it learns, infer, and decide. Tampering with this data can lead to erroneous results and unprecedented behavior and decision making of AI. So it is suggested that we have to take the data from a source that is secure and reliable. Here comes the importance of the integration of Blockchain in AI. The blockchain can serve as a distributed ledger on which data can be stored and used through(Salah, Rehman, Nizamuddin, & Al-Fuqaha, 2019). The data on this blockchain as in the process should be accepted, signed, and validated by all the miners. We know the immutability of blockchain. Hence it cannot be tampered with. The problem with Machine Learning algorithms is that they are disputable and less trustable. The inclusion of smart contracts can make this Trustworthy and undisputed. So including the blockchain to AI can make AI learn, infer, and make decisions of data from a secure, immutable, and decentralized Peer to peer storage system. In practice, this data can emerge from various sources such as IoT devices, buildings, robots, etc., which are considered to be miners in the blockchain. The inclusion of cloud to this particular integration can make the systems more efficient, viable, and highly practical and useful. Some changes that the AI system goes through due to the integration of blockchain can be as mentioned below.

3.1.1. Data Security

The main drawback of AI as previously mentioned is the security of the data used for training, learning, and inferring purposes to make decisions. Blockchain can be used as a highly secured diskless data storage. The data needed to be written in every block of blockchain must be signed. Also due to the data being digitally signed, the only thing that has to be kept secure will be the respective private keys (Marr, 2018). And we know the data cannot be manipulated or tampered with once it is stored in a blockchain. This leads the AI to train, learn and infer data from highly secured and immutable data storage.

3.1.2. Trustworthiness

The decisions and data given by an AI algorithm fail to get the trust of users. The main reason for the loss of trust by users over an AI program is since the data given by the user might have been tampered with. Blockchain is immutable in nature. The immutability gives the user the confidence that the data given is not tampered. Also for most AI algorithms, the learning process never stops, and thus even the decisions after training must be stored and the algorithm needs to learn through this decision again for future purposes. Once the decision is shown to the user, the AI will be storing the data in blockchain with the acceptance of the user and this can solve make the user gain more trust in future transactions and decisions too. Also, by recording the process of decision making of the AI in a blockchain can help in improving the trust of the users as the whole process is publicly accessible (Campbell, 2018). Also, this renders the usage of a third party to audit the decisions unnecessary, as the decentralization can make any miner or the user who is in the network, an auditor for their own purposes and reasons.

3.1.3. Decision Making

Decision making in AI now is necessarily coordinated in an environment or an ecosystem of multiple devices. Any decision made is better if it's a collective decision; to achieve a goal in a shared system, each of the machines should co-ordinately come to a specific decision (Ferrer, 2016; Brambilla, Ferrante, Birattari & Dorigo, 2013; Strobel, Castelló Ferrer & Dorigo, 2018). This is called Collaborative/Collective decision making. The decentralization of the blockchain can help AI in this collective decision making and also, this removes the need for a central authority. In practice, each machine in the ecosystem will be an identified user for the network. For the collective decisions, each robot votes for a certain decision in the blockchain, and the decision is made by the majority rule. The vote here is taken as a transaction as blockchain works in transactions for processes and the process will repeat till all the machines agree on a certain decision. The decentralization can give democratic structure for an ecosystem while having a central authority runs around the decisions made by the central system alone.

3.1.4. Decentralization

The problem with centralization in AI is that when the central system or central authority is tampered, the whole system may misbehave. As mentioned before the inclusion of blockchain can give decentralization to the system. The decentralization is not just restricted to the data storage and security. Blockchain can also induce the

AI, the concept of decentralized intelligence. The decentralization of the decision making procedure can improve the system performance altogether. For example in a case where the system needs to take a high-level decision, the algorithm can be split into parts to various machines connected in the system through the same data for training. Different machines can take different steps of the process and execute the decision-making process to come to a decision that is taken by the collaboration of all the systems. This can lead to less workload on all the systems by decentralizing the whole procedure and make the decision more precise as during the procedure if a few decisions seem to be out of the loop, they can rerun the procedure. Consider for individual security of all the systems in a network, the security can be fully coordinated among the agents of the systems underlying in the network for a higher levels of security (Brambilla, Ferrante, Birattari & Dorigo, 2013; Janson, Merkle & Middendorf, 2008).

3.1.5 Efficiency

The AI schemes as such can be less efficient when the data that need to be processed and trained for the decision-making process is very high. The same is the case when the decision that has to be taken has multiple parameters. The efficiency can be exponentially increased by integrating the AI with blockchain. The smart contracts can make the AI more efficient. Considering a scheme where the data and procedures to be authorized by multiple parties such as individual users or independent IoT devices or even different organizations, the inefficiency increases due to the need of each party to accept the transaction or procedure. This can be addressed by integrating AI and blockchain to increase efficiency as the integration can lead to the development of devices called Decentralized Autonomous Agents that can evaluate the data, values or asset transfers among different users or stakeholders and also without the intervention of a centralized authority (Magazzeni, McBurney & Nash, 2017).

3.2 Blockchain Transformed by AI

The structure and operation of blockchain, to achieve its postulates, had to trade-off for security, scalability, governance, and personalization. The integration of AI to the blockchain can improve the governance and performance along with including the concepts of security, confidentiality, and privacy to the chains. The following are the few improvements that the integration of AI can do to blockchains.

3.2.1. Security

Blockchains are almost immune to hacking. The hacking of a blockchain can only happen when the adversary has the highest mining power. If we consider that the adversary does have the highest mining power, that also means that he was the one who designed most of the blockchain. The reason for this being the mining power of each user depends on the number of transactions he made and the number of blocks he was able to build in the blockchain. As we discussed in the above section, the concept of stakeholders for proof-of-stake. If one thinks this makes the blockchain secure, they are wrong. Though the structure and procedure of blockchain seem secure, the problem comes with the fundamental and building blocks of the blockchain which are not that secure.

The best example of this scenario is the exploit of Ether, a blockchain-based cryptocurrency. It was one of the largest crowdfunded cryptocurrency and was exploited for a $50Million theft (Myers, Bazinet & Cummings, 2008). The hacker was able to manipulate the smart contract such that it repeats the transactions and was able to withdraw more money from the transactions. The building blocks such as smart contracts and other applications used for building a blockchain are not that secure and thus makes it easy to exploit.

These kinds of issues can be addressed by tracing down the transactions happening and validating the transactions. Also one has to be able to stop if something like this is happening as soon as possible or remove the specific block where the irregularity is happening. The problem with this is we cannot manually trace each and every transaction occurring on a blockchain. This is where the integration of AI comes into the picture. The AI machines as of now, with the advent of machine learning, if we can develop a blockchain governed by AI the possibility of detecting and defending such irregularities in the blockchain might be possible. Even if the damage is unavoidable, one can fairly remove the current block from the blockchain, as losing a block doesn't affect the blockchain and the other part of blockchain can be free from the attack.

3.2.2 Scalability

Apart from the security, another important drawback of blockchain is that it is not scalable. The above-discussed system not only is useful for the increase in security of the system, but making few changes to it can make the blockchain scalable and robust too. A normal blockchain has a specified or constant rate of creation for blocks. By including an intelligent system to govern the blockchain, during a higher transaction rate, the governing machine might be intelligent enough to increase the rate of creation of the blocks thereby increasing the overall throughput. Though it may lead to longer confirmation rates, the creation of blocks and transactions will be done fast. Being just acknowledgments of transaction successes, longer confirmation periods don't have much effect on the blockchain as it cannot even be compared to the advantages of the blockchain being scalable.

3.2.3 Privacy and Personalization

Privacy and personalization are interlinked. To be more precise the more one concentrates on privacy, the less personalization they would be able to get. For example, social networking, e-commerce, and streaming sites and services would personalize the recommendations according to your tastes and your friends' tastes and previous search and views. The personalization is possible due to the storage of your private data at the server's end. If we want our privacy to be completely non-negotiable, that would end up with no or unrelated recommendations and such. The personal data can be controlled by using blockchains. This makes the user's personal data as much private as possible, but that comes at the cost of losing the personalized processes. Well, the ideal system would be one with the best privacy and the highest amount of personalization possible. Philosophy says that most of the theoretical ideal systems are not possible in practice.

So to address this issue, the integration of AI and blockchain seems necessary. The creation of content selection models come into the picture for this specific application. Let us consider the possibility of it and name it as a decentralized content provider. The best example of this can be a social networking website on a blockchain. The idea is to leverage the AI on the user's side to personalize the content on the website. Running an AI algorithm on the user's device to store the habits and behaviors and analyze this data and personalize it. In a normal social network, the data will be stored at the server for each user and the data is pushed to the user's device to be shown. But in the current scheme, the AI will pull the data from the server's side and then shown to the user. The only important thing to note down is that the user's system operates and thus the hardware requirements for such a website might be more than what is required for current social networking sites. Thus the personal data of the user never leaves his device. The whole procedure and AI decision making will be done at the client-side rather than on the server-side, maintaining the privacy of the user and also the personalizing for the user. Issue in the current social networks like filtering of users by the content providers leads to a lot of privacy issues. This can also be reduced by the scheme mentioned.

3.2.4 Advanced Smart Contracts

Smart contracts are the programs or piece of code which will decide who wins the transaction. In a blockchain, during a transaction, the resolving of contracts among various users of the blockchain is, as of now decided by these smart contracts. This shows the ability of machines to govern the rules for the resolutions of complex tasks such as contracts. Though it seems the machines are advanced to a place where they can govern the complex things as such, the most important aspect to remember is that these are just some predefined simple contracts and the parameters of the contract are mostly predefined.

To advance these smart contracts and take machines to a higher dimension integration of AI to the smart contracts might be taken as a necessity. The AI, developing now at a very high pace might be soon able to handle highly complex situations. One might even be able to resolve certain disputes on-chain without attending a court-room (Nummenmaa, Glerean, Hari & Hietanen, 2014). The advancement of AI and integrating it into the process of smart contracts can make it possible. With certain evidence and documents, the AI linked with smart contracts might be able to clear the dispute in an unbiased manner. The evidence and documents cannot be tampered with due to the beautiful immutable property of our blockchain. The decision made is purely data-driven and thus can be considered as justified and consistent.

3.3. Evolution of Blockchain

The evolution of blockchain is categorized into phases. Each of those phases added features while keeping the disadvantages of the previous phase in check. Having a good idea of the evolution can help in understanding the basic idea behind the process of integrating thinking to the blockchain process as a whole.

3.3.1. Blockchain 1.0

The blockchain emerged explaining a distributed ledger as a virtual currency or coin, known as a Bitcoin (Nakamoto, 2019). The new currency or called as Internet cash or cryptocurrency allowed users to do the financial transaction under a different medium. The reason for the currency being called cryptocurrency is that it follows cryptographic procedures of signing and verifying. Each coin is signed using a private key by the sender while is verified using the private key by the receiver. It proposed using the Finite State Transition Automata as a ledger, in where each state acts as ownership of users and all transactions between users to be a transaction between the states (auth).

Blockchain 1.0 succeeded in providing an electronic payment channel with lower transaction costs while assuring the security, anonymity, and transparency of transactions, with a finite supply of currency. Advantages come with disadvantages and the same was the case for the Bitcoin. With the added advantages, the approvals of transactions were slow in comparison to other channels and due to the anonymity and absence of a third party Bitcoin had to go through various fraud schemes and mining scams (Hajdarbegovic, 2014). Thought to be only a cryptocurrency the idea of integrating AI and blockchain was not taken into consideration.

3.3.2. Blockchain 2.0

The introduction of Ethereum as blockchain currency in 2013 (Buterin, 2014), addressing numerous problems in Bitcoin led to the first evolution of the blockchain as a whole and adding a new feature called smart contracts. Also, it was this time around when Bitcoin was also unable to address the shifting of blockchain towards the decentralization. The Bitcoin had limited capabilities making it unable to answer the requirements of decentralization, developing the necessity to build a general-purpose platform. This requirement can be considered as the most important factor for the evolution of blockchain and the introduction of Ethereum, built-in Turing Complete programming language (Srivastava, Bhattacharya, Singh, Mathur, 2018).

Unlike the predecessor Ethereum stayed on the faster side while maintaining the advantages using the smart contracts, which are interpretable scripts, making them faster to run. The smart contracts seemed to be so useful didn't come with advantages alone. Starting from the difficulty to write and implement the smart contracts, there were many vulnerabilities such as re-entrance, transaction ordering dependency, exception, and timestamp detection vulnerabilities (Natoli, Gramoli, 2016; Luu, Chu, Olickel, Saxena, Hobor, 2016). It was also practically hard and infeasible to modify or cancel a smart contract once the execution started and due to the decentralized structure feasibility of leveraging smart contracts by anonymous persons and transactional privacy and trust issues led to limited usage of the technology (Juels, Kosba, Shi, 2016).

The introduction of smart contracts and decentralization of the model can be considered the main reason for making the integration of blockchain with various fields possible and profitable. One such field was AI. The advantages of integrating the decentralization and smart contracts in AI were already discussed above. The security of the blockchains along with additional benefits of smart contracts and decentralization of the system can evolve AI and the applicability of AI to various systems.

3.3.3. Blockchain 3.0

The speed of Ethereum was no longer enough due to the heavy usage of smart contracts for microtransactions. This led to an increase in decentralization further and the internet started to shift to a decentralized system integrating open standard platforms and data storage. This led to the development of DApp (Decentralized Applications). The backend of these systems run on a blockchain network and made it possible for the front-end to be developed in any language with the only prerequisite that it should be able to call the blockchains in the backend. The development of these types of applications can lead to the creation of Decentralized Autonomous Organisations (DAO) (Green, 2016). The profits of such organizations are shared among all the users.

Due to the heavy decentralization structure of blockchain in this phase, the single points of failures are no longer to be found and the position of central authority became unnecessary. Also due to the decentralization the transaction speed increase about a hundred times (Srivastava, Bhattacharya, Singh, Mathur, 2018). On the other side, it takes more time to update any bug fixes as it has to update every node in the system. The integration of AI became important to address this, which in turn can also help the AI to be improved as mentioned above. Also one can say that AI evolved along with blockchain, as every aspect of the evolution of blockchain came as a helping hand in improving the AI itself.

Now that we have seen what can AI and blockchain do to each other and how we can improve our technologies by integrating these two, let us discuss the application of blockchain to the process of thinking itself.

4. THINKING THROUGH BLOCKCHAIN

With all the improvements in blockchain and an increase in the number of areas where this technology is applicable, one of the important applications of this technology in the future can be in the area of thinking itself (Swan, 2015). Improvement in the area of thinking can improve not only AI but also the human enhancement. Blockchain thinking is explained in the following sections as an IPO model. The research in this area and the improvement of thinking with blockchain can make unfathomable improvements in the integration of human and AI. This can help in humans being able to upload the data in the brain as files in an artificial intelligent environment and even can fathom the concept of Friendly AIs. The following sections are dedicated to explain about the process of thinking and how blockchain can help in improving the thinking.

4.1 Thinking

Before we start with how blockchain can help to improve thinking, let us have a brief review of the process called thinking. Thinking in psychology is defined as a mental process in which one form models and psychological assumptions of the real-world entities. Also, it is considered as, the art of manipulating information and reaching a decision accordingly. In the field of AI or for any research prospect, thinking is considered as a computational process. Fundamentally, one can define thinking as a process of acquiring outputs by processing inputs. This is the reason why we are going to formulate thinking as an IPO (Input-Processing-Output) model with the integration of blockchain. There are other functional requirements needed to completely investigate and understand the process of thinking apart from the computational aspect. These can be brought out by applying blockchain to the process. For this context, we are going to assume the situations that involve cognitive and mental, processing, and understanding along with thinking, not limited to humans but machines as well.

In the case of the thinking, as we discussed above, the process of thinking is considered as an IPO model, where the inputs are both the data from outside the system and inside the system. Memory of the system is the main internal data while sensory data and such can be considered as external data. The processing of the data then takes place inside the system and stored to achieve our outputs. These outputs can be anything like action that needs to take place, store the data, complete the transaction, or chose a winner of the current transaction. The outputs are what we are interested in and inputs might be either provided or already present in memory. Before we dwell deep into the IPO architecture, let us see the vision of the mission to integrate blockchain with thinking.

4.2 The Vision

The objective we're discussing here is to instantiate thinking on a blockchain. That is we are going build thinking machines using the architecture of the blockchain. From a broader perspective, this can lead to improvements in both human and AI. In both the fields, the decentralized structure of blockchain can lead to expansion in domains such as freedom, expressions, actualization, realization, liberty, possibility, and many others (Swan, 2015). Let us consider some fields where blockchain thinking can prosper.

4.2.1 Personal Thinking Chains

This will be one of the, if not the most important application of blockchain thinking. The possibility in the near future where a person's mind can be uploaded as a file or a group of files to a system can change the basic structure of our technology and advance it to a level far from what it is now. Blockchains working with digital mind files as such can actualize this future. The personal thinking chains are the data stored in some storage in a compressed format that has all of a person's thinking encoded. So, while storing this data by using methodologies such as brain-computer interfaces or some tracking devices, we can make a log of transactions or the specific data to be stored in a blockchain. This makes the blockchain to constitute a person's thinking process or even the consciousness of the person. Now as the whole data is stored in a blockchain we can transact data and use the person's thinking to achieve at certain decisions for some problems, in a way that the original person might respond. This can also be used to restore data in case the person's memory might need to be restored.

The reason why these personal thinking chains are not currently practiced is due to the issues in the privacy of storage of one's memories or thinking. The inclusion of blockchain can make sure the security to be well answered as the stored thinking or consciousness will be in an immutable storage and can obviously be designed in such a state that only the person will be able to see what is happening in the blockchain. The blockchains thus can be used to track not only the person's thought process; but will also help in understanding health conditions in the medical field and can be used mainly for understanding the mental health of a person.

4.2.2 Personal Genome Files

Another use of blockchains might be the creation and maintenance of personal genome files. Personal genome files or more precisely personal connectome files that contain both personal genome files and Electronic Medical Records, can be created and maintained using blockchains(Swan, 2015). This PCF is nothing but the structural and functional mappings of one's brain. The research in this field will go on for quite long periods as the experiences such as feelings and emotions do not have computational and mathematical decisions yet. Also, another claim for the application of blockchain to these PCFs is that blockchain would not store all the data; instead, it stores the locations of PCFs of each person, while the PCFs are stored at the person himself or a unified secure storage. Some claim these mind files and personal genome files are not only used as a backup but can be provided to the next generations of the person to know about their ancestor's life and experiences.

Also, the mind files can be used to gain some experiences about certain situations and be trained. This can lead to a person experiencing one as a normal human and other experience being accumulated by the digital version of the person. By using processes such as version control and such, the digital version can be synced with the person to accumulate all experiences of both in the person himself along with upgrading the digital version.

4.2.3 Blockchain Advocating

As mentioned before the smart contracts of blockchain are both a boon and bane at the same time. If we can improve the security of the smart contracts, they might manage our future. They might be able to serve as our independent personal advocates for unprecedented futures. They can be coded in such a way that they can advocate on behalf of us. In the case of digital court hearings and negotiations, the mind files on blockchains can be used for advocating on our behalf with the usage of smart contracts. Digitalization of the mind using such blockchains and such can actualize the future where the machines and humans coexist along with digitalized humans for their own purposes.

Now that we have seen where the thinking enhanced by blockchain can take us into and how it might reshape our futures, let us discuss the theoretical architecture for the implementation of blockchain in the area of thinking in the following section.

4.3 Architecture

We have seen various possibilities that blockchain thinking can unveil in the future, we are yet to discuss the architecture of such a system. As the actual perfected architecture for this system is yet to be developed, we will go through a possible basic architecture and idea that can help the researchers to develop it further. One of the main reasons for the blockchain to be able to handle the enhancement of thinking is the built-in accountability and tracking features. All the users of the network, let them be persons in the network, the smart contracts, or the machine codes will be able to access this data at any given time. The architecture is as mentioned before, an IPO model, with input, processing, and output model, which are Memory, storage, and file-serving as inputs, utility functions, and such as processing units and outputs(Swan, 2015) are briefly explained here.

4.3.1 Input

The basic requirement of thinking is memory. Memory usually is distinct. Let us consider that the memory is divided into units and all the distinct units of the memory are encoded and stored at someplace. In the case of overlapping memory units, they can be stored as separate distinct units. Just like any digital file has arbitrarily many copies, the memories too will have arbitrarily many copies stored at different places. The optimization of the number of and locations of these stored copies dynamically for system operation. This is the principal step in blockchain thinking. Though the memory is yet to be split into units or so-called modules, various researches are going on in both digital and biological fields. Let us see how the memory architecture in blockchain thinking.

Blockchain thinking needs the IPFS, spoken about in the earlier sections. It is a file system that implements various functionalities like versioning from GitHub, peer-to-peer file serving system, and unique identifier and hashing functionalities of a blockchain. IPFS tries to serve any file request that is possible in a system connected to the internet, to the user. The possibility of this IPFS system came from the defined architecture of the internet, in which each file is stored at certain storage for access. Once requested the file is broken into packets and then those packets are sent to the user and reassembled at the user's end.

Torrent system changed this basic architecture. It started a peer-to-peer serving system and each file will have multiple copies at multiple users and whoever is willing and has the file can share the packets to the one requesting it and the reassemble of the packets from different places is done at user's end. IPFS follows the same peer-to-peer exchange system. Though IPFS follows this, the functionality of the IPFS is far higher and complicated than a normal torrent client. Unlike the torrents which share only music, videos, and games, the IPFS will share any file from any peer to any peer depending on the request. Any digital file can be uploaded into the blockchain. Using the distributing property the user might get the packets of the same file from different sources.

One of the main issues of the torrent system is that the packets one receiving might not be secure. Someone on the network might have modified the packets and add some virus in it. The addition of Blockchain to this peer-to-peer exchange scheme in IPFS can answer this problem. The immutability property of blockchain kicks in and any user who downloaded it will not be able to manipulate and share the file. Also, the inclusion of blockchain will make it easy to validate the transactions and transmissions. Also due to IPFS being able to integrate torrent and git, the availability of resources in git might increase and will be easy to access than as of now. This makes IPFS the best option to store the memory files and other prerequisites for the processing to start in blockchain thinking.

Now that we came to know where and how our memories can be stored, there is one more important thing about human beings we are forgetting. People are biased. It doesn't matter to us what they are biased towards, but for us, we need unbiased memories to let the machines do the decision making properly. So the care should be taken to check the biased nature of one before ascertaining that a machine's decision was true based on a person's memory and experience. On the other hand, if we are talking about how a specific person whose memory is getting accessed for decision making would respond in a certain situation, the blockchain should also store the bias nature of the person. This is easier said than done. The memory in blockchain can be used as an input to assess the biased nature of a person and on the other hand, implement the smart contracts and make adjustments based on the respective decisions.

4.3.2 Processing

Processing is the next step in our architecture for blockchain thinking. The decentralization of blockchain and the internet helps to process in more ways than assumed. The decentralized processing can help this step to execute faster than it normally would on a single system. This is the case for any process under decentralization. Also, it helps in removing the redundancy in processes. In blockchain, we can take advantage of this decentralization and implement that to our thinking. Decentralized processing would normally split the data into packets, process at different nodes, and recombine the output. In our case, we have to deal with packetized thoughts. Before we even get into the application, the aspect of packetized thoughts can change the technologies. This packetized thinking can be implemented using our blockchain. Digitized thinking is nothing but in reality collection of data and code. It is not hard for a digitized thinker to packetize his thinking. So we can make the digitized thinker as a collection of decentralized processing nodes and assemble the data after all the units have processed.

The current super-computers can do this packetizing of processing by similarly-structured parallelizable computational nodes. If we just consider need to consider the computing power alone for processing, AI applications should have already been at the level of human intelligence. But this is not the case, as intelligence is not computational power. Some of the territories related to the reasons why human being is intelligent are still uncharted. Even though with faster computational capacities than humans, supercomputers are still can't be considered intelligent for this reason. Also, digital systems might never become as intelligent as humans, as our bodies work like analog systems with many analog parameters. For a digital thinker to come close to human intelligence and thinking, it might have analog processing and non-linear architectures and be complex. Some researches and algorithms which try to emulate human brain thinking might come close but they are still too far away from human intelligence. Blockchains can help in those researches to reduce the complexity by adding the decentralized processing techniques and make more efficient use of resources.

The inclusion of smart contracts can help in breaking down of tasks by such supercomputers. Blockchain might facilitate the issue of tackling complex tasks that supercomputers might face and improve the level of problems that supercomputers can solve. The complex problems can be changed into a format where they can be solved using mining to reduce the load on the resources and utilize the otherwise wasted processing cycles of a supercomputer. Also instead of using proof of stake, we might implement psychological proofs like proof of intelligence, digitizing it in the blockchain for the mining process. The proof of intelligence can judge the miner with the best intelligence and gives priority to that miner's decision, just like how a normal blockchain would give the transaction to the miner with the highest stake.

4.3.3 Output

Outputs are what we require for almost any procedure. There can be a variety of outputs for our architecture. They might be actions taken or needed to be taken, feedbacks or notifications, or even some smart contracts for the future. Our digitized thinker might have to write data to files or files to storage might even have to conduct transactions. One of the most important outputs can be the assessment of the system or a utility function or some other higher-order goal that has to be included in the system. The smart contracts can help in tracking, ordering, monitoring, and fine-tuning such operations, goals, and objectives. The claim in the architecture is that, let it be any kind of digital processing or thinking, blockchain can be coordinate and govern them(Swan, 2015). The higher-level goals mentioned before are particularly to improve the utility functions of these smart contracts. These functions might become part of the constitutional set up for various blockchain thinkers, but will always remain specialized for thinking specific operations.

The utility functions so far mentioned are not easy to understand or implement. One choice is to use the mathematics of complexity science to define and derive these functions. Also, the implementation of these blockchain thinkers, utility functions, and smart contracts can lead to the development of Friendly AI, AI which can benefit humans. Blockchain might actualize the concepts of Friendly AIs.

4.4. Industry 4.0 and Blockchain 4.0

The digital industrial revolution is considered as the fourth industrial revolution or Industry 4.0(Lasi, Fettke, Kemper, Feld, Hoffmann, 2014) is the ability of gathering and analyzing data across machines. Unlike in the previous era these are handled in fast flexible and efficient manners. These changes made it possible for the productions were less costly than before. Big Data and analytics, autonomous robots, simulation, system integration, Industrial IoT, Cybersecurity, Cloud, additive manufacturing and augmented reality are considered to be the nine most important technologies of Industry 4.0(Vaidya, Ambad, Bhosle, 2018). Though each of them represents a field of its own, AI is used in almost each of these fields. Blockchain is considered to be a provider of security in the Industry 4.0 due to the decentralized, and security features it provides. Though blockchain is considered as a part of the cybersecurity, it is undeniable that it has various applications in most of, if not every other the field.

The autonomous robots(Fahimi, 2009) are the product of highly trustable and heavily researched AI. The discussion given above about how the thinking can be established as a process using blockchain stands as a path for advancement in the robotic industry. The ever-growing fields of both AI and blockchain are fated to be integrated for the betterment of the robotic industry as a whole. Though AI has strayed from its path of understanding a human brain a little due to the overly complex nature of the brain and the neurons, including the blockchain in the thinking process can lead to the development of artificial systems and thinking on a functional perspective. This can be seen by the new technological advancements in blockchain such as the EOS.IO(IO, 2017), which is a cryptocurrency that tried to emulate attributes of practical CPU and GPUs, making the possibility of using blockchain as a decentralized operating system. Having many uncharted areas as such blockchain can seem to improve the technology in many ways.

5. FUTURE DIRECTIONS

From the above sections, it is almost certain that there are way too many opportunities for future research. As a matter of fact, most of the discussions in the chapter deal with future directions and assumptions of what might happen in the future and how the integration can be explained. One might get a lot of future directions in various fields just by going through the chapter. Let us list a few possible and notable foreseeable challenges.

- The integration of Blockchain and AI still is not perfected yet, there are too many undefined variables and issues to check with, like, a publicly available blockchain ledger, which is used for training AI might lead to privacy issues. The privacy in this case has to be controlled according to the data and application.
- Smart contracts are still not perfected as specified above. The issue at Ethereum is one of the examples of it. Making smart contracts secure is going to be a big challenge with the increase in the availability of computational power to the common man.

- IPFS system is yet to be completely developed. The peer-to-peer serving though seems identical; the received packets might still be a concern and have to be checked for packet manipulation.
- Coming to the blockchain thinking, storing of memories in a blockchain or the storage positions of memories in the blockchain bring out possibilities of open challenges on how to digitalize memories and thinking procedure. This will not just be a challenge in the digital environment but also, biological advancements are necessary to actualize the memories and thought process in digital forms.
- Though the memories would be stored in some other storage and the blockchain would store the locations of these memories, privacy issue might still raise, as a whole the blockchain is public and these locations being made public can lead any adversary having even limited access of blockchain to visit the securely stored memories.
- Proof-of-stake though is researched for the current blockchain stakeholders and transactions; the proof-of-intelligence still has to be studied heavily before implementation. The evaluation of intelligence and levels of intelligence of a system has to be numerated before proof-of-intelligence can chose a miner to be intelligent.
- The IPO model discussed above for thinking procedure through blockchain is just a high-level architecture and has a lot of challenges in all three steps of Input, Processing, and Output.
- This might be into seeing far into the future, but the challenge of designing an analog machine and processing the analog data might be the biggest of all with a lot of uncharted territory. Succeeding in this might lead to actualizing the thought of AI being close to human intelligence.
- Implementation of blockchain to supercomputers for extra processing speed, decentralization of supercomputers, and improving their performance is still a research area with a lot of opportunities.
- Friendly AI, though just mentioned in the chapter, is still an uncertainty and has to be made sure before developing such systems as these can either exponentially improve human lives or destroy it altogether.

6. CONCLUSION

AI became the most important technological advancement in the digital industry and also is studied and used heavily in almost all of the industries. Blockchain, though is still mostly uncharted, the fundamental concept of this being integrated with AI can make much progress compared to what both can do individually. Also, the integration of these two can open many other paths that are yet to be studied and researched. In this chapter, the discussions of the basics of what AI and blockchain are and how each of them can help the other when integrated are presented. Blockchain thinking, the idea of applying the procedure of thinking inside a blockchain, originated from the idea of integration of AI and blockchain can revolutionize the progress in both machine and human intelligence. The chapter also covers what is thinking and how blockchain can help in improving thinking, and how one can implement thinking as a process using blockchain is presented along with the very-high level architecture of how the process of blockchain thinking can be carried out in future. Researching while integrating these two can even help in solving the problems that might still exist in both systems even after integration, as they seem to be complementing each other. Though the chapter is specifically about how AI and blockchain can improve the future, many future challenges have to be addressed and some of them are mentioned in the above section, which can actualize the dreamed future of co-existence of artificial and human beings.

REFERENCES

Baynham-Herd, Z. (2017). Enlist blockchain to boost conservation. *Nature*, *548*(7669), 523–523. doi:10.1038/548523c PMID:28858318

Benet, J. (2014). *Ipfs-content addressed, versioned, p2p file system.* arXiv preprint arXiv:1407.3561

Brambilla, M., Ferrante, E., Birattari, M., & Dorigo, M. (2013). Swarm robotics: A review from the swarm engineering perspective. *Swarm Intelligence*, *7*(1), 1–41. doi:10.100711721-012-0075-2

Buterin, V. (2014). Ethereum white paper: a next-generation smart contract & decentralized application platform. *First version, 53.*

Campbell, D. (2018). *Combining AI and Blockchain to Push Frontiers in Healthcare.* Available: https://www.macadamian.com/2018/03/16/combining-ai-and-blockchain-in-healthcare

Dinh, T. N., & Thai, M. T. (2018). Ai and blockchain: A disruptive integration. *Computer*, *51*(9), 48–53. doi:10.1109/MC.2018.3620971

Fahimi, F. (2009). Autonomous robots. *Modeling, Path Planning and Control.*

Ferrer, E. C. (2016). *The blockchain: A new framework for robotic swarm systems.* Available: https://arxiv.org/abs/1608.00695

Green, H. (2016). Introducing the DAO: The organisation that will kill corporations. City AM, 3.

Hajdarbegovic, N. (2014). *Bitcoin Miners Ditch Ghash. io Pool Over Fears of 51% Attack.* Academic Press.

IO. E. (2017). *EOS. IO technical white paper.* EOS. IO (accessed 18 December 2017) https://github. com/EOSIO/Documentation

Janson, S., Merkle, D., & Middendorf, M. (2008). A decentralization approach for swarm intelligence algorithms in networks applied to multi swarm PSO. *International Journal of Intelligent Computing and Cybernetics.*

Juels, A., Kosba, A., & Shi, E. (2016, October). The ring of gyges: Investigating the future of criminal smart contracts. In *Proceedings of the 2016 ACM SIGSAC Conference on Computer and Communications Security* (pp. 283-295). 10.1145/2976749.2978362

Kahneman, D. (2011). *Thinking, fast and slow.* Macmillan.

Kaku, M. (2015). *The future of the mind: The scientific quest to understand, enhance, and empower the mind.* Anchor Books.

Lasi, H., Fettke, P., Kemper, H. G., Feld, T., & Hoffmann, M. (2014). Industry 4.0. *Business & Information Systems Engineering*, *6*(4), 239–242. doi:10.100712599-014-0334-4

Lin, C., He, D., Huang, X., Choo, K. K. R., & Vasilakos, A. V. (2018). BSeIn: A blockchain-based secure mutual authentication with fine-grained access control system for industry 4.0. *Journal of Network and Computer Applications*, *116*, 42–52. doi:10.1016/j.jnca.2018.05.005

Luu, L., Chu, D. H., Olickel, H., Saxena, P., & Hobor, A. (2016, October). Making smart contracts smarter. In *Proceedings of the 2016 ACM SIGSAC conference on computer and communications security* (pp. 254-269). 10.1145/2976749.2978309

Magazzeni, D., McBurney, P., & Nash, W. (2017). Validation and verification of smart contracts: A research agenda. *Computer*, *50*(9), 50–57. doi:10.1109/MC.2017.3571045

Mamoshina, P., Ojomoko, L., Yanovich, Y., Ostrovski, A., Botezatu, A., Prikhodko, P., ... Ogu, I. O. (2018). Converging blockchain and next-generation artificial intelligence technologies to decentralize and accelerate biomedical research and healthcare. *Oncotarget*, *9*(5), 5665–5690. doi:10.18632/oncotarget.22345 PMID:29464026

Marr, B. (2018). Artificial intelligence and blockchain: 3 major benefits of combining these two mega-trends. *Forbes*.

Maxmen, A. (2018). AI researchers embrace Bitcoin technology to share medical data. *Nature, 555*(7696), 293–294. doi:10.1038/d41586-018-02641-7

Morris, D. (2014). Bitcoin is Not Just Digital Currency. It's Napster for Finance. *Fortune, 21*.

Morris, D. Z. (2016). Leaderless, blockchain-based venture capital fund raises $100 million, and counting. *Fortune*, 5-23.

Myers, D. S., Bazinet, A. L., & Cummings, M. P. (2008). Expanding the reach of Grid computing: combining Globus-and BOINC-based systems. *Grids for Bioinformatics and Computational Biology*, 71-85.

Nakamoto, S. (2019). *Bitcoin: A peer-to-peer electronic cash system*. Manubot.

Natoli, C., & Gramoli, V. (2016, October). The blockchain anomaly. In *2016 IEEE 15th International Symposium on Network Computing and Applications (NCA)* (pp. 310-317). IEEE. 10.1109/NCA.2016.7778635

Panarello, A., Tapas, N., Merlino, G., Longo, F., & Puliafito, A. (2018). Blockchain and iot integration: A systematic survey. *Sensors (Basel), 18*(8), 2575. doi:10.339018082575 PMID:30082633

Rothblatt, M. (2014). *Virtually Human: The Promise---and the Peril---of Digital Immortality*. Macmillan.

Salah, K., Alfalasi, A., & Alfalasi, M. (2019, April). A Blockchain-based System for Online Consumer Reviews. In *IEEE INFOCOM 2019-IEEE Conference on Computer Communications Workshops (INFOCOM WKSHPS)* (pp. 853-858). IEEE. 10.1109/INFCOMW.2019.8845186

Srivastava, A., Bhattacharya, P., Singh, A., & Mathur, A. (2018). *A Systematic Review on Evolution of Blockchain Generations*. Academic Press.

Strobel, V., Castelló Ferrer, E., & Dorigo, M. (2018, July). Managing byzantine robots via blockchain technology in a swarm robotics collective decision making scenario. In *Proceedings of the 17th International Conference on Autonomous Agents and MultiAgent Systems* (pp. 541-549). International Foundation for Autonomous Agents and Multiagent Systems.

Swan, M. (2014). *Blockchain AI: Consensus as the mechanism to foster 'friendly' AI*. Institute for Ethics and Emerging Technologies.

Swan, M. (2015). Blockchain thinking: The brain as a decentralized autonomous corporation [commentary]. *IEEE Technology and Society Magazine, 34*(4), 41–52. doi:10.1109/MTS.2015.2494358

Swan, M. (2015). *Blockchain: Blueprint for a new economy.* O'Reilly Media, Inc.

Team, N. A. (2018). *NEBULA AI (NBAI)—Decentralized Ai Blockchain Whitepaper.* Academic Press.

Vaidya, S., Ambad, P., & Bhosle, S. (2018). Industry 4.0–a glimpse. *Procedia Manufacturing, 20,* 233–238. doi:10.1016/j.promfg.2018.02.034

Wood, G. (2014). Ethereum: A secure decentralised generalised transaction ledger. *Ethereum project yellow paper, 151*(2014), 1-32.

Zhang, G., Li, T., Li, Y., Hui, P., & Jin, D. (2018). Blockchain-based data sharing system for ai-powered network operations. *Journal of Communications and Information Networks, 3*(3), 1–8. doi:10.100741650-018-0024-3

ADDITIONAL READING

Salah, K., Rehman, M. H. U., Nizamuddin, N., & Al-Fuqaha, A. (2019). Blockchain for AI: Review and open research challenges. *IEEE Access: Practical Innovations, Open Solutions, 7,* 10127–10149. doi:10.1109/ACCESS.2018.2890507

Swan, M. (2015). Blockchain thinking: The brain as a decentralized autonomous corporation [commentary]. *IEEE Technology and Society Magazine, 34*(4), 41–52. doi:10.1109/MTS.2015.2494358

Zheng, Z., & Dai, H. N. (2019). *Blockchain Intelligence: When Blockchain Meets Artificial Intelligence.* arXiv preprint arXiv:1912.06485

Chapter 2
Study of Risk Analysis in the Internet of Things

Manoj Kumar Srivastav
https://orcid.org/0000-0002-5080-6796
Champdani Adarsh Sharmik Vidyamandir, India

ABSTRACT

The internet of things (IoT) refers to a network comprised of physical objects capable of gathering and sharing electronic information. Internet of things will be connected with physical objects that are accessible through the internet. In general, IoT is a collection of all things in the world and that should be connected over internet. But in any technology, there exist some risk factor which will diminish the performance of an organization. In IoT, security of information is always a challenging task. Security is an essential pillar of the internet, 'the' most significant challenge for the IoT. When the number of connected devices increases, the opportunity of risk factor in positive and negative side will work to implement the IoT. Risk analysis is the review of the risks associated with a particular event or action. In this chapter, challenges of security and analysis of risk have discussed to reduce the problems.

1.0 INTRODUCTION

Risk analysis is a mechanism to identify and analyze the issue related to the negative impact on an organization. It is used to study the different aspects of a security issue related to information technology on a quantitative and qualitative basis. An organization always takes a management issue related to risk of the security issue, project and information technology etc. Risk analysis is a component of risk management. Risk management is a process that allows obtaining minimum risk and

DOI: 10.4018/978-1-7998-5876-8.ch002

maximum profit in a system (Aven, 2015).The Internet of things or IoT refers to the billions of physical devices around the world that are now connected to the Internet, all collecting and sharing data. IoT(Internet of things) is an advanced automation and analytic system. It is based on networking, automation and analytic system. IoT increase performance when it is applied to any industry or system. Generally, IoT collects and exchange data without human interaction by Connecting everyday thing embedded with electronics software and sensors to the Internet.The term "things" in the Internet of things refers to anything and everything in day to day life which is accessed or connected through the Internet.

In the Internet of Things, all the things that are being connected to the Internet can be put into three categories:

1. Things that collect information and then send it.
2. Things that receive information and then act on it.
3. Things that do both.

By collecting information from an external source, IoT can make some intelligence decision. For example, sensors like temperature etc. can collect information from the environment. In IoT, it is possible that the machine receives information and act upon it. For example, a printer receives a document, and it prints it. The most important features of IoT on which it works are connectivity, analyzing, integrating, sensing and making endpoint engagement etc. Internet of things facilitates the several advantages in day-to-day life in the business sector like the use of efficient resource utilization, minimum human effort with saving time. Though IoT assigned with many benefits, it also creates significant challenges like security and privacy(Mohammeda et. Al, 2017). Since the IoT systems are interconnected and communicate over networks, so there exists risk related to security challenge and privacy of data from various kind of network attack. During the study of risk analysis in IoT, it is required to identify the risk, analyze the risk, evaluate the risk, treat the risk and monitor and review the risk respectively. It is required to uncover, recognize and describe the risk that will be harmful to IoT. When the risk is identified, it is required to analyze the nature of the risk and potential of the risk. After making an analysis of the risk it is required to level a risk which is acceptable or not acceptable to make changes. It is further steps is to treat the risk, and finally, it is required to monitor risk and reviews the risk.

2.0 SECURITY CHALLENGES FOR THE FUTURE OF THE INTERNET OF THINGS

2.1 Outdated Hardware and Software

As the use of IoT devices is increasing, the production and manufacture company are focusing on making a new device. They are not giving more attention to security. Updating of hardware and software is required with the passage of time, but the majority of company do not give major attention regarding updating. There exists a challenge regarding its security features as it becomes vulnerable to attacks when the hackers find some bugs or security issues.(Shah,2019)

. IoT can be updated on the basis of sampling. There is some object which is needed to be updated with the passage of time, and some object does not need to be updated. Concept of sampling can be applicable to introduce for updating hardware and software. Collection of the object whose elements are examined in view of their individual characteristics is called a population. The sample is a subset of the population. The process of selecting a sample is known as sampling. The number of elements in the sample is the sample size. For a finite population, there are two types of random samplings:

1.   Simple random sampling with replacement
2.   Simple random sampling without replacement. (Gupta & Kapoor, 2001)

   Definition

- *Sampling with Replacement*: Sampling with replacement is used to find probability with replacement. In other words, you want to find the probability of some event where there are a number of balls, cards or other objects, and you replace the item each time you choose one.
- *Sampling without Replacement*: Sampling without Replacement is a way to figure out probability without replacement. In other words, you don't replace the first item you choose before you choose a second. This dramatically changes the odds of choosing sample items.

Simple random sampling with replacement is a type of random sampling in which units are drawn one by one and are returned to the population before the next selection or drawing.

   Simple random sampling without replacement is a type of random sampling in which The units are drawn one by one and not returned to the population before the next selection or drawing. There is a need to predict the service of IoT based device.

For example, hardware and software should be updated with the passage of time in such a way that there is no need to wait for a machine to fail, IoT sensors on a production line can track the requirement like heat, humidity, vibration, oil viscosity and other data points. Providing alerts in advance allows a company to alert for maintenance, and the company will be ready to schedule repairs on the requirement of the machine device. There is a need to gather data regarding the performance of IoT based technology so that manufacture will be able to provide guidance when equipment needs service, and this will save manufacturers' maintenance costs. But there are some challenges related to the reliability of the sensor. When a sensor malfunctions and fails to trigger a maintenance warning, it can compromise the quality of the finished product. Regular updates of hardware and software have always been an important concern for security in the IoT system. Security is an essential factor in IoT. There is a need to update hardware and software; otherwise, there exist chances to data breach of not only customers but also of the companies that manufacture them.

Sampling will play an important role in the study of those IoT devices. Sampling will be helpful to understand which device hardware or software is required to make changes. It may be useful to make some IoT devices should be replaced with the passage of time, or some IoT device are made little changes with little modification in it.

2.2 Use of Weak and Default Credentials

Many IoT systems are poorly designed. Many IoT companies are selling device with providing default credentials to consumers. Many IoT companies provide consumer default username and Password. Hackers need just the username and Password to attack the device. When they know the username, they carry out brute-force attacks to infect the devices. Consumers should prepare to change the default credentials as soon as they get the device. Generally, Manufacturer does not give instruction and guide to change the default credentials. Not making an update in the instruction guides leaves all of the devices open to attack. Generally, the manufacture does not give proper guidance related to IoT devices. They give limited guidance for life cycle maintenance and management of IoT devices.

For the security purpose, the following thing should be maintained

Password Management

Password plays an import role in any security features. Generally, there are two types of Password: (i) Weak Password and (ii) Strong Password. *Weak passwords* always play a major role in any hack. Some time application does not enforce password complexity, and as a result, the user uses simple Password like name@123, own mobile number, abc@123 Password @ 123 etc. Weak Password does not always mean length and the characters used, and it should be tried to avoid the Password related to name, place, or mobile number. Weak passwords can be guessable or attacker cans brute force if the length of the Password is very small. There is a need to develop strong Password.

Security in any system generally starts from authenticating the user (commonly with a username and a password). Password may be in text form, fingerprint, mobile verification, ATM card etc. Password should be strong for the security purpose. If a system user uses weak passwords, it is possible that could be discovered by brute force.(Nagpal,2014)

Working System of IoT System Design

Design of the IoT system should be made in a proper way. Sometimes IoT system is designed in default way to grant a permit to access the system/program. Such design of IoT should be avoided. Authenticated process of IoT system should follow properly. Lack of mature IoT technologies and business processes lead to risk zone with respect to security.

Audit and logging standards are not defined for IoT components.

Audit and Logging system standard should be maintained for the security purpose. There should be a focus on awareness and identifying methods for achieving security in the IoT system.

2.3 Security From Malware and Ransomware

Ransomware has become one of most serious cyber threats these years. All the user of IoT devices wants to protect and secure them from encryption viruses. IoT ransomware is more dangerous than traditional ransomware. IoT ransomware does not encrypt your data. The well-known and most active crypto viruses like Locky and Cerber lock down important files on infected machines. The victims are forced to pay money for obtaining the decryption key or prepare to lose their data or file in case there are no backups. Generally, it is assumed that files and important data are given valuation in the sense of money. Hackers want to earn money on attacking the IoT device. By locking some file, IoT viruses may lock and get complete control over many devices and even networks. IoT malware may stop vehicles, disconnect the electricity, even stop production lines. Such programs can do much more harm, and therefore hackers may demand much larger ransom amounts.

Although there is no universal solution, many experts believe that the observance of certain guidelines and methodologies can help organizations and manufacturers better protect their IoT systems from ransomware.

Upgrade the Firmware of the Smart Device

It is required to develop such a system in which a smart device should be upgraded to make the system secure. Up-gradation process should be simple, safe and secure.

Reliable Authentication

A reliable authentication mechanism poses another important protection measure. It may be possible to face an insecure condition when most of the devices are connected to the Internet without any authentication at all. This paves the way for spoofing. If lack of authentication becomes a mass phenomenon, it will be possible to disable millions of devices. Spoofing is particularly dangerous when a server with millions of connected machines is infected. To avoid the entire dangerous situation, it is required to make a reliable authentication process in the system.(Khurana 2014)

2.4 Predicting and Preventing Attack

Prediction of security of Iot object can be implemented by either in a statistical approach or in the classical approach. With the passage of time, the development of IoT device makes cyber attacks very unpredictable. The attacks and attackers used modern methods to breach security, which is a significant concern for almost everybody. It is necessary to find all the weak point in network combination of IoT devices to prevent from attack. The security of devices is a long term concern. Repeated experiment and making an observation on the working frequency of IoT devices will help to predict the weak point in security in the IoT system. The favourable result will help the IoT system. AI-powered monitoring and other such analytical tools are definitely going to help in predicting the security issues, but it is also complex to adopt such kind of techniques. The reason for this is because, in IoT, connected devices need processing of data instantly, which is hurdled by such processes.[Broder et al, 2012].

2.5 Difficult to Find if a Device Is Affected

The Internet of things is a rapidly growing technology which aims to connect all devices to the existing Internet infrastructure. Internet of things (Device(s) that have sensors, that are programmed to act in a certain way, are connected together to achieve a certain result.)It is not possible to make practically 100% security from security threats and breaches. Many user do not know about the status of their devices is hacked.(Cheruvu et.al, 2019)

In mathematical form let us represent that if the device is connected over a network and A_{ij} represent that device Ai is connected with device Aj over internet network and there are two conditions are--

As Aij =1 if connected devices over the network are working properly.

And Aij =0 if connected devices over the network are not working properly or any device has been hacked.

When the number of connected devices is small, it will be possible to sort out the problem, but when the number of connecting devices is increasing and becomes in large scale, it is difficult to monitor all of them. It is because an IoT device needs apps, services, and protocols for communication.

2.6 Protection of Data and Security Challenges

Data protection and security challenges are a major issue. Data generated from connected device may be high to handle concerning the network point of view. There is a need for AI tools and automation. It is required to set new rules and methods by IoT admins to solve the problem.

Correlation means association - more precisely, it is a measure of the extent to which two variables are related. There are three possible results of a correlation study: a positive correlation, a negative correlation, and no correlation(Ross, 2010). A **positive correlation** is a relationship between two variables in which both variables move in the same direction. Therefore, when one variable increases as the other variable increases or one variable decreases while the other decreases. For example, when proper risk and security measure will be taken in the IoT device system, the performance of the IoT system will increase. A **negative correlation** is a relationship between two variables in which an increase in one variable is associated with a decrease in the other. An example, when the IoT devices are not working properly, but the organization is using lots of IoT device without taking and security measure, the performance of the IoT device will decreases. A **zero correlation** exists when there is no relationship between two variables. The concept of correlation theory can be implemented in the study of risk analysis in IoT. Proper use of security measure will lead to handle the security challenge.

3. STEPS IN THE RISK ANALYSIS PROCESS IN IoT

3.1 Conduct Risk Assessment Survey

A Survey is defined as a research method used for collecting data from a pre-defined group of respondents to gain information and insights on various topics of interest. It is required to collect data and make an assessment regarding security or threats in IoT based organization or system. The risk assessment survey is a way to begin documenting specific risks or threats within each device. (Rouse 2020)

3.2 Identify the Risk

It is necessary to identify the different types of risk during the use of software, hardware, data and employee in IoT based system. The risk assessment will be helpful to evaluate the working potential of different types of devices used in IoT.

3.3 Analyze the Risk

Once the risk is identified, there is a need to make an investigation of available information to identify hazard and estimation of risk. Risk analysis process should determine the likelihood that each risk will occur, as well as the consequences linked to each risk and how they might affect the objectives of a project.

3.4 Develop a Risk Management

Risk management is the process of selecting and implementing security countermeasure to achieve an acceptable level of risk at an acceptable cost. It is necessary to study the working method of devices which will probably reduce the effect of those devices which negatively impact the IoT system.

3.5 Implement the Risk Management Plan

The ultimate goal of risk assessment is to implement measures to remove or reduce the risks. Based on the result of risk assessment and the decision taken by the risk manager/admin, risk management policy are implemented in IoT.

Figure 1. Diagram showing implementation of risk

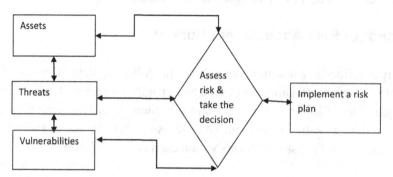

3.6 Monitor the Risk

The ongoing process of identifying, treating and managing risks should be an important part of any risk analysis process. It is important to continue monitoring in IoT in order to accurately discover attacks, identifying vulnerabilities and analyze the behaviour of all network-connected device.

4. QUALITATIVE AND QUANTITATIVE RISK ANALYSIS IN IoT

Two main approaches to risk analysis in IoT are qualitative and quantitative. (Goodrich)]

4.1 Qualitative Risk Analysis

Qualitative risk analysis is a technique used to quantify risk associated with a particular hazard. Risk assessment is used for uncertain events that could have many outcomes and for which there could be significant consequences. Qualitative risk analysis typically means assessing the likelihood that a risk will occur based on subjective qualities and the impact it could have on an organization using pre-defined ranking scales.

Qualitative techniques of risk analysis in IoT:

4.1.1. Observation Techniques

observation may be defined as a systematic method of analyzing and recording behaviours of IoT devices. It is the techniques which deal with external or overt behaviour of IoT devices inappropriate situation controlled or uncontrolled.

4.1.2. Checklist

The checklist consists of a prepared list of items which are prepared by the company /organization. The checklist is used to record the presence or absence or frequency of occurrence of IoT devices.

4.1.3 Rating Scale

The rating scale record opinions or judgment and degree or amount of working response of IoT. By rating means the judgment of any device by some person or system.

4.1.4 Cumulative Record

The cumulative record is an individual device record. It serves as a comprehensive measure of the effectiveness of the organization's service in guiding the growth of the IoT device.

4.1.5 Questionnaire

A questionnaire is a device consisting of a series of question dealing with some problems related to IoT devices or systems. It is scientifically and systematically classified and intelligently generalized and analyzed. A questionnaire serves as an important tool of research to obtain certain qualities and practices of IoT based devices.

4.2 Quantitative Techniques of Risk Analysis in IoT

Quantitative risk analysis is a numeric estimate of the overall effect of risk on the project objectives such as cost and schedule objectives. The results provide insight into the likelihood of project success and are used to develop contingency reserves.

Individual risks are evaluated in the qualitative risk analysis. But the quantitative analysis allows us to evaluate the overall project risk from the individual risks plus other sources of risks. Business decisions are rarely made with all the information or data we desire. For more critical decisions, quantitative risk analysis provides more objective information and data than qualitative analysis. Risk analysis is a systematic process to determine the working functioning of the whole system. It works on the analysis of available information which will be helpful to determine the occurrence of events and their consequence. Risk is generally treated in negative events, and it may be defined as variability of returns that are expected from a given investment. But there are positive aspects of risk analysis. Continue evaluation of risk analysis in any system will identify the problem and helpful to manage in a good result in future with new opportunities. In the sense of financial management, an organization always wants to run the system with the help of modern technology which will be helpful to make a better profit. Generally, an information-based organization is implementing IoT based technology to get maximum profit. IoT based technology in an organization may work in the Worst case scenario, Best case scenario, most likely scenario.

- *Worst case scenario:* All IoT based technology are paid at a higher cost to run an organization, but the performance of system or output in the sense of cost is lowest. The outcome is losing money.
- *Best case scenario*: All IoT based technology are paid with minimum cost to run an organization, but the performance of system or output in the sense of cost is highest. The outcome is gaining maximum profit.
- *Most likely scenario:* All IoT based technology paid cost to run an organization is more or less equivalent to the output of money.

Quantitative Risk Assessment Tools and Techniques

Quantitative Risk Analysis tools and techniques include but are not limited to:

4.2.1 Three Point Estimate

A technique that uses the optimistic, most likely, and pessimistic values to determine the best estimate. Three-point estimation looks at three values –

- the most optimistic estimate (O),
- a most likely estimate (M), and
- a pessimistic estimate (least likely estimate (L)).

Three-point Estimate (E) is based on the simple average and follows the triangular distribution.

$$E = (O + M + L) / 3$$

Figure 2. In triangular form representation of O,M,L.

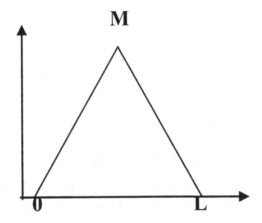

In Triangular Distribution,

Mean = (O + M + L) / 3

Standard Deviation = $\sqrt{[((O - E)^2 + (M - E)^2 + (L - E)^2) / 2]}$

Three-point Estimation Steps

Step 1 – Arrive at the Work Breakdown Structure

Step 2 – For each task, find three values – most optimistic estimate (O), a most likely estimate (M), and a pessimistic estimate (L).

Step 3 – Calculate the Mean of the three values.

Mean = (O + M + L) / 3

Step 4 – Calculate the Three-point Estimate of the task. Three-point Estimate is the Mean. Hence,

E = Mean = (O + M + L) / 3

Step 5 – Calculate the Standard Deviation of the task.

Standard Deviation (SD) = $\sqrt{[((O - E)^2 + (M - E)^2 + (L - E)^2)/2]}$

Step 6 – Repeat Steps 2, 3, 4 for all the Tasks in the WBS.

Step 7 – Calculate the Three-point Estimate of the project.

$$E \text{ (Project)} = \sum E \text{ (Task)}$$

Step 8 – Calculate the Standard Deviation of the project.

$$SD \text{ (Project)} = \sqrt{(\sum SD \text{ (Task)}^2)}$$

Convert the Project Estimates to Confidence Levels

The Three-point Estimate (E) and the Standard Deviation (SD) thus calculated are used to convert the project estimates to "Confidence Levels".
  The conversion is based such that –

- Confidence Level in E +/– SD is approximately 68%.
- Confidence Level in E value +/– 1.645 × SD is approximately 90%.
- Confidence Level in E value +/– 2 × SD is approximately 95%.
- Confidence Level in E value +/– 3 × SD is approximately 99.7%.

Commonly, the 95% Confidence Level, i.e., E Value + 2 × SD, is used for all project and task estimate.
  The above mathematical formula can be applied to the study of project related to risk analysis of IoT.

4.2.2 Decision Tree Analysis

A diagram that shows the implications of choosing one or other alternatives. Risk analysis is a term used in many industries. By risk analysis, we mean applying analytical tools to identify, describe, quantify, and explain uncertainty and its consequences for Implementation in IoT based organization's projects. A decision tree is a visual model consisting of nodes and branches. A **decision tree** is a decision support tool that uses a tree-like model of decisions and their possible consequences, including chance event outcomes, resource costs, and utility. It is one way to display an algorithm that only contains conditional control statements.(*Kamiński et.al, 2017*)

4.2.2 Expected Monetary Value (EMV)

A method used to establish the contingency reserves for a project budget and schedule. The expected monetary value is how much money you can expect to make from a certain decision.

4.2.3 Monte Carlo Analysis

A better way to perform quantitative risk analysis is by using **Monte Carlo simulation**. In Monte Carlo simulation, uncertain inputs in a model are represented using ranges of possible values known as probability distributions. By using probability distributions, variables can have different probabilities of different outcomes occurring. Probability distributions are a much more realistic way of describing uncertainty in variables of a risk analysis. Monte Carlo simulation is a computerized mathematical technique to generate random sample data based on some known distribution for numerical experiments. This method is applied to risk quantitative analysis and decision making problems. This method is used by the professionals of various profiles such as finance, project management, energy, manufacturing, engineering, research & development, insurance, oil & gas, transportation, etc.

4.2.4 Sensitivity Analysis

A technique used to determine which risks have the most significant impact on a project. Sensitivity analysis is a financial model that determines how to target variables are affected based on changes in other variables known as input variables. This model is also referred to as what-if or simulation analysis. It is a way to predict the outcome of a decision given a certain range of variables. By creating a given set of variables, an analyst can determine how changes in one variable affect the outcome. Application of the concept of Sensitivity analysis will be helpful to determine the effects of changes in working IoT system when working behaviour of one device to many devices changes.

4.2.5 Fault Tree Analysis (FMEA)

The analysis of a structured diagram which identifies elements that can cause a system failure. It is a deductive procedure used to determine the various combinations of hardware and software failures and human errors that could cause undesired events (referred to as top events) at the system level. The primary purpose of the fault tree analysis is to help identify potential causes of system failures before the failures occur. It can also be used to evaluate the probability of the top event using analytical or statistical methods. These calculations involve system quantitative reliability and maintainability information, such as failure probability, failure rate and repair rate.

4.3 Difference Between Qualitative and Quantitative Risk Analysis in IoT

Quantitative data is information about quantities, and therefore numbers and qualitative data is descriptive and regards phenomenon which can be observed but not measured, such as language.

Table 1. Comparative study of Qualitative and Quantitative Risk Analysis

Qualitative Risk Analysis	Quantitative Risk Analysis
Qualitative risk analysis typically means assessing the likelihood that a risk will occur based on subjective qualities and the impact it could have on an organization using pre-defined ranking scales. This risk is required to always perform.	Quantitative risk analysis attempts to assign a specific financial amount to adverse events, representing the potential cost to an organization if that event occurs, as well as the likelihood that the event will occur in a given year. This risk is required to perform in optional.
A qualitative risk analysis produces subjective results because it gathers data from participants in the risk analysis process based on their perceptions of the probability of a risk and the risk's likely consequences.	A quantitative risk analysis examines the overall risk of a project and generally is conducted after a qualitative risk analysis. The quantitative risk analysis numerically analyzes the probability of each risk and its consequences.

5. ADVANTAGES OF STUDY OF RISK ANALYSIS IN IoT

The term Internet of Things (IoT) refers to the interconnection of uniquely identifiable devices within the existing Internet infrastructure. In more simple terms, it's an environment where Internet-connected devices and sensors communicate with each other to perform a designated task. IoT devices are designed to help consumers save money, reduce energy, and eliminate some hassles of everyday life, among other benefits. Study of risk analysis in IoT will give benefit to its user. Some advantages are given below:

Improvement in Customer Role

By making time to time monitoring on risk in IoT customer increasingly expect that their IoT devices will securely connect with different devices. Risk analysis will help the customer to understand the functioning of IoT devices. Customer will be aware to access their devices with the proper way.

Improvement in Technology

Assessment of risk analysis with updated technologies and data will improve the customer experience. Improvement of Technology will help to make faith in the use of technology. Use of IoT based technology is increasing day by day. It is useful to tackle the complex task in a simple way. Improvement in IoT device in a secure manner will increase its use in an organization.

Reduce Waste

Risk analysis will help the management to use the IoT based in a proper way. It will be helpful to work more effectively in an organization to use resources. IoT makes areas of improvement clear. Current analytics give us superficial insight, but IoT provides real-world information leading to the more effective management of resources.

Enhanced Data Collection

Modern data collection suffers from its limitations and its design for passive use. Assessment of risk analysis in IoT will help to find those spaces and places it exactly where humans want to go to analyze our world.

6. CONCLUSION

Security is a significant concern in an organization. The use of Internet of thing is growing in different organization rapidly. The organization must understand the risk associated with the use of their IoT devices effectively and efficiently to protect their assets. Risk analysis can help an organization improve its security in several ways. There is a need to identify the overall impact of risk in IoT based technology system. It is required to identify gaps in security and take necessary steps to eliminate the weaknesses and strengthen security. The improved security policy should implement in the organization. Study of risk analysis in IoT will help to take proper decision in implementing in an organization. The employee may be able to understand the different security measures and risks by giving proper guidance. Study of risk analysis in IoT will help to work as an essential tool and techniques for managing costs associated with risks. IoT applications have brought great changes in human lives. Nowadays, IoT is used in integrating into many industries and personal life. An IoT application aims at minimizing trouble spots such as delays, interruption and production in an organization with the help of coordinating various works. But the current rapid growth of Internet of things (IoT) will lead to a significant increase in Cyber attacks and security challenges in the IoT devices. Security measures in IoT are particularly crucial because of the numerous weak points. Due to different types of devices present in the market, data protection and security is falling behind. The first step in finding better IoT security is risk analysis. Risk analysis is a review of the risk associated with a particular event or action. In this chapter, it will try to study different types of security challenges in IoT. Security challenges in IoT will help to reduce the problems. Uses of IoT face risk every day. Managing risk is critical, and that process starts with risk assessment. A proper risk analysis process will help to reduce the negative factor in an organization. Implementation of proper steps of the risk analysis process will bring a significant change in IoT. In general, the risk is analyzed on a quantitative and qualitative basis. Study of Qualitative and Quantitative risk analysis in IoT will help to tackle the different challenging issue in the system. Risk analysis will help to protect our values with IoT security. Reliability, Privacy and Safety are three major pillars in security. By accepting and solving different types of security challenges will help to overcome the security problem in IoT. Security for IoT based network is different for all kind of situation. A small office would only require basic security, while the large business will require high maintenance and advanced software and hardware to prevent malicious attacks from hacking and spamming. Finding the solution of different types of security challenging problem will help to run a system in a smooth way. A qualitative and quantitative method in a risk analysis will help to minimize the risk factor in an organization.

REFERENCES

Aven, T. (2015). *Risk Analysis. John Wiley & Sons Ltd*. doi:10.1002/9781119057819

Aven, T. (2015). Risk assessment and risk management: Review of recent advances on their foundation. *European Journal of Operational Research*, 1–13. doi:10.1016/j. ejor.2015.12.023

Boeckl, K., Fagan, M., Fisher, W., Lefkovitz, N., Megas, K. N., Nadeau, E., & Piccarreta, B. (2018). *Draft NIST Internal Report 8228: Considerations for Managing Internet of Things (IoT) Cybersecurity and Privacy Risks*. Applied Cybersecurity Division, Information Technology Laboratory. doi:10.6028/NIST.IR.8228-draft

Broder, J. F., & Tucker, E. (2012). Risk analysis and security Survey (4th ed.). Butterworth-Heinemann. doi:10.1016/C2009-0-63855-1

Chauhan, S., & Panda, N. K. (2015). *In Hacking Web Intelligence.* https://www. sciencedirect.com/topics/computer-science/weak-password

Cheruvu, S., Kumar, A., Smith, N., & Wheeler, D. (2019). Demystifying Internet of Things Security: Successful IoT Device/Edge and Platform Security Deployment. Apress.

Decision tree. (2003, May 23). *Wikipedia, the free encyclopedia.* Retrieved May 30, 2020, https://en.wikipedia.org/wiki/Decision_tree

Difference between quantitative and qualitative risk analysis. (2020, May 23). *Projectcubicle.* https://www.projectcubicle.com/difference-between-quantitative-and-qualitative-risk-analysis/

Estimation techniques - Three point. (n.d.). *RxJS, ggplot2, Python Data Persistence, Caffe2, PyBrain, Python Data Access, H2O, Colab, Theano, Flutter, KNime, Mean.js, Weka, Solidity.* https://www.tutorialspoint.com/estimation_techniques/ estimation_techniques_three_point.htm

Goodrich, B. (n.d.). *Qualitative Risk Analysis vs Quantitative Risk Analysis.* PMP Concepts Learning Series.

Gupta, S. C., & Kapoor, V. K. (2001). *Fundamental of Mathematical Statistics.* Sultan Chand & Sons.

How to perform a qualitative risk analysis. (2020, March 9). *TechRepublic.* https:// www.techrepublic.com/article/how-to-perform-a-qualitative-risk-analysis/

How to recover files recently deleted from a computer? (n.d.). *Best Windows Data Recovery Software 2020 Free Download.* https://hetmanrecovery.com/recovery_news/ how-to-recover-files-recently-deleted-from-a-computer.htm

Internet of Things (IoT). (2020, April 6). *Mobio Solutions.* https://mobiosolutions. com/internet-of-things-iot/

Kamiński, B., Jakubczyk, M., & Szufel, P. (2017). A framework for sensitivity analysis of decision trees". *Central European Journal of Operations Research, 26*(1), 135–159. doi:10.100710100-017-0479-6 PMID:29375266

Khurana, R. (2014). *Operating System.* Vikas Publishing House Pvt Ltd.

Kulshrestha, A. K. (2003). Teaching of mathematics. R. Lall Book Dept.

Mohammeda, Z. K. A., & Ahmedb, E. S. A. (2017). Internet of Things Applications, Challenges and Related Future Technologies. *World Scientific News, 67*(2), 126-148.

Monte Carlo simulation. (n.d.). *RxJS, ggplot2, Python Data Persistence, Caffe2, PyBrain, Python Data Access, H2O, Colab, Theano, Flutter, KNime, Mean.js, Weka, Solidity.* https://www.tutorialspoint.com/modelling_and_simulation/modelling_and_simulation_monte_carlo_simulation.htm

Nagpal, D. P. (2014). Data Communications and Networking. S. Chand & Company Pvt. Ltd.

Palisade. (n.d.). *What is Monte Carlo Simulation?Monte Carlo simulation: What is It and How does It work?-Palisade.* https://www.palisade.com/risk/monte_carlo_simulation.asp

Pereira, T., & Santos, H. (2014). Challenges in Information Security Protection. In *Conference: 13th European Conference on Cyber Warfare and Security (ECCWS-2014).* The University of Piraeus.

Reuven, Rubinstein, & Kroese. (2016). Simulation and the Monte Carlo Method. DOI: doi:10.1002/9781118631980

Risk management: 7 steps of risk management process. (2019, October 3). *iEduNote. com.* https://www.iedunote.com/risk-management

RMstudy-Risk Management Certification Courses. (n.d.). http://www.rmstudy.com/ rmdocs /Identify%20Risks.pdf

Roman, Najera, & Lopez. (2011). Securing the Internet of Things. *IEEE Computer, 44,* 51-58.

Ross, S. (2010). *A first course in Probability Theory.* Pearson Publication.

Rouse, M. (2020). *What is Risk analysis.* https://searchsecurity.techtarget.com/ definition/risk-analysis

Sensitivity analysis. (2003, November 26). *Investopedia.* https://www.investopedia. com/terms/s/sensitivityanalysis.asp

Shah, V. (2019). *9 Main Security Challenges for the Future of the Internet Of Things (IoT).* https://readwrite.com/2019/09/05/9-main-security-challenges-for-the-future-of-the-internet-of-things-iot/

Singh, D., Singh, N., & Sharma, D. (n.d.). *NCERT Solutions books Model Test Papers Question Pdf.* https://ncerthelp.com/

What are the 5 risk management process steps? (2018, June 26). *Continuing Professional Development*. https://continuingprofessionaldevelopment.org/risk-management-steps-in-risk-management-process/

What is the Internet of things? | IoT technology. (n.d.). *SAP*. https://www.sap.com/india/trends/internet-of-things.html

Chapter 3
Supply Chain Management for Agri Foods Using Blockchain Technology

Niranjan Dandekar
Birla Institute of Technology and Science, Pilani, India

Amit Dua
Birla Institute of Technology and Science, Pilani, India

Manik Lal Das

Dhirubhai Ambani Institute of Information and Communication Technology, India

Viral A. Shah
Dhirubhai Ambani Institute of Information and Communication Technology, India

ABSTRACT

The agricultural supply chain consists of many participants like producer (generally farmer), consumer (people who buy the product and consume them), wholesalers, and retailers. This system consists of many levels of mediator parties as well which have different policies of the commission. Due to the difference in these policies, the producers do not get their fair share of price. Due to the varying prices, consumers also suffer as they do not get the right quality of the product for the right price. There are no central records maintained regarding the transactions between the participants which could lead to many serious problems. To tackle the above-mentioned issues, we need a holistic approach that can provide solutions to most of the above issues. Here, blockchain-based solution can be used to achieve traceability (we can trace the whereabouts of the product, the origin of the product, etc.), transparency (so that a sense of trust is achieved), fairness (by removing the intermediaries), assurance of food safety and pricing (so that nobody has to bear the loss).

DOI: 10.4018/978-1-7998-5876-8.ch003

1. INTRODUCTION

1.1 A Brief Overview of Blockchain

Blockchain is an immutable ledger which is shared and visible to all the participants of that specific system. Blockchain consists of blocks of transactions which are arranged in some specific order. The addition of transactions into the block is based on some consensus algorithm. Thus, the transactions to be added into the block and order of those transactions is decided based on the consensus algorithm. Once the data is inserted into the blockchain as a block, its subsequent block contains a hash of its previous block. Thus, making it hard to change any intermediate blocks.

Initially, blockchain was thought to be used only in cryptocurrency systems like Bitcoin, Ethereum, etc. But nowadays, Blockchain is used in various sectors to provide transparency and security to the data.

1.1.1 Data Structures

Linked list can be thought of as a list of nodes chained together using the address of the next node. The following diagram shows a singly linked list. Here, the elements are stored in a linear fashion but unlike arrays these do not facilitate spatial locality. That means, even though the elements can be accessed in a linear form, but the memory locations in which these are stored are not necessarily contiguous. To take an example, Node A in the diagram is location 0x100, but Node B which is the next node in the linked list is stored at a memory location 0x900.

The number mentioned below each node is the address of that node.

Figure 1. Linked List

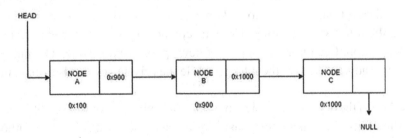

This data structure forms the basis of blockchain technology. Although, in blockchain technology, addresses are not used as a chaining tool because in the

Internet scenario these addresses become obsolete, i.e. when a machine B is used, addresses specific to machine A will be of no use to it.

Thus, we now need to fix upon a mechanism which can be used globally without becoming obsolete. To ensure this, Hashing is used to connect one node to the other in case of blockchain. The details of Hashing will be provided in the subsequent sections.

1.1.2 Cryptography

Cryptography is used to protect the information, be it of any kind, so that only the person intended can have access to the information in a meaningful form. This protection is done using a technique called hidden writing. Here, codes are used to convert the information into something which seems meaningless to the rest of the world, but with proper use of a tool called a KEY, this information can be converted back into a meaningful one by the intended person (Stallings, 2013).

The following terms will be used in the subsequent sections.

- Plaintext: The original message
- Ciphertext: The coded meaningless message
- Encryption: The process of converting from plaintext to ciphertext using an encryption key
- Decryption: The process of converting from ciphertext to plaintext using a decryption key.

Now, based on the key used the encryption algorithms can be classified into two main categories:

- **Private key Cryptography**: Here, the key used is the same for both encryption and decryption. So, it has to be kept a secret from the rest of the world.
- **Public key Cryptography**: Here, a separate key is used for encryption and decryption. Each user has a pair of keys, public and private. The public key can be advertised over the internet while the private key needs to be kept safe.

Security of the data basically depends on 3 main pillars: Confidentiality, Integrity and Availability. Confidentiality basically means that to be secure, unauthorized access to the information must be prevented. Similarly, the information also needs to be protected from unauthorized changes which are made to it, which is maintaining Integrity of the data. Availability as the word suggests means that the information must always be available for access to its authorized users. To implement the above pillars of security, various techniques are used which provide one or more of the above services. In this section we are only interested in Cryptographic Hashing because of its use in the implementation of the blockchain. Hashing is used to provide integrity. Hashing basically uses a hash function to convert any form of data into a fixed size output which is called Message Digest or fingerprint of the data. The advantage of using this is even if 1 bit of input data is changed, its corresponding Message Digest is completely different. Another advantage is that it is very less likely that the Message Digest of two non-identical messages are the same, which is collision resistance. So, it is not feasible to guess the data given its Message Digest.

1.2 Game Theory

The basic goal of Game Theory in cryptocurrencies is to build a network by modelling human reasoning into it yet, it requires no human intervention and produces positive outcomes every time. It basically means that a cryptocurrency needs to function consistently without any existence of a third party. Let us understand this concept more clearly by taking an example of Bitcoin, a cryptocurrency which makes the actors (miners) do the verification part of it by incentivizing them. Here, miners are supposed to use their computing power to secure the Bitcoin network in a way, which in return awards them with Bitcoins. So, the goal of doing the work without involving a third party is achieved.

The Bitcoin creators also had to ensure that all the players were following certain protocols and rules. These protocols are used to punish or reward the players of the game for their behaviour. In Bitcoin, this protocol is implemented by making the mining process extremely difficult and inefficient. For proposing their block, miners need to solve a hash puzzle and attach the proof of its solution which exhausts a high amount of computing resources of miners. This is the mechanism implemented by Bitcoin to ensure consensus among the system, which is PoW(Proof of Work). Various other mechanisms which make use of such incentives are also implemented in other cryptocurrencies.

1.3 Consensus and Redundancy

- **Consensus**: As we saw in the last subsection, every cryptocurrency has implemented a consensus mechanism. Now, the question is what Consensus is and why is it so important which will be answered in this subsection. Consensus is basically a fault-tolerant mechanism which is used in computer science to agree on a particular value or a particular state of the network. This process is only required in decentralized systems like Cryptocurrencies because in a centralized system, the value or the state can be obtained through a central entity and hence is guaranteed to be the same if that entity is not compromised. So, it is an important aspect to keep the system consistent so that all players get the same value or the state.

- **Replication:** As the name suggests, replication is making a copy of any and every data and sending it to every other node in the system through the network.

So as a result, every transaction made in the network, however small it maybe, is reflected in the entire network. Let us take an example to understand the role of Replication in Blockchain. Bitcoin consists of two main types of nodes: Full nodes and Light nodes. As the name suggests, Full nodes are the ones with every transaction made in the network since the Genesis Block. There are multiple Full Nodes present at different locations in the system. These nodes act as a verifier to authenticate each transaction made in that blockchain network. Full nodes receive the data through replication. The second type of nodes are the Light nodes which do have to maintain the entire copy of the transactions.

1.4 Merkle Hash Tree

As we are familiar with the normal tree data structure in computer science, Merkle Hash Tree is a variant of it which has hashes of data as its non-leaf nodes. Rest of the concepts remain the same where the number of children for a node can vary. Here, the main point to be nodes is that all the leaf nodes are at the same height (depth) and are as far left as possible.

As seen in the previous section, the hash functions are used to check integrity of the data. Merkle Hash Tree is basically a data structure which uses hashing for better data synchronization and to check its integrity.Let us see the example of a binary merkle tree to understand the concept better.

Now consider a scenario where you must check a transaction that was made let's say 2 years ago. Now, checking the hashes of the entire transaction list right from the genesis block is not a feasible option. So, we use Merkle Trees instead where for the verification part, we just have to check a part of the tree and not the entire list of transactions.

Another significant advantage that it provides is that it can map huge data efficiently and identify small changes made to any data with minimal effort. To do this, we must check the root hash of the tree, if it does not match, then the data is changed. One more thing that we can gain from the above discussion is that the root of the tree can be used as the fingerprint for the entire data.

Figure 2. Merkle Tree

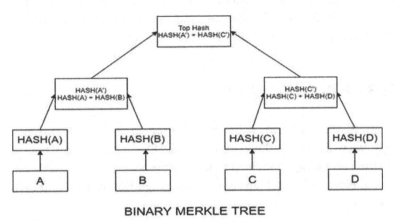

BINARY MERKLE TREE

1.5 Digital Signature

Digital Signature is a cryptographic approach to provide authenticity and integrity of the data. Here data can be anything software, images, videos, etc. With the above-mentioned services, it also provides one more important service, non-repudiation which was previously unknown to us (Stallings, 2013). Non-repudiation in layman's terms means that if I send a document to person X, then after some time I cannot deny sending the document.

The Digital Signature is divided into three main parts, Key Generation Algorithm, Signing Algorithm and Signature Verification Algorithm. The basic functionality of Digital Signature as mentioned above is providing authenticity, integrity, and non-repudiation. We will understand the process of Digital Signature through the following steps:

1. Firstly, we compute the hash of the data to be signed. The used hash function is mentioned in the information of Digital Signature as it will be used by the receiver as well.
2. Then we encrypt this hash using our private key which is also called the Signature Key. The encrypted hash along with other information is the digital signature of that data. This is appended with the data and is sent.
3. The receiver receives the data along with its digital signature. The data itself is encrypted but let's not get into that for now.
4. Receiver decrypts the received Digital Signature using the public key of the sender and gets the hash of the data.

5.   Then using the algorithm mentioned in the information, the receiver computes the hash of the data sent. If this hash matches the one obtained from decryption, then we can guarantee that the data is not changed.

2. TYPES OF BLOCKCHAINS

As we saw all the background details required to understand the blockchain technology, we will now see the various types of blockchains that exist which have been classified according to their uses and their properties.

Two main types of blockchains are Permissioned Blockchains and Permission-less Blockchains.

- **Permissioned Blockchains**: Also known as Private blockchains, these act as a closed ecosystem where access is restricted to a group of people only. The transactions made by these people are not visible to the outside world. Typically, these types of blockchains are used within an organization where it thinks that the data is too sensitive to be public. To verify the transactions made in these types of blockchains you are required to have the permission of a central authority controlling that blockchain. Thus, because of the presence of a central entity, these blockchains are more centralized in nature (Nadir, 2019; Medium, 2020). Ripple can be thought of a perfect example of a permissioned blockchain. Also, Hyperledger and Corda are private blockchains. There are certain advantages of using a private blockchain, which are as follows,
  - These blockchains have more scalability as compared to the public blockchains.
  - Due to the presence of central authority, various levels or steps of governance can be implemented according to the rules of that particular organization.
  - Clearly, because of a smaller number of participants, the speed of the overall blockchain network is high and thus more efficient performance.
- **Permissionless Blockchains:** Also known as public blockchains, are the open source variant of blockchains where anyone is allowed to participate as full nodes, light nodes, community members, etc. Here, all the transactions made are fully transparent in nature. Anyone from the outside world can view the transaction. These blockchains are fully decentralized in nature unlike the private ones and so do not have any central authority controlling them. Now, because of the absence of a central authority, these blockchains need to have some sort of tokens (currency of that blockchain) to incentivize and

reward the participants. Now, certain characteristics of public blockchain are as follows:

- ○ Currency / Token Requirement: As mentioned earlier, public blockchains require incentives or rewards as there is no central entity and the verification part is to be done by the participants only. One purpose served by introducing a token is that trust can be built in the blockchain network.
- ○ Transparency: This property states that the participants can know every detail in the system. Let us take an example of Bitcoin to understand the transparency in it. To access any Bitcoin account, you need to have private keys (related to each of the accounts) with you, without which the access is not possible. So, we can consider this as a default, which needs to be provided to the users in any case. But transparency here enables the users to also get addresses (of accounts) and see all the transactions that have been done till that point of time.
- ○ Presence of Decentralization: There is no central entity present in this type of blockchain as mentioned earlier. So theoretically to modify any protocol, make any changes to the network, or for any sort of malicious activity, 51% of the users need to agree on it, which is very difficult practically.

Now, as we saw the major characteristics/advantages of the two types of blockchains (Public and Private), there are also a few disadvantages of both. From the above points we can note that we not only require privacy from the Private or Permissioned one, but also transparency and security from the Public one. So, to combine the above benefits, there exists a Hybrid blockchain. A perfect example of a hybrid blockchain is Dragon-chain. This provides the businesses with significant flexibility.

3. THE PROPOSED AGRI-CHAIN SYSTEM

In this section, we will look at the detailed working of the system including all the algorithms. It also gives a basic idea about the process flows happening between different participants in the system.

As mentioned in the diagram, the various participants in the system are farmers (producing the goods), wholesaler, end consumer, retailer and the APMCs (I.E.S, 2016). Here, APMCs is the government appointed committee which trades in certain products based on the acts issued by the government. Here, transaction is defined by the following entities:

Transaction = { Transaction$_{id}$, Product$_{id}$, Product$_{type}$, Product$_{Qty}$, Seller$_{ID}$, Seller$_{Signature}$,

Buyer$_{id}$, Buyer$_{signature}$, Product$_{Status}$, PreviousBlock$_{Number}$, Product$_{Details}$, Price }

Transaction$_{id}$: ID of the transaction
Product$_{id}$: ID of the product
Product$_{type}$: Type of the product
Product$_{Qty}$: Qty of the product
Seller$_{ID}$: Identity of seller
Seller$_{Signature}$: Signature of the seller
Buyer$_{id}$: Identity of Buyer
Buyer$_{Signature}$: Signature of the buyer
Product$_{Status}$: Status of the product
PreviousBlock$_{Number}$: Previous block for this transaction
Product$_{Details}$: Other product details
Price: Price of the product being transacted

We can divide the process of communication between all these entities into three main parts:

1.   Farmer - APMC process flow
2.   APMC - Wholesaler process flow
3.   Seller - Buyer Process Flow

We will start with the Farmer - APMC process flow.

This part depicts the communication between the farmer and APMC admin and also with the other entities in the APMC, which include Publisher, Assaying Operator and Entry Operator.

Here, whenever a farmer wants his products to be published so that they get purchased, he will need to advertise it first by sending the details to APMC Admin. This is done by the Sending Product Details algorithm. Here, the farmer supplies the required information associated with the product like Type of the Product, Quantity of the product produced, and ID of the farmer. This is converted into a transaction and is digitally signed using Farmer's ID. We have already seen what Digital Signature is and how it is used. Then this will be sent to the APMC Admin (Viral Shah, n.d.).

Now, once the farmer has sent the details of the product he wishes to sell, it needs to be verified. This is to avoid any fraudulent transactions. So, the APMC Admin executes this algorithm to verify the transaction. APMC Admin checks whether

Figure 3. Farmer-APMC Process Flow

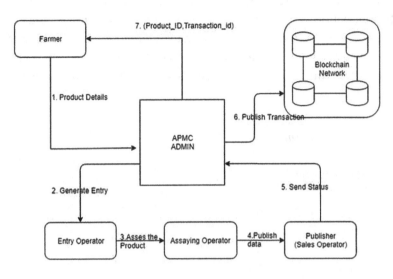

Algorithm 1. Sending Product details

```
Inputs: Product_Type, Product_Qty, Farmer_id
Output: Transaction txn
1 Transaction txn = new Transaction(Product_Type, Product_Qty, Farme
r_id);
2 Sig_sk f id(txn);
3 Send txn to APMC Admin;
```

Algorithm 2. Send for Entry

```
Inputs: Transaction txn
Output: Transaction updated_txn
1 if Farmer id is registered && Signature is valid then
2     txn.Product Status = "New";
3     Sig_sk admin (txn);
4     Send txn to Entry Operator;
5 else
6     txn.Product Status = "Rejected";
7     return Error;
8 end
```

the provided ID is registered, and the signature is valid, if both check out, Admin labels the transaction as New and sends it to the Entry Operator. If either the ID is not registered, or the signature is not valid then the transaction is rejected and error is returned. As a result, the product is not entered, and the transaction is invalid. As mentioned earlier, this is a necessary precaution to curb malicious activities (Viral Shah, n.d.).

Algorithm 3. Generate Entry

```
Inputs: Transaction txn
Output: Product id
1 if Signatures are valid then
2       Product_id = SHA_256 (Farmer id, Product Type, Product Qty,
timestamp);
3       txn.Product_Status = "Generated";
4       Sig_skEO(txn);
5       Send txn to Assaying Operator;
6 else
7       txn.Product Status = "Rejected";
8       return Error;
9 end
```

Now, once the transaction is sent to the Entry Operator after verification, the Entry Operator would carry out the necessary steps like vehicle entry management (for the farmer's actual vehicle), Farmer's ID verification. Then Entry Operator will generate a Product ID which will be associated with the product as a unique identifier. Product ID is a hash of product details and farmer ID. SHA_{256} is used here. Then the relevant status is associated with the product. If successful, signature of Entry Operator will be marked on the transaction and then the transaction is forwarded to the Assaying Operator (Viral Shah, n.d.).

When the Assaying Operator receives the product from the Entry Operator, he needs to check the quality of the product so that the product is compatible with the quality guidelines. To do so, the Assaying Operator will get a sample of the product and perform the required quality tests in the APMC premises itself. The values will be compared with predefined ranges for acceptance. If the value obtained from the sample is within the predefined ranges, then it is accepted and the required parameters like Quality and Status are updated. The status here is updated to "Verified". Then to prove that the Assaying Operator was indeed genuine, his signature is also captured in the transaction. Then this transaction is forwarded to the Sales Operator (Viral Shah, n.d.).

Algorithm 4. Assess Product

```
Inputs: Transaction Product id txn
Output: Product Quality Results
1 if Product id is valid then
2      if results is in ranges then
3            txn.product quality = results;
4            txn.Product Status = "Verified";
5            Sig_{skAO}(txn);
6            Send txn to Sales Operator;
7      else
8            txn.Product Status = "Rejected";
9            return Error;
10    end
11 else
12    txn.Product Status = "Rejected";
13    return Error;
14 end
```

Algorithm 5. Sales Approval

```
Inputs:Transaction_{Productid}txn
Output: Transaction_{Productid}updated_txn
1 if Signatures are valid then
2      Get the weight of the product;
3      Get the current price for Producttype;
4      txn.price = price;
5      txn.ProductStatus = "Approved";
6      Generate the sales agreement;
7      Sig_{skSO}(txn);
8      Send txn to APMC Admin;
9  else
10     txn.ProductStatus = "Rejected";
11     return Error;
12 end
```

Once the Sales Operator receives the transaction from the Assaying Operator, the Sales Operator would calculate the weight of the product and acquire the price details of the product. This information would be updated into the transaction. Then the status of the product would be updated as "Approved". After updating the status, an agreement would be generated between buyer and the seller of the product. Once again to verify the identity of the operator, his signature is captured into the transaction. Then this transaction is sent to APMC Admin for approval. If the rest of the signatures from the previous processes are not valid, then this transaction is "Rejected" (Viral Shah, n.d.).

Algorithm 6. Publish Transaction

```
Inputs:Transaction_Productid txn
Output: Transaction_Productid txn, Transaction_id
1    if (Signatures are valid) && (Sales Agreement is valid)
then
2        txn.transaction_id = SHA256(txn);
3        txn.Product_Status = "Available";
4        Sig_sk admin (txn);
5        Add Transaction to Block(txn);
6        Send (Product_id, Transaction_id) to Farmer_id;
7    else
8        txn.Product_Status = "Rejected";
9        return Error;
10 end
```

After completion of all the above steps, the APMC receives the transaction with all the required details including Sales Agreement. APMC Admin verifies the signatures of all the entities. It also verifies the Sales Agreement made in the last algorithm. If all the details check out, APMC Admin updates the product transaction to "Available" and signs the transaction. Then this is added to the block which will be eventually added to the blockchain. Then the transaction status is sent to the farmer (Viral Shah, n.d.).

Now coming to the APMC - Wholesaler process flow,

This subsection of algorithms gives an idea about the basic process flow which takes place from APMC to the wholesaler who wants to buy the product. In order to do so, the details can be obtained from the blockchain. Then a buy request is generated. The step by step explanation of this process will be given as algorithms implemented to do their respective functions. The name of the algorithm will be intuitive enough to just like the ones mentioned in the previous subsection of the algorithms.

Figure 4. APMC-wholesaler Process Flow

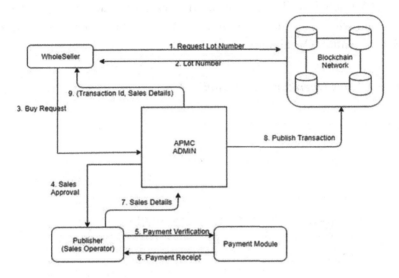

Algorithm 7. Buy Request

```
Inputs: Product_id
Output: Transaction txn
1 Transaction txn = new Transaction(Product_Id);
2 txn.previous_block = Get-BlockNumber (Product_id);
3 Sig_sk buyer(txn);
4 Send (txn) to APMC Admin;
```

Algorithm 8. Sales Operator Approval

```
Inputs:Transaction_Productid txn
1 if txn is valid and Sig_sk buyer is valid then
2      send txn to Sales Operator;
3 else
4      return ERROR;
5 end
```

Now as introduced, to buy the product, the wholesaler needs to fetch the data from the blockchain. To do so, the wholesaler gives the input as product $_{ID}$ and it creates a new transaction. Then the product is searched in the blockchain and details of it are sent to the APMC admin. As usually done, the transaction is signed with the Buyer's signature (Viral Shah, n.d.).

Now, APMC admin will receive the newly created transaction from the previous algorithm and will verify the signature of Buyer (wholesaler) and sends it further to the Sales Operator (Viral Shah, n.d.).

Algorithm 9. Sales Operator Verification

```
Inputs:Transaction_Productid txn
Output: Transaction_Productid updated_txn
1 if Product_id status is "Available" then
2       receipt = Payment-Verification (Product_id, Buyer_id);
3       if receipt is valid then
4            txn.payment - receipt = receipt;
5            txn.Product_Status = "Approved for Sale";
6            Sig_skSO(txn);
7            send txn to APMC Admin;
8       else
9            txn.ProductStatus = "Rejected";
10           return ERROR;
11      end
12 else
13      txn.ProductStatus = "Rejected";
14      return ERROR;
15 end
```

The main aim of this algorithm is to verify whether the payment done is genuine and valid or not. To verify, the Sales Operator will call the payment module and get the receipt of the payment. Now if the payment is verified, the operator would update the same in the transaction. Operator also changes the status of the transaction to "Approved for Sale". Now operator signature is included like the previous algorithms, and then it is sent to APMC Admin (Viral Shah, n.d.).

Algorithm 10. Payment Verification

```
Inputs: Product_id, Buyer_id
Output: Payment - Receipt
1 if Product_id status is "Available" then
2      calculate Price for the Product_id;
3      Get Payment from Buyerid;
4      if Payment is successful then
5           Generate Payment - Receipt;
6           send Payment - Receipt to Sales Operator;
7      else
8           return ERROR;
9      end
10 else
11     return ERROR;
12 end
```

This is the payment verification module that we talked about in the previous algorithm. The input to this algorithm will be the $Product_{id}$ and the $Buyer_{id}$. This module will first check the availability of the product and get the current price for the product from the market. Then that amount will be debited from the buyer's account and a receipt will be generated. This receipt will be sent to APMC Admin which will be used by it for the verification (Viral Shah, n.d.).

Algorithm 11. Publish Transaction

```
Inputs:Transaction_Productid txn
1 if Signatures are valid then
2      txn.transaction_id = SHA256(txn);
3      txn.Product_status = "Sold-to-WH(Buyer_id)";
4      Sig_sk admin (txn);
5      Add Transaction to Block(txn);
6      Send (Transaction_id, Payment - Receipt,) to Buyer_id;
7 else
8      return Error;
9 end
```

Figure 5. Buyer Seller Process Flow

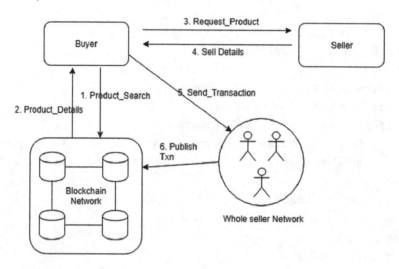

Algorithm 12. Buyer Buy Request

```
Inputs: Product id
Output: Transaction txn
1 Transaction txn = new Transaction(Product_id, Buyer_id,
Seller_id);
2 Sig_sk bid (txn);
3 Send txn to Seller S_id ;
```

Algorithm 13. Seller Response

```
Inputs: Transaction txn
Output: Transaction updated_txn
1 if Signature is valid & Product_id is available then
2     txn.price = price txn.status = "Available to Sell" Sig_sksid
(txn);
3     Send txn to Buyer S_id ;
4 else
5     txn.status = "Not Available";
6 end
7 Send txn to Buyer B_id ;
```

Algorithm 14. Buyer Approval

```
Inputs: Transaction txn
Output: Transaction updated_txn
1 if Signature is valid & agreed on the details then
2     txn.status = "Available With Seller_id ";
3     Sig_sk bid (txn);
4     Send txn to Wholesaler Network;
5 else
6     Update the details;
7     send back to Seller S_id ;
8 end
```

Now after the "Sales Operator Verification" algorithm, it sends the signed transaction to APMC Admin. Admin would verify all the signatures included in the transactions and change the transaction status to "SOLD-TO-WHOLESALER(ID)". The transaction will be signed by the APMC Admin and then added to the blockchain. The transaction details will be sent to the buyer (Viral Shah, n.d.).

Now coming to Buyer-Seller process flow,

As covered in the last subsections of algorithms, the product now is available with the wholesaler. Here, the wholesaler is the one who has direct contact with the producer of the product. After that, the wholesaler can supply it to anybody right from retailers to industries using it as a raw material. To do so, the buyer needs to get the product details from the blockchain. Both the participants of the transaction have A Mutual Agreement signed between them. This Mutual Agreement will be available in the transaction itself. The next subsection of algorithms will depict how these processes are carried out.

As mentioned above, to buy the product, the buyer would fetch the details of the product from the blockchain. So, the input to this algorithm will be Product$_{id}$. Now as mentioned in the algorithm, a new transaction will be created which will have the details of the product, buyer and seller. This transaction will also include the signature of the buyer. This transaction is further sent to the Seller (Viral Shah, n.d.).

When the seller receives the request forwarded in the last transaction, it updates the price of the product based on the current price in the market. It will subsequently also update the status of the product to "Available to Sell (Buyer ID)". The transaction will also include the signature of the Seller and will be sent back to the Buyer (Viral Shah, n.d.).

After the Buyer receives the details related to the product from the Seller, the details are verified by the Buyer. If they match with the ones mentioned in the transaction, then the transaction is forwarded to the wholesaler network for approval (Viral Shah, n.d.).

Algorithm 15. Wholesaler Approval

```
Inputs: Transaction txn
Output: Transaction updated_txn
1 if Signatures are valid then
2       receipt = Payment-Verification (Product_id, Buyer_id);
3       if receipt is valid then
4           txn.payment - receipt = receipt;
5           txn.Product Status = "Available with B_id ";
6           Sig sk WH-ID (txn);
7           Add Transaction to Block(txn);
8           Send (Transaction id, Payment - Receipt) to Buyer id
;
9       else
10          txn.Product Status = "Rejected";
11          return ERROR;
12      end
13 else
14      txn.Product Status = "Rejected";
15      return ERROR;
16end
```

This is the last part of the process before the product is owned by the Buyer. The wholesaler will verify all the signatures on the transaction and will check for the payment by the Buyer. After the payment is confirmed, the ownership of the product will be changed to the Buyer. Also, the amount transferred by the Buyer will be credited into the Seller's account (Viral Shah, n.d.).

4. IMPLEMENTATION DETAILS

In the previous section we saw all the underlying algorithms in the system. Now, to simulate these algorithms and turn it into an actual working system various steps will be followed. These steps will be discussed here in detail. First of all we will be using Hyperledger Fabric, which as we discussed earlier is a Private Blockchain. The main aim of using Hyperledger here is that the network will be limited to the participants (like farmers, APMC, etc.) and the data shared between them will not be visible outside the blockchain. So the overall business network will be developed in the Hyperledger Fabric itself. Now, all the algorithms that we proposed and discussed above are implemented in Hyperledger Composer Modeling Language (CTO) and the transactions which will be initiated by the parties among themselves are implemented in JavaScript. These files will contain transaction logic which would be executed by transaction processor functions on the fabric peers.

Figure 6. System Setup Diagram

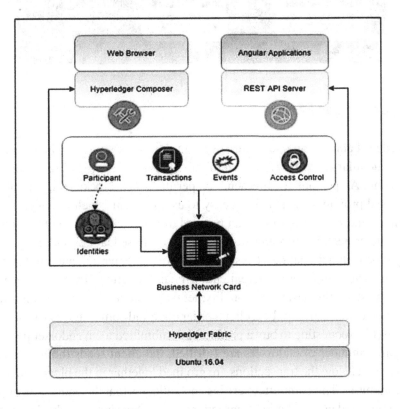

The above diagram describes how the system setup is done. The 3 key aspects that we need to understand in the above diagram are Hyperledger Fabric, Hyperledger Composer and Business Network Card. Now we will see the importance of these three components and the role that they will play in setting up our system (Viral Shah, n.d.).

Figure 7. ComposerArchitecture

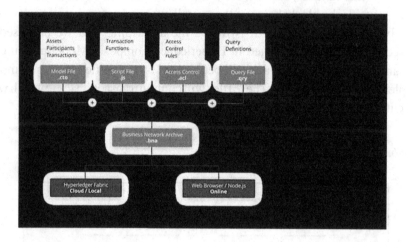

4.1 Hyperledger Fabric

Hyperledger Fabric is an open source system developed by Linux Foundations. It acts as a modular and extensible system for deploying and operating permissioned blockchains. As per our requirements of permissioned blockchain, this platform will be used prominently. This is an easy to use platform which provides a variety of modules and functions which can be used directly without implementing them again in the project. So, this enables easy reuse of those features and integration of already existing functionalities. It also allows us to specify participants on the network which can have completely different authority and functionality over the network.

To understand the basic functionality, let us consider an example consisting of an endorser, endorsement policy, client, order node and committer. The transactions proposed (like requesting to buy a product) are submitted to an endorser peer. After the required number of endorsers are fulfilled, the client sends the transaction to the order node. Now the transactions are grouped together in the block and are sent to the committer. The committer verifies and validates that the endorsement policy was satisfied, and no conflicting transactions exist. Once both the checks are made, the transactions are committed to the ledger (H Fabric, 2019).

4.2 Hyperledger Composer

Hyperledger Composer is an open source development framework which facilitates development of blockchain applications on top of the Hyperledger Fabric environment. It also helps to implement the idea in terms of a business network containing participants, assets, and business rules combinedly known as Transactions (H Composer, 2019).

Now as mentioned above, we can define participants, assets and business rules using Modeling Language (CTO) which is provided by the Hyperledger Composer. The composer assigns each participant with a unique identity which consists of a Public and a Private key to interact with the system and other participants in it.

4.3 Business Network Card

Business Network Card is an important component in the system, as the only possible way to access the blockchain is through a valid business card. For the sake of simplicity, we can relate the Business Network Card to a government approved identification card, like a Driving License. Just as a valid Govt ID allows the participant to avail various services, the Business Network Card allows the participants to connect to the network. Based on this Card, the access control rules are decided for the participant. The admin is responsible for creating business card associated with each participant. When the card is used for the first time, a public key and a private key are associated with the card for unique identification of each participant. The business network archive consists of model, transaction, permission, and event files.

4.4 System Methodology

This subsection will combine all the above components and give detailed steps which are followed by the system using all the components mentioned above.

- Initially Hyperledger Fabric is to be installed with all the necessary docker images such that all the modules that are required like organization, peer, Couch DB, orderer, etc. All these components will be running in the background and the Hyperledger composer will be initialized.
- The composer will contain a model.cto file which is used to define Participants, Transactions and Assets.

Participants of our system will include Farmer, APMC, Entry Operator, Assaying Operator, Sales Operator, Wholesaler, Retailer and Customer.
Assets will be Products, Shipments and OrderContract.
Transactions are defined as and when required in each algorithm.

- After the above step, a business network is deployed, and a business network archive file is created which is a complete package of the business network.

- After the network is established, we will need to create a connection file for the fabric connection and also identify public and private keys for the admin user. This way we create a business card for the admin user which is responsible for creating network cards for all the participants. This Admin card is registered with the network using the **import** command.
- Eventually, based on the reputation of APMC, wholesaler, etc. the Admin role can be passed on to them. So, once a new participant is added in the system identities are issued to this user by the Admin. Identities include assigning of public and private keys.
- As per the roles assigned to the participants in the system, they perform certain tasks. Each transaction created in doing those tasks is stored permanently in the ledger using transaction id and timestamp.

5. CONCLUSION

In this chapter we discussed about the traditional agricultural supply chain system's issues and shown how blockchain can overcome the problems associated with the existing supply chain. To learn more about the Blockchain technology, we have provided an overview of all the basics required to understand how Blockchain technology works. Transparency, Traceability and Fairness are the most prominent challenge in the existing agricultural supply chain. We proposed a blockchain-empowered Agri-chain system with detailed operation flow along with algorithms pertaining to various transactions and participant entities involved in the system. We have provided the implementation details of the proposed system.

REFERENCES

Androulaki, E. (2018). *Hyperledger Fabric: A Distributed Operating System for Permissioned Blockchains*. Academic Press.

Buterin, V. (n.d.). *A next-generation smart contract and decentralized application platform*. https://github.com/ethereum/wiki/wiki/White-Paper

Composer, H. (2019). *Welcome to hyperledger composer*. https://hyperledger.github.io/composer/latest/introduction/introduction.html

Fabric, H. (2019). *Business network cards*. https://hyperledger.github.io/composer/v0.16/playground/id-cards-playground

I.E.S. (2016). *Agricultural produce market committee (APMC)*. http://www.arthapedia. in/index.php%3Ftitle%3DAgricultural_Produce_Market_Committee_(APMC)

Malik, S., Dedeoglu, V., Kanhere, S. S., & Jurdak, R. (2019). TrustChain: Trust Management in Blockchain and IoT Supported Supply Chains. *2019 IEEE International Conference on Blockchain (Blockchain)*, 184-193. 10.1109/Blockchain.2019.00032

Nadir, R. M. (2019). Comparative study of permissioned blockchain solutions for enterprises. *2019 International Conference on Innovative Computing (ICIC)*, 1-6. 10.1109/ICIC48496.2019.8966735

Nakamoto, S. (n.d.). *Bitcoin: A peer-to-peer electronic cash system*. https://bitcoin. org/bitcoin.pdf

Pourmajidi, W., & Miranskyy, A. V. (n.d.). *Logchain: Blockchain-assisted log storage*. Available: https://arxiv.org/abs/1805.08868

Private vs Public Blockchain in a nutshell. (n.d.). https://medium.com/coinmonks/ public-vs-private-blockchain-in-a-nutshell-c9fe284fa39f#:~:text=Public%20 blockchains%20are%20decentralised%2C%20no,Blockchain%20is%20a%20 permissioned%20blockchain

Shah, V. (2019). *AgriChain: Supply-Chain Management for Agri Foods using Block-chain Technology* (Master Thesis). DA-IICT, Gandhinagar.

Stallings, W. (2013). *Cryptography and Network Security: Principles and Practice* (6th ed.). Prentice Hall Press.

Yang, X., Chen, Y., & Chen, X. (2019). Effective Scheme against 51% Attack on Proof-of-Work Blockchain with History Weighted Information. *2019 IEEE International Conference on Blockchain (Blockchain)*, 261-265. 10.1109/Blockchain.2019.00041

Chapter 4
Google Stock Movement:
A Time Series Study Using LSTM Network

Nishu Sethi
Amity School of Engineering and Technology, Amity University, Gurugram, India

Shalini Bhaskar Bajaj
Amity School of Engineering and Technology, Amity University, Gurugram, India

Jitendra Kumar Verma
 https://orcid.org/0000-0003-4103-4218
Amity School of Engineering and Technology, Amity University, Gurugram, India

Utpal Shrivastava
Amity School of Engineering and Technology, Amity University, Gurugram, India

ABSTRACT

Human beings tend to make predictions about future events irrespective of probability of occurrence. We are fascinated to solve puzzles and patterns. One such area which intrigues many, full of complexity and unpredicted behavior, is the stock market. For the last decade or so, we have been trying to find patterns and understand the behavior of the stock market with the help of robust computation systems and new approaches to extract and analyze the huge amount of data. In this chapter, the authors have tried to understand stock price movement using a long short-term memory (LSTM) network and predict future behavior of stock price.

DOI: 10.4018/978-1-7998-5876-8.ch004

INTRODUCTION

Stock market prediction is pretty complex even in today's technologically advanced world. Generally, it's being said that a stock picked in a random fashion can perform better than a stock chosen by a sophisticated algorithm. Curious minds and investors always try to find patterns in the stock market via different methods of predictions, such as ARIMA, Time Series or the latest trending and advanced methods like Neural Networks and Deep learning models (Javier et al., 2003) (Fama, 1995) (Kim, 2003) (Boettiger & Hastings, 2013).

The history of stock market prediction dated back to the 1980s using simple spreadsheets and registers which held the crucial information about the selling and buying of shares for a particular company. Later on these methods were abandoned due to poor performance on larger datasets and rapid changes occurring in the stock market became a difficult task to solve just by the spreadsheets, then we witnessed time series analysis and fundamental analysis for the companies which helped up to a great extend to predict market behavior back in those days.

Recent years have witnessed changed dynamics in the behavior of the stock market. Stock market is becoming more unpredictable due to various factors involved in the fluctuation of the stock market which in turn raised concern about the methods used by investors and researchers to predict stock market behavior.

LITERATURE REVIEW

In (Lee, 2015) author said that crypto securities market does not require any changes in traditional stock market but there idea of the Blockchain for the crypto securities can be an alternative. According to author there may be need of both the system in parallel. In (Yoo, 2017) author analyzed the Blockchain technology by the cases of different country like Korea and others and concluded that the Blockchain technology from the customer certification field is appropriate. Author also stated that before using this technology it security, safety as well as the cost for the implementation should be first analyzed. In (Lee et al., 2019) author analyzed that previous model made by different researchers is for a single country, they had not considered the global market. The author proposed a model considering the global market using artificial neural network and better results were obtained. In (Janková & Dostál, 2019) author used artificial intelligence for the analysis of the US stock market. A fuzzy model was created by considering the influence of investor, economic optimism, the index of political stability and other sentiment in the market. The results obtained by them showed a good control and supervision of the financial markets. In (Lussange et al., 2019) author used a multi-agent system model for the portfolio management.

A strategy of long term only equity autonomous reinforcement learning algorithms for the forecasting of price and stock trading was followed. The results showed that the rates of agent bankruptcy reduced by a good percentage of greedy agents.

This is when machine learning and neural networks come in handy (De Oliveira et al., 2013). Neural networks are great at learning like a human brain and even on a huge scale compared to the as of the human brain.

Figure 1. Structure of a simple RNN

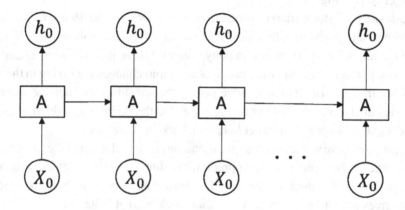

GOOGL STOCK PRICE PREDICTION

Googl has been established since 1998 in the technology field and evolving at a lightning speed. Stock prices for big tech giants like Googl vary a lot in a short timespan which makes it more difficult to predict stock movement (Fama, 1965).

Here we have used **LSTM Neural Network** (one kind of Recurrent Neural Network figure 2) to train it on Googl Stocks (GOOGL) data and predict future prices (Finance, n.d.) (Shah et al., 2018). LSTM is better at learning from big chunks of data and produces a sustainable model to predict the future of stock prices.

RNN: A Brief Overview

As mentioned above LSTM Network is a special type of Recurrent Neural (RNN) Network as shown in figure 1 (Rather et al., 2015). In a simple recurrent neural network, there is a set of repetitive neural units. As the network forwards it passes the data from starting units to the end units i.e. all the units are connected to each other. Initially RNN looks good for all sort of problems ranging from speech recognition to text classification but later on various researchers found drawbacks in the structure of the neural network as well as it performed poorly when compared to benchmark results (Yoshihara et al., 2014).

In this network:

A = One unit of the Neural Network

X_i = Inputs for the units of neural network

h_i = Output from these Units

Main Issues in the RNN

- **Short-Term Memory -** When forwarded too many steps, RNN generally discards the earlier available information which is a huge setback in certain work areas, e.g. text classification.
- **Vanishing Gradient –** Gradient is used to moderate the values of weights to a given neural network, if it gets too small the network neglects it for future learning (LeCun et al., 1998).
- **Exploding Gradient -** Complete opposite of the vanishing gradient, i.e. extra importance to the gradient.

The Solution: Long-Short Term Memory Networks

Both LSTM and RNN work similarly, as the passes data to the upcoming units and LSTM have one improved feature, gates: helps to decide whether to take the information or not (Hochreiter & Schmidhuber, 1997).

Components Of LSTM

- **Cell State:** Acts as a relay to pass the info in the sequence.
- **Forget Gate:** Selector for the information passing between units.
- **Input Gate:** Controls the cell state, by deciding which information to keep.
- **Output Gate:** Selects next hidden state to be activated.
- **Sigmoid:** It helps to regulate the information feed to the LSTM cells.
- **Tanh Function:** Helps to normalize the output from LSTM cells.

Working of LSTM

Step 1: Rectifying the information

Figure 2. Structure of a LSTM Network

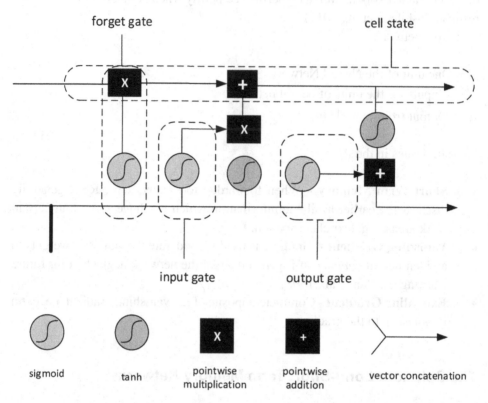

In this step we decide what information to pass on through the cell state and which information should be omitted out from the LSTM network.

At each cell we will have a sigmoid function to help us in the process. Here the output from the last cell is fed to new cell $h_t - 1$ and also new input for the current cell (X_t) is passed through sigmoid function and determines upto what extent we need to keep the information.

This gate is referred to as the forget gate (f_t) as the name suggests it helps to rectify the information.

$$f_t = \sigma (W_{fg} [h_{t-1}, X_t] + b_{fg}) \tag{1}$$

Here W_{fg} and b_{fg} are weights and bias for our forget gate.

Step 2: Feeding the new information

This step involves a two-step process involving sigmoid function to decide if new information needs to be updated or not. Then the tanh layer regulates the old output and current input by giving it an importance on the scale of -1 to 1.

Finally, overall information for the cell state is updated in the last step.

$$\text{info}_t = \sigma \, (W_{in} \, [\, h_{t-1}, X_t \,] + b_{in}) \tag{2}$$

$$New_t = \tanh \, (W_{in} \, [\, h_{t-1}, X_t \,] + b_{in}) \tag{3}$$

$$CS_t = (CS_{t-1} * f_t) + (New_t * \text{info}_t) \tag{4}$$

Here info_t is the information obtained from the sigmoid layer. New_t is the new information obtained from the tanh layer.

CS_t represents the cell state at time t, and CS_{t-1} at time t-1 respectively.

W_{in} and b_{in} are weights and bias values for the input gate.

Step 3: Final cell output

The cell output (h_t) is computed as the filtered version of the output from the current cell (OUT_t).

It's a two-step process where the cell output (OUT_t) is passed through sigmoid to decide which part to keep in the final cell output.

Then the final output is calculated when the tanh layer regulates the current cell state (CS_t).

This whole process is known as output gate.

$$OUT_t = \sigma \, (W_{out} \, [\, h_{t-1}, X_t \,] + b_{out}) \tag{5}$$

$$h_t = OUT_t \, \tanh(CS_t) \tag{6}$$

This process continues for the complete LSTM network. Every cell in the LSTM has the same process for dealing with the information.

Googl Stocks Data

In our research we have considered GOOGL stocks data for 5 years (from June 2010 to June 2015) in the training phase of our LSTM network.

Source: Dataset is obtained from Yahoo Finance Website, which stores Historical data for the stock market. In the training dataset there are a total 1259 rows and 7 columns of data.

In the training dataset as shown in Figure 3, Date on which stock traded, Opening price (Open), highest price on that day (High), Lowest price on that day (Low), Closing price for the day (Close), Adjusted Closing price (Adj Close) and the volume of stocks traded (Volume) is given.

Figure 3. Sample data from the training dataset

```
In [4]:  training_data
Out[4]:
```

	Date	Open	High	Low	Close	Adj Close	Volume
0	2010-06-08	242.348755	242.840561	237.227066	240.823669	240.823669	5405000
1	2010-06-09	242.035797	242.860428	234.474960	235.478439	235.478439	5493300
2	2010-06-10	238.632919	242.671661	236.382553	241.931473	241.931473	5189200
3	2010-06-11	239.691040	242.775970	239.253891	242.671661	242.671661	3586400
4	2010-06-14	245.642334	245.652267	240.033813	240.033813	240.033813	4107200
5	2010-06-15	239.979172	248.583206	239.532074	247.385986	247.385986	8574600
6	2010-06-16	246.481873	250.371567	246.452072	249.015396	249.015396	4608200
7	2010-06-17	250.098358	251.300537	246.740189	248.424240	248.424240	3980200
8	2010-06-18	249.631393	250.108292	247.455536	248.399399	248.399399	5783000
9	2010-06-21	248.334824	248.866364	240.878311	242.701462	242.701462	6005600
10	2010-06-22	243.367126	246.695480	241.295609	241.553925	241.553925	4468200
11	2010-06-23	241.871857	241.871857	237.535065	239.467499	239.467499	4084500
12	2010-06-24	238.280212	239.815231	235.100891	236.014954	236.014954	3811700
13	2010-06-25	236.988617	237.281708	233.759613	234.812775	234.812775	4519500
14	2010-06-28	234.768066	237.232040	232.989624	234.514709	234.514709	3547400

Training Methodology

Step 1: Importing required libraries and loading the training dataset

Here we have two csv files 1) training_set.csv for the model training and 2) testing_set.csv for the testing of our model. Sample data from the training dataset is shown in figure 3.

Training_set contains five years data from 08/06/2010 to 08/06/2015 for the stock movement. For the testing phase we have taken two years of data from 09/06/2015 to 09/06/2017.

Step 2: Plotting the data points

In the graph we can show how the data points are scattered over the years. Initial graph compares the Opening, Closing, High, Low and Adjusted Closing Price for the given day. The graph below(figure 4) represents these parameters.

Figure 4. Graph showing GOOGL stock prices over time period

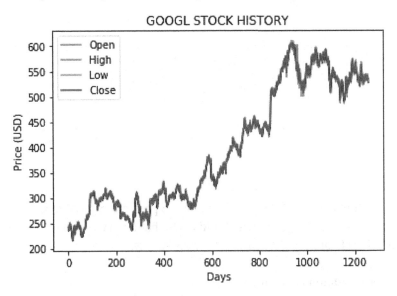

As observable, on the Y-axis the stock price is taken and X-axis represents the days. From the graph it's quite clear that all the prices for any given day are pretty close to each other, which shows that prices varied very slightly on the particular days.

But one more thing to note is the fluctuation in the prices over time period of days to weeks is pretty random and difficult to observe a normal pattern. This graph also validates randomness in the stock movement.

Next thing is the volume graph which shows the total number of stocks traded on a particular day figure 5.

Figure 5. Graph showing number of stocks traded on a given day

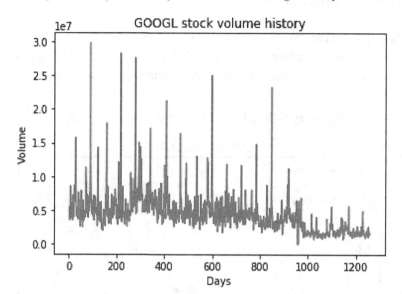

This graph may be useful while deciding the prediction strategies. As there are some high spikes in the graph which indicates that a very high number of shares were traded back and forth during that particular day.

Step 3: Normalization of the training set

These stock prices vary from 240 to maybe up to 470 and so on; hence it's a bit messy to deal with the data points, for better clarity and ease we need to normalize it down to the scale of 0 to 1. It will be better for computation and during the training phase. Unscaled and scaled date sample is shown in figure 6.

Step 4: Creating timestamps

As earlier mentioned, that, LSTM network relies on previous information for future learning, hence we need to decide our timestamp which we will be using in the model while training.

Timestamp: Simply number of characters/data points your network will take into consideration during model run. For example, if you want to keep 60 data points in the memory then set your timestamp = 60.

Step 5: Developing LSTM model

Figure 6. unscaled vs. scaled data

```
In [12]:  train_set
Out[12]:  array([[242.348755],
                 [242.035797],
                 [238.632919],
                 ...,
                 [537.76001 ],
                 [536.349976],
                 [533.309998]])
```

```
In [14]:  scaled_train_set
Out[14]:  array([[0.06282896],
                 [0.06202998],
                 [0.05334246],
                 ...,
                 [0.81701128],
                 [0.81341147],
                 [0.80565043]])
```

In our model we have used Keras for the creation of the neural network. For our network we have the following configuration:

1. Sequential Layer - To initialize our neural network
2. LSTM Layer - This for Long Short-Term Memory layer in the model
3. Dropout - This defines number of connections to be dropped if the model is over fitting
4. Optimizer - We have used 'adam' optimizer for our network
5. Loss type - In our model it has mean square error metrics for evaluation of the error
6. Output Layer - Simply one output neuron layer is connected to the network i.e. for the predicted price

In our network we have three LSTM layers of dimensionality varying different for finding better accuracy. Dropout rate was initially taken as 0.2 that means 20%

of the network connections will be dropped randomly when overfitting occurs in the network (Srivastava et al., 2014).

ANALYSIS AND OPTIMIZATION

In our system setup we have considered **Mean Squared Error** loss function for our LSTM model (Janocha & Czarnecki, 2017). This loss function is as follow.

$$\frac{1}{n}\sum_{i=0}^{n}\left(x_i - y_i\right)^2$$

Here x_i is target value i.e. actual share price and y_i is predicted value i.e. estimated share price using our model. Based on this we try to minimize our loss function and improve predictions.

Another interesting factor to consider is optimization of network. In this model we have selected **Adam Optimizer** as because it's an improved variant of stochastic gradient descent (Kingma & Ba, 2014).

Adam optimizer takes following parameters:

Alpha: Learning rate for the network. It helps to decide when to tune weights for the network.

Beta1 and **Beta2** are decay helps to manage decay rates of moving averages of gradient and squared gradient respectively.

Adam Optimizer is slightly better than other optimization methods as it has bias correction in place (Ruder, 2016).

Table 1. For accuracy of network on different configuration

S. No.	Batch Size	Epochs	Accuracy (MSE)
1	42	100	0.0060
2	32	100	0.0014
3	36	85	0.0072
4	32	75	0.0057
5	30	50	0.0083
6	28	70	0.0062
7	26	65	0.0034
8	24	65	0.0020

Figure 7. Overfitting model

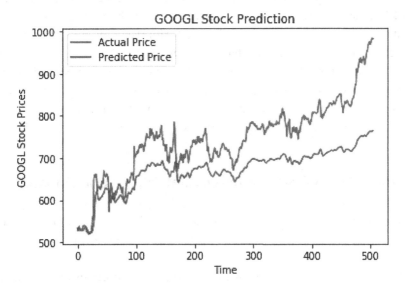

Epochs are the number of times you re-run your network on the data set for better accuracy. If Epoch = 50, it means your network will run 50 times on the same dataset with varied parameters and weights in the network. Batch Size represents the number of data points after which your network will change the bias weights for finding more accurate results. Batch Size = 32 indicates that your model will rearrange the bias weights for the layers after 32 data points. Table 1 shows the accuracy of network on different configurations done during the simulation. For different batch size, Eprochs accuracy is obtained. The results shows that when batch size is 32 where Eprochs are 100, an accuracy of 0.0014 is obtained, When batch size is of 36 and Eprochs are 85, an accuracy of 0.0072 is obtained. For other configuration of batch size and Eprochs, the accuracy lies in the rage of 0.0072 to 0.0014 (Table 1).

RESULTS AND FINDINGS

As we trained initially our model on the standard LSTM network it performed very poorly on the testing dataset. Its accuracy was pretty low. Then we tried changing the number of Epochs and Batch Size for the network. Below is a chart showing accuracy over different configuration of the Epochs and Batch Size.

After trying different configurations, it was clear that model is improving but not up to a good extent. Even when it showed better accuracy it was not predicting prices so well on the testing dataset.

For instance, on **batch size = 32** and **Epochs = 100** it gave a pretty good accuracy of **0.0014** and when tested on the testing data set, the results of Table 1 were obtained.

As it can observed, this model is failing badly for the prediction, despite showing great accuracy during the training phase. It's a sign of an overfitting model (figure 7).

Changing the number of neurons in the LSTM layer as well affected the accuracy of the model. We reduced our hidden layer neurons of LSTM layer as comparable to our inputs. On further investigating and tuning up the **hyperparameters** (bias, batch size, epochs, dropout) for the network we got better results (Loshchilov & Hutter, 2016).

Deciding a Good Combination of Batch Size and Epochs

It's quite difficult to get a great combination of both, in earlier training phase we observed if the batch size was big (> 40) the network performed very poorly on the testing dataset.

Below is a graph (figure 8) showing training and testing results for Batch size = 40 and Epochs = 100.

Figure 8. Poor learning when batch size is too big

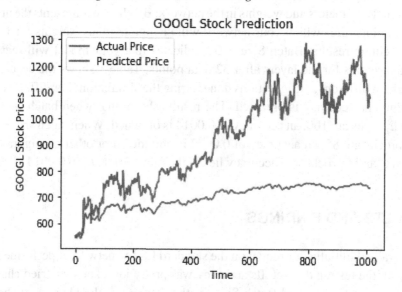

As batch size is big, then the learning curve becomes flat and model trains very poorly on the training data (figure 8), this is entirely because as the batch processes through the model it changes bias values on new batch and if the batch size is too big the dataset is processed way too fast and hence poor results.

Even if we try to make very small batch sizes it will have its own demerits and then model's learning rate will be very slow thus reaching the optimum value will be very hard and also one more threat is of over learning,

Overall batch size should be comparable and medium sized so that learning won't be affected and good results will be obtained.

Epochs also has to be selected properly to avoid over learning or very low training on the dataset.

CONCLUSION

For our training model the hyper parameter selection was crucial. In multiple runs we tried different hidden layer sizes, batch sizes and no. of epochs and one more thing came into play which is Dropout rate: to deal with the overfitting issue (Merity et al., 2017). When we increased the dropout rate to 30% and our LSTM layers size to 50 neurons each, we got better results, for batch size of **24** and **65** Epochs we got an accuracy of **0.0020** and it performed well on the testing data as well. The graph below (figure 9) shows the final results:

Figure 9. Well-trained model performance

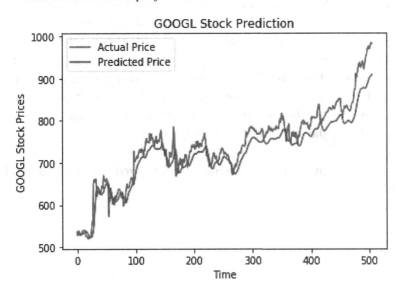

In conclusion, the results obtained from the model are good but not completely accurate because there are still chances of overfitting and predicting the stock prices entirely on its historic data will be pretty naive.

Using a LSTM network is a beginning step to a more sophisticated model which will be more accurate and applicable for various companies. Inflammation in the stock market is the result of various factors including the nation's economic condition, trade regulations, company policies and stockholder's behavior etc.

This model can be comprised with sentimental analysis and study of other market indicators such as fundamental analysis, technical analysis etc. (Li et al., 2014). To make the model more accurate we need to find better hyperparameters for the model and the network architecture can be altered to find if there is any chance of improvement.

The proposed work involves time series analysis of the Googl Stock data. In this study we studied the historic movement and predicted the future price only based on the previous provided stock prices.

Further the outcome of proposed work act as the foundation for a more advanced model for stock price prediction. The aspects to be considered are as follows.

- **Fundamentals and Technical Aspects:** The Company's fundamentals and how the company is operating, corporate governance, company leadership and technical analysis of the stock can help to improve the accuracy.
- **Sentimental Analysis of recent news:** News plays a crucial role in our daily lives. Analyzing the news related to trade deals between different nations, news related to company's progress and performance and also competitors related information can be analyzed to build an optimized prediction model. The sentimental analysis (Bhardwaj et al., 2015) can help to evaluate the stock movement and market opinions with respect to the particular stock.
- **Cross Stock Analysis:** Though it seems that two companies' stocks aren't related to each other but analyzing the stocks related to same sector companies help you to decide how the sector is performing and how the overall market is affected from the recent news, events and work in general.

These aspects may help to build a more sophisticated model for the stock price prediction.

REFERENCES

Bhardwaj, A., Narayan, Y., Vanraj, Pawan, & Dutta, M. (2015). Sentiment Analysis for Indian Stock Market Prediction Using Sensex and Nifty. *Procedia Computer Science, 70*, 85–91. doi:10.1016/j.procs.2015.10.043

Boettiger, C., & Hastings, A. (2013). Tipping points: From patterns to predictions. *Nature, 493*(7431), 157–158. doi:10.1038/493157a PMID:23302842

De Oliveira, F. A., Nobre, C. N., & Zárate, L. E. (2013). Applying Artificial Neural Networks to prediction of stock price and improvement of the directional prediction index - Case study of PETR4, Petrobras, Brazil. *Expert Systems with Applications, 40*(18), 7596–7606. doi:10.1016/j.eswa.2013.06.071

Fama, E. (1965). The Behavior of Stock-Market Prices. *The Journal of Business, 38*(1), 34–105. doi:10.1086/294743

Fama, E. (1995). Random Walks in Stock Market Prices. *Financial Analysts Journal, 51*(1), 75–80. doi:10.2469/faj.v51.n1.1861

Finance. (n.d.). https://in.finance.yahoo.com/

Gao, Z. (2020). The application of artificial intelligence in stock investment. *Journal of Physics: Conference Series, 1453*, 012069. doi:10.1088/1742-6596/1453/1/012069

Hochreiter, S., & Schmidhuber, J. (1997). Long short-term memory. *Neural Computation, 9*(8), 1735–1780. doi:10.1162/neco.1997.9.8.1735 PMID:9377276

Janková, Z., & Dostál, P. (2019). Utilization of Artificial Intelligence for Sensitivity Analysis in the Stock Market. *Acta Universitatis Agriculturae et Silviculturae Mendelianae Brunensis, 67*(5), 1269–1283. doi:10.11118/actaun201967051269

Janocha, K., & Czarnecki, W. (2017). *On Loss Functions for Deep Neural Networks in Classification.* ArXiv, abs/1702.05659

Javier, C., Rosario, E., Francisco, J. N., & Antonio, J. C. (2003). ARIMA Models to Predict Next Electricity Price. *IEEE Transactions on Power Systems, 18*(3), 1014–1020. doi:10.1109/TPWRS.2002.804943

Kim, K.-J. (2003). Financial time series forecasting using support vector machines,". *Neurocomputing, 55*(1-2), 307–319. doi:10.1016/S0925-2312(03)00372-2

Kingma, D. P., & Ba, J. (2014). *Adam: A Method for Stochastic Optimization.* Paper at the 3rd International Conference for Learning Representations, San Diego, CA.

LeCun, Y., Bottou, L., Bengio, Y., & Haffner, P. (1998). Gradient-based learning applied to document recognition. *Proceedings of the IEEE, 86*(11), 2278–2323. doi:10.1109/5.726791

Lee, J., Kim, R., Koh, Y., & Kang, J. (2019). Global stock market prediction based on stock chart images using deep Q-network. *IEEE Access: Practical Innovations, Open Solutions, 7*, 167260–167277. doi:10.1109/ACCESS.2019.2953542

Lee, L. (2015). New kids on the blockchain: How bitcoin's technology could reinvent the stock market. *Hastings Bus. LJ, 12*, 81.

Li, X., Huang, X., Deng, X., & Zhu, S. (2014). Enhancing quantitative intra-day stock return prediction by integrating both market news and stock prices information,". *Neurocomputing, 142*, 228–238. doi:10.1016/j.neucom.2014.04.043

Loshchilov, I., & Hutter, F. (2016). CMA-ES for hyperparameter optimization of deep neural networks. *International Conference on Learning Representations Workshop Track.*

Lussange, J., Palminteri, S., Bourgeois-Gironde, S., & Gutkin, B. (2019). *Mesoscale impact of trader psychology on stock markets: a multi-agent AI approach.* arXiv preprint arXiv:1910.10099

Merity, S., Keskar, N., & Socher, R. (2017). *Regularizing and Optimizing LSTM Language Models.* Academic Press.

Rather, A. M., Agarwal, A., & Sastry, V. N. (2015). Recurrent neural network and a hybrid model for prediction of stock returns,". *Expert Systems with Applications, 42*(6), 3234–3241. doi:10.1016/j.eswa.2014.12.003

Ruder, S. (2016). *An overview of gradient descent optimization algorithms.* Academic Press.

Shah, D., Campbell, W., & Zulkernine, F. (2018). *A Comparative Study of LSTM and DNN for Stock Market Forecasting.* doi:10.1109/BigData.2018.8622462

Srivastava, N., Hinton, G. E., Krizhevsky, A., Sutskever, I., & Salakhutdinov, R. R. (2014). Dropout: A simple way to prevent neural networks from overfitting. *Journal of Machine Learning Research, 15*, 1929–1958.

Yoo, S. (2017). *Blockchain based financial case analysis and its implications. Asia Pacific Journal of Innovation and Entrepreneurship.* doi:10.1108/APJIE-12-2017-036

Yoshihara, A., Fujikawa, K., Seki, K., & Uehara, K. (2014). Predicting Stock Market Trends by Recurrent Deep Neural Networks. In PRICAI 2014: Trends in Artificial Intelligence, vol. 8862 of Lecture Notes in Computer Science (pp. 759–769). Springer International Publishing. doi:10.1007/978-3-319-13560-1_60

Chapter 5

Internet of Things (IoT) in Agriculture

Muralidhar Kurni

https://orcid.org/0000-0002-3324-893X

Jawaharlal Nehru Technological University, Anantapuramu, India

Somasena Reddy K.

Jawaharlal Nehru Technological University, Anantapuramu, India

ABSTRACT

Connected devices have access to every part of our lives with the increasing implementation of the internet of things (IoT), from home automation, health and fitness, automobile, logistics, to smart cities, and industrial IoT. Therefore, it is only natural that IoT, connected devices, and automation find their application in agriculture, and as such, greatly enhance almost every facet of it. In recent decades, farming has undergone a variety of technological changes, becoming more industrialized and powered by technology. Farmers have gained effective control and efficiency over the process of raising livestock and growing crops through the use of various smart farming devices. Within this chapter, the authors discuss and analyze the advantages of using IoT within agriculture. They present the IoT system architecture to allow smart farming. This chapter also covers the advantages of integrating the blockchain into the agricultural field. Case studies are included in the end for your reference.

DOI: 10.4018/978-1-7998-5876-8.ch005

1. INTRODUCTION

The field of Internet of Things (IoT) is a prominent standard that establishes a connection between various sensors and electronic devices using the internet to assist the progress of our livelihood. IoT provides creative solutions to several problems and challenges concerned with government organizations, both public sector and private organizations and several business enterprises present throughout the globe through intelligent devices and the internet (Sfar et al., 2017).

The rapid growth of IoT makes it a significant aspect of our daily activities and even we realize its presence ubiquitously. Simply, IoT can be defined as a modernized technology that comprises widespread smart devices, architectures, sensors and various smart devices (Figure 1). Additionally, IoT utilizes nanotechnology and quantum technology, which provides assured benefits regarding storage space, sensing capabilities and processing speed which were not conceived initially (Gatsis & Pappas, 2017).

We can perceive a significant change in our daily life activities together with the growing participation of IoT technology and devices. By expanding the information available with the production value chain, IoT technology provides enhanced opportunities to reconstruct agriculture, manufacturing industries, energy construction and dissemination through networked sensors. The possibility of IoT in various aspects of technology and our living is massive. Still, a significant challenge is to address the data/information security and equip to make it much more advantageous. Nevertheless, IoT delivers its best practicable efforts to manage the concerns related to data/information security.

1.1 What Is the Internet of Things?

"Internet of Things" (IoT) is a phrase first used by a British Techie Kevin Ashton in the year 1999 to interpret a model where real-world objects were connected to the sensors through the internet (Lee & Lee, 2015). Nowadays, IoT is a prominent phrase in explaining the frameworks that contain connectivity to the internet along with computing abilities that expands to various devices, objects, sensors and daily use items.

Figure 1. An overview of IoT

In the IT sphere, IoT is a rapidly developing model. IoT can be summarized as a technique of establishing a connection to any specific device with an ON/OFF switch for internet connectivity and other linked devices it is connected. Internet of Things (IoT) is a massive network where an enormous number of devices with varying sizes and shapes are interconnected with people, wherein every object gathers data and distributes it among themselves and connected environments. These objects could range from microwave systems meant to cook food automatically for the devised period, to self-driven cars with complex sensors to identify the drive path, to wearable smart fitness devices which collects health data of the individual such as heart rate, exercise records, the number of steps taken every day, the stress level and many more and utilizes these data to advise the exercise plans accordingly. It is also possible to track the behaviour aspects of a football through an application to understand the speed, distance and trajectory of the football based on the velocity of the kick. This information and statistics can be used to train players in the future.

1.2 Defining IoT

Despite the global buzz around the Internet of Things, defining the phrase IoT using one and a globally recognized definition is not available. Hence, several groups have defined IoT in several ways to encourage a broader perspective on the meaning of the Internet of Things and its major features (Madakam et al., 2015). Through a strong understanding of those definitions, one can extract a prevalent aim from them and contemplate the initial and final versions of the internet where the initial version provides information about the creation of data by people whereas the final version states about the creation of data by objects (things). Conclusively, (Madakam et al., 2015) can be recognized as the optimal definition on the Internet of Things stated as follows.

"An open and comprehensive network of intelligent objects that have the capacity to auto-organize, share information, data and resources, reacting and acting in face of situations and changes in the environment."

Rather than curtailing the phrases "IoT" and the "Internet of Things" to considering them commonly as computers, these phrases can be stated extensively as the expansion of network connectivity as well as the computing capacity against various devices, things, and sensors to serve the scope of this chapter. Such "intelligent objects" do not need more human monitoring for creating, sharing and consuming data and in fact, they establish quality connections for collecting distant data, investigation and managing abilities.

1.3 Advantages of IoT to Organizations

IoT establishes several advantages for organizations. Such advantages can be categorized as advantages for specific industries and some of them were suitable across for many industries. Few of the customary advantages of IoT which facilitates businesses to:

- Observe their complete business methods;
- Enhance the experiences of the consumer (cx);
- Preserve money as well as time;
- Improve the efficiency of the employee;
- Blend and accustom various available business models;
- Generate enhanced business resolutions; and
- Produce larger profits.

The emergence of IoT paved the way for companies to reconsider the methods they follow for their business ventures and provides them the necessary tools to enhance their business plans. Since IoT utilizes sensors and various IoT devices, the application of IoT is rich in various organizations, namely manufacturing, utility and transport; but IoT has identified benefits for industries such as agriculture, home automation and infrastructure which gives scope to these industries to transform their businesses digitally. IoT helps farmers involved in agriculture to complete their jobs easily through automated farming methods by collecting various environmental data using sensors that gather temperature, humidity, rainfall, soil content and various other aspects that can, in turn, result in a more efficient harvest.

1.4 Applications of IoT in Real-Time

Internet of Things (IoT) provides an enormous number of real-time applications such as Industrial IoT (IIoT) for organizations to manage their production and for an individual consumer. The application of IoT stretches to broader sectors like energy, telecom and automotive. Smartphones and computers can be automated to access various appliances in smart homes that contain intelligent thermostats, appliances, connected devices for lighting, heating and electronic appliances in the consumer segment. This provides enhanced comfort to various users to improve their lifestyle via wearable devices that contain sensing devices and software which gathers and evaluates the user data and forwards it to various other technologies for optimizing the best results. Such devices can be also made use in ensuring the safety of the public, for instance, enhancing the response times in case of emergencies by furnishing the best routes to the intended locations or by tracing the essential indications of firefighters or workers involved in constructions during the situations that threaten human lives.

Similar to other important sectors, IoT extends its support and provides enormous advantages towards for health care. The intended benefits include close observation of the patients, monitoring their care workflow, machine to machine communication, inventory management of medical instruments, etc. A smart building can use IoT for sensing temperature levels in conference halls, home or office, and automatically switch ON/OFF the air conditioners by identifying the number of people in that room. The deployment of IoT devices and sensors in the case of a smart city will support for decreasing the traffic, preserving energy, observe and present various challenges in the environment and enhance sanitation. In the field of agriculture, the role of IoT-based intelligent farming systems will be handy. They can support monitoring the agriculture field by gathering various environmental data such as temperature, humidity, the moisture content in the soil, light, etc. IoT also contributes to automating the systems used in irrigation.

2. AGRICULTURE AND ITS IMPORTANCE

In history, efforts have been made to improve agriculture yield with lesser resources and human work through various modernized techniques. However, the requirement and supply never matched because of the rapid population increase rate. The population of the world is foreseen to cross 9.8 billion by the year 2050, which is nearly a 25% increase from the present population (Affairs, 2020). To meet the consumption needs for such an increasing population, food production must be doubled (Un, 2009), (B22B-01: Improving Nitrogen and Water Management in Crop Production on a National Scale (Invited), 2020). Also, the production of crops is equally important to food production since the role of certain crops such as rubber, cotton, and gum, etc., are contributing to the economy of various countries. Ensuring food security is also critical because of their demand in the production bio-energy, bio-fuel and several other industrial requirements. Such demands could further lead to the scarcity of the available agricultural resources.

Regrettably, it is possible to utilize only a finite part of the earth's area for agriculture due to constraints such as climate, topography, temperature, and soil quality which is not homogeneous. Furthermore, several other factors such as the economic, political, increase in population, varying climatic conditions, land patterns, urbanization, etc., are heavily challenging to utilize the available agricultural land for cropping. The overall agricultural land made use in the production of food had seen a severe downturn in the past years (Bruinsma, 2017). Hence, there exists an inconsistency in the food demand-supply chain causing fear to the near future.

Additionally, investigations reported that each agricultural field carries contrasting characteristics that have to be evaluated independently. The type of the soil, availability of nutrients, irrigation flow and resistance to the pest are some of the important characteristics that determine the ability to harvest a particular crop to a field. In many circumstances, many variations prevail in a single cultivable field, though that agricultural land is cultivated with the same crop every season. Therefore, field-specific evaluations are needed to understand the temporal and biological variations that can potentially lead to an increase in the agricultural yield and production of various crops. To address these various challenges, farmers require advanced technological assistance to meet such requirements that can generate higher yields from small lands with lesser labor.

2.1 Need for Smart Agriculture

With the traditional farming procedure, farmers have to supervise the crops growing in their agricultural field quite often to get a clear view of the conditions of crops. To understand the condition of the crops, around 70% of the time gets wasted in supervising the crops rather than undergoing fieldwork. This necessitates the need for Smart Agriculture (Navulur et al., 2017). Though the agriculture industry is broad and widespread, there is a requirement to create sustainability that puts lesser influence on the environment. This can be attained through technology-based accurate solutions.

Modern-day technology that uses sensing devices and communication allows farmers to monitor the crop fields without being physically present at the field. This can be stated as 'eye in the field' ability, i.e., observing the field remotely. Wireless sensing devices can observe the crops continuously with larger accuracy and are capable of identifying unwanted states prematurely (A list of IoT Devices for Smart Agriculture can be found in Appendix-A).

That is why the contemporary agricultural methods utilize intelligent kits and tools that take care of the entire life cycle from sowing the seeds to harvesting the crops and provides support until storing those crops and transporting them. Various sensors are utilized to report data in real-time, which facilitates the overall process of analyzing the data and provide accurate supervising abilities resulting in a cost-effective process. Presently, the agriculture equipment is well supported by a large number of self-governing tractors, drones, robot-based weeders, harvesting equipment and satellites. The installation of the sensors can be made in a short time. Those sensors gather data and make it accessible online for future assessment instantly. Further, the modern-day technology-based sensors also facilitate field-specific or crop-specific agriculture since they aid in the accurate collection of data from each site.

2.2 Role of IoT in Agriculture

Currently, the Internet-of-Things (IoT) influences on a broad range of domains and industries such as health, manufacturing, communication, energy, agriculture and many more to decrease their inabilities and enhance the efficiency in various markets (Sisinni et al., 2018)(Ayaz et al., 2018)(Lin et al., 2017)(Shi et al., 2019) (Elijah et al., 2018). Quite shortly, it is foreseeable that IoT technology will play a vital role in a large number of applications that will be used in the agriculture industry. The reason behind such a possibility is because the IoT technology with its abundant infrastructure for communication links intelligent systems, namely sensors, smartphones, vehicles, etc., through the internet and also provides variety of services in cloud-dependent, smart data analysis (local or distant data) and decision making, through an automated user interface thus enhancing the agricultural processes. These abilities of IoT technology could transform the agriculture sector that is considered as one of the incompetent domain of our economic value chain currently.

To encourage intelligent solutions in farming, a remarkable proportion of research has been carried out in the agricultural sector. Various approaches and architectures have been put forward by several engineers and research scholars across the world recommending different types of equipment to observe and collect data regarding the status of crops at various stages taking into consideration the types of crop and agricultural land. Various top industries provide a variety of sensors, robots, drones, communication equipment and several other heavy types of machinery to deliver the appropriate analysis of the collected data. To manage and monitor the environmental and food safety measures with the use of technology, several government organizations and commissions, are establishing codes and policies (COGECA, 2018) (Monitor, 2017) (King et al., 2017) (Blockchain & Safety, 2020) for the agriculture, and food industries. IoT has transformed the agriculture industry and its environment by investigating various issues/obstacles in farming and providing an optimal solution.

3. IoT IN AGRICULTURE

Every aspect of conventional farming practice can be rudimentarily modified by applying the IoT technology in agricultural practices. Various IoT applications are now available to build highly efficient resources that increase the productivity of agriculture. Important IoT applications that are used in agriculture and their advantages are analysed below.

3.1 Notable IoT Applications in Agriculture

3.1.1. Climate Monitoring

Climatic conditions are crucial for agriculture. Inappropriate knowledge about the climate could largely degrade the quality and quantity of the crop yield. However, the real-time conditions of weather can be known through IoT solutions (Talavera et al., 2017). Various sensing devices can be kept in and out of the farming field to gather environmental data and help the farmer to select which particular crop can be grown in that particular climate. The entire ecosystem of IoT comprises various sensors aimed to understand the weather conditions such as temperature, humidity, rainfall, etc., in real-time. To predict these environmental parameters, various sensors are configured appropriately to match the intelligent farming needs. Such sensors observe the crop conditions as well as the weather encompassing them. Sensors predict bad or inappropriate weather and send alerts through messages instantly. Such a facility offered by IoT technology avoids the farmer's physical monitoring of the conditions which ultimately improves the yield to get larger benefits in agriculture.

A climate sensing and reporting equipment that works via Bluetooth within a range of 200m are available with Grofit, which can be placed over the entire harvest area. Such a device collects data that saves up to 30 days of work involving observation of air temperature, humidity and radiations from the sun in real-time, Growers can be used (Grofit, 2020).

A various number of IoT applications are available to predict climate changes for intelligent agriculture. A device called allMETEO that contains Meteoshield along with Smart City intelligent weather sensors provide (Stokes, 2018) intelligent handling of crops along with warning signs to take appropriate precautionary steps and to save the plants. Indeed, the incorporation of this smart management system remarkably enhances the abilities of precise farming methods.

3.1.2. Precision Farming

Precision farming can be otherwise stated as precision agriculture (Khanna & Kaur, 2019), concerning the growing of crops and raising livestock through a controlled and precise manner. The Precision Farming method utilizes information technology along with sensing devices, robotics, control systems, self-governing vehicles, variable rate technology, and automated hardware, to provide precise processed information. The incorporation of smartphones, uninterrupted high-speed internet access and dependable cost-effective satellites used for positioning and image capture plays a significant role in precision farming. The precision farming method is considered a popular and widely used IoT application in the agricultural domain and a large number of organizations across the globe have adopted this method.

CropMetrics is an organization that adopts precision agriculture, which aims at providing innovative and trendy agrarian solutions for practicing precision agriculture management. CropMetrics offers various services and products such as soil moisture probes, virtual optimizer PRO, VRI optimization, etc., for agriculture. Variable Rate Irrigation (VRI) optimization increases the revenue over irrigated agricultural lands by providing vital information on the difference in soil or topography and effective usage of water resources thus improving the yield. The soil moisture probe technology furnishes seasonal and local agricultural assistance and directions to perfectly utilize water. The virtual optimizer PRO provides an easy user interface for water management through a single centralized, cloud-based and robust location designed for farmers and consulting executives to utilize the advantages of precision agriculture.

3.1.3. Smart Greenhouses

Smart Greenhouses is a technique used to improve the productivity of fruits, crops, vegetables, etc. Greenhouses control environmental parameters either by human monitoring or by a method of proportional control mechanisms. Since, human monitoring leads to various losses in productivity, energy and labour costs, such a technique is not feasible. To resolve these issues, smart greenhouses were modelled using IoT devices (Ibrahim et al., 2019) with climate control sensors, thus removing the need for human monitoring and providing a cost-efficient process with improved accuracy as well.

To manage the environment in the modelled smart greenhouse, various sensing devices are used to understand the needs of the varied type of plants. A cloud server connected to the IoT can be constructed to access the system remotely. The cloud server allows processing the real-time data and establish a proportional control method within the greenhouse. This model is cost-effective and furnishes the best solutions for agriculture with lesser human monitoring.

Illuminum Greenhouses is a drip-irrigated Agri-Tech greenhouse organization that makes use of the latest innovative technologies to furnish optimized services. With the advent of IoT sensors that are powered using solar energy, these systems construct innovative and cost-effective smart greenhouses. Sensing devices attached to the IoT monitor the current status of the greenhouses and also observes the utilization of water and alerts the farmers through SMS through an online portal. Such smart greenhouses also accomplish cultivation automatically. The smart greenhouses equipped with sensors that follow IoT technology furnish information about the temperature, humidity, pressure and light. Such sensing devices automatically command actuators that perform various functions, namely switching the lights ON/OFF, turning a fan or mister ON, controlling the temperature levels of a heater, opening a window, etc., through a Wi-Fi signal.

As a representation of IoT applications in smart farming, Farmapp offers farmers an Integrated Pest Management platform with tracking features, sensors and fumigation. Specifically, it includes a scouting app with satellite maps, comparative maps, charts and reports at hand for quick recording and enforcing the necessary steps. Also, data on weather and soil conditions can be obtained in real-time via direct access to satellite images and algorithmic calculations. Additionally, the Farmapp's functionality allows monitoring of the quantity of water used on plants for optimal irrigation.

Growlink enables real-time monitoring to improve quality and yield efficiency in greenhouses. In particular, this solution for IoT agriculture focuses on automating the work with operational data including planning, managing, tracking and monitoring. Farmers, therefore, get an excellent opportunity to produce the best long-term results possible.

3.1.4. Agricultural Drones

Agriculture drones are the result of modern technologies and innovations in the agriculture sector. Drones are largely utilized in the field of agriculture currently to facilitate various benefits and to improve the conventional practices in agriculture (Giacomo & David, 2017). Aerial-based and Ground-based agricultural drones are used for farming, monitoring the crops, spraying of crops, evaluating the health of the crops, assessing the agricultural land, soil assessment and planting of seeds.

The incorporation of drones in agriculture offers various advantages, namely GIS mapping that provides crop health imaging capturing, consumes less time, is easy to handle and use and improves productivity. Drone technology in the field of agriculture systematically collects real-time data and processes them through structured planning hence improving the quality of work in the field of agriculture.

PrecisionHawk is a firm that makes use of agricultural drones to collect sensitive information through various numbers of sensors that capture images, maps the crop field and the area of interest and surveys the crop field. Such drones are capable of performing indoor aviation tracking and monitoring. The role of the farmers is to select which crop field has to be surveyed and he has to choose the height of the drone for a clear resolution of the ground.

Making use of the data collected by the drones, we can collect the observations regarding the plant's health, plants count, productivity predictions, the height of the plants, canopy cover mapping, scouting reports, field water ponding mapping stockpile measuring, nitrogen content in wheat, chlorophyll measurement, drainage mapping, weed pressure mapping, etc. Drones also collect thermal, multi-spectral and visual imagery of the lands. Simply put, agricultural drones will manage the entire life-cycle of crops from seeding to cultivation.

3.1.5. Monitoring Livestock

Farmers who have larger farms can utilize wireless IoT applications to gather information about the geographical location, count, health status, etc., about their livestock (Zhang et al., 2016). Such data support the farmers to predict which animals are sick and isolate them from other animals avoiding the spread of disease. This method reduces the manual labor charges for owners and they could be able to identify them through IoT based sensors.

JMB North America is a firm that provides cow monitoring solutions for livestock owners. These solutions support the livestock owners to monitor the cows that are pregnant and that are about to deliver by making the farmers more focused on the health aspects of the cow. Allflex SCR provides cow, milking, and herd intelligence services. The services involve monitoring all information about each herd participant (heat, safety, and nutrition), optimizing the milking process (simplifying and streamlining), and collecting data into an integrated herd growth plan that can be actioned. Cowlar is a company that addresses similar needs to optimize milking, maximize efficiency, cut labour costs and improve reproduction.

Also, to overcome the problem of long-term animal health tracking, Symphony Link is an application that prevents mesh networking and effectively completes the mission of full integration. As a ground-breaking innovation in agriculture's IoT world, it links wide-area IoT networks with modules (including RXR-27), gateways, and conductors.

3.1.6. Data Analytics

The data gathered by the IoT sensors require a good size of storage space but the traditional database model does not carry that much space. Storage of data in the cloud space and the end-to-end IoT environment enjoys a significant role in the modern-day intelligent agriculture system (Elijah et al., 2018). (Brief on notable opensource and other popular IoT cloud platforms can be found in Appendix-B). Such systems were foreseen to play a significant role since they are capable of delivering their best. Indeed, sensors are the chief source to collect a large quantity of data. Data analytics tools are used for assessing and reconstructing substantial information. Data analytics supports in evaluating the conditions of weather, livestock and the plants. Such data gathered from various sources helps us to make optimal decisions. The real-time crop conditions can be known from the sensor data through the support rendered by IoT devices. This provides a better understanding of the situation to make optimal decisions through predictive analysis. The forthcoming conditions of weather and the details about reaping the crops can be assessed through data analysis. The incorporation of IoT technology in the agriculture sector assists farmers to manage the crop quality as well as the productivity of the lands which further improves the volume and quality of the products.

3.1.7. Entire Supply Chain Management

In connection with logistics, the incorporation of IoT technology in agriculture supports the utilization of RFID, GPS and other location-based sensing devices to curb plant storage and transportation. In this context, the entire supply chain can increase its effectiveness, meaning the enhancements regarding awareness of the consumer (precisely, in terms of food safety) and transparency.

End-to-End farm management systems is an area of interest for the growth of IoT software in the agriculture industry. There is a possibility to add sensors and software in this context which will provide data for analytics, reporting and accounting. FarmLogs and Cropio are the exact solutions with certain functions for this sector.

FarmLogs provides tools for the agricultural sector to promote marketing decisions regarding food crops. Specifically, it includes a toolkit required to build a marketing plan (which carries the value of unsold crops, list of contacts and objective setting), as well as observations on profitability. Farmers can order marketing reports, automated recording of activities, crop health imaging, and rainfall tracing among the concrete products.

As for Cropio, the approach applies to the features of the field management and the plant control system. In particular, it facilitates the monitoring of the status of various fields, provides data on the requisite changes in real-time and assists in forecasting. The ability to offer field history, instant warnings, vegetation charts, soil moisture and harvest forecasts are impressive among its main features.

3.2 Advantages of IoT in Agriculture

The primary advantages of the application of IoT technology in agriculture are listed below:

- Community agriculture applied in villages as well as cities benefit from the huge availability of precise data with the existing software and hardware resources.
- Logistic and subjective delectability in producing the food supports in cost reduction and prevents inputs wastage using real-time information in making decisions.
- Generating business models (Dolci, 2017) in the agricultural context, which enables to establish an explicit connection with the customer.
- Plant monitoring along with preventing machine thefts.
- Automatic farming systems (Kaewmard & Saiyod, 2014) functions by taking the input values from the sensors. This data gets collected automatically about the environmental parameters (namely temperature, humidity, soil moisture, etc.,) for further processing and evaluation.
- The huge content of data will be evaluated using decision support systems to enhance the crop yield as well as efficiency in the operations performed (Nandyala & Kim, 2016) (Cambra et al., 2017).

3.3 Endless Possibilities of IoT Application in Agriculture

What is the role and significance of IoT in agriculture? Regrettably, it is not possible to provide one satisfying answer to this question. To enhance comfort to the industries and to carry out tests to know about their uses, farmers try various applications. More commonly, applications that provide support to manage pests, supervise the animals, limit water utilization and various other use cases are implemented throughout the world. With the advent of modern-day smart farming methods and IoT technology, it is possible to enhance productivity, preserve money and many other factors without much human monitoring.

The probability of technological advancements and innovations in the field of agriculture is immense in the IoT domain. This IoT technology provides many possibilities that were not visualized previously by the farmers. Thanks to modern-day advanced sensors, cameras and various other devices, farmers get a comprehensive view of their agricultural land and diagnose everything through real-time monitoring. Further, IoT technology is capable of immediately adapting to modifications and varying its operations to accomplish beneficial results. In the case of farmers, their main aim is to provide fresh and wholesome produce and not only profit.

Agricultural work is very tough but modern-day technology allows smart farming methods that simplify the agricultural processes by providing access to important information and assure a smoother unification with IoT.

4. IoT SYSTEM ARCHITECTURE FOR AGRICULTURE

This section outlines an IoT system architecture for smart agriculture. According to (Elijah et al., 2018), the architecture of IoT contains four important components namely IoT devices, communication technology, internet, storage of data and processing components. The architecture of the proposed IoT model is shown in Figure 2.

4.1 IoT Devices

The devices in the IoT system contains an embedded system that communicates with sensing devices and actuators through a wireless link. Such devices in the IoT system are occasionally termed as IoT sensors. The embedded system present in the IoT system contains Microprocessors or FPGA (Field Programmable Gate Array), memory units, I/O units and communicating modules. The role of IoT sensors is to supervise and to measure various environmental parameters in the field such as temperature, weather conditions, nutrients in the soil, etc., and determinants that influence productivity. Various sensors are used to collect data in the crop field, namely electrochemical, mechanical, location, optical, airflow sensors to name a few (Li et al., 2010). These IoT sensors collect data namely temperature in the air, the temperature in the soil at different depths, rainfall prediction, wetness in the leaves, chlorophyll content, the temperature of dew point, direction of the wind, solar radiation, atmospheric pressure, and relative humidity. The significant features present in the IoT devices enables them to fit for various agricultural needs. Some of the features of IoT devices are effectiveness in computing, power, memory, mobility, endurance, dependability, coverage and effective costs.

Figure 2. An IoT system architecture for agriculture
(Elijah et al., 2018).

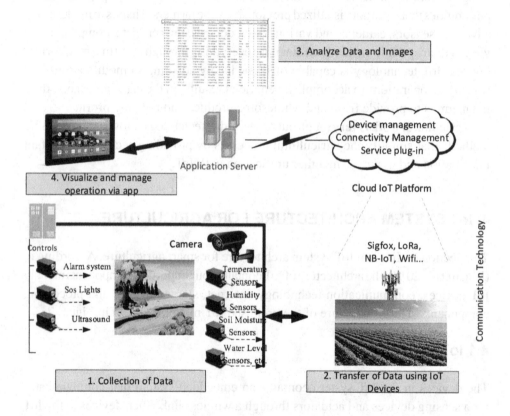

4.2 Communication Technology

To implement IoT systems successfully, the role of communication technology is vital (Feng et al., 2019). The improvements in providing seamless connectivity are considered as the absolute victory of deploying IoT systems in the agriculture sector. The absolute objective is not possible without having protected links across several competing IoT objects. To accomplish a dependable connection, telecommunication engineers play a critical part in the field of agriculture. To execute the IoT technology on a massive scale in the field of agriculture accurately, we require to establish an appropriate architecture on a large scale. Before selecting the medium of communication, we need to contemplate vital components such as coverage, costs, energy utilization and dependability. Low-energy networks could only establish links on one field and usually are not capable of providing services to distant places where the collected data is to be forwarded to the farm management systems (FMS). As per the needs of scalability, availability, and application requirements, several modes of communication models have to be incorporated simultaneously. Some of the available technologies that suit to serve the large scale implementation are Zigbee, Bluetooth, Cellular Mobile Links, Sigfox, LoRa and many more.

4.3 Internet

With internet connectivity, IoT devices make sure that data is available at all times and wherever in need. The objective of establishing internet connectivity is to build a centralized network layer where routing is established to transport and share the network information among various subnetworks. Because of the emergence of smartphones, wireless communication systems, and pervasive services it gives rise to the need for extensive internet connectivity. Still, data transferring through the internet needs enough real-time data support, security and ease of access feature. Thus, Cloud computing is a viable solution that is established through the internet to store and process huge volumes of collected data.

The IoT middleware and linking protocols were established to accomplish the linkage with devices and heterogeneous systems through internet connectivity (Al-fuqaha et al., 2015). Some of the examples of IoT middleware are cloud-based IoT middleware, actor-based IoT middleware and service-oriented architecture (SOA). These are accomplished to provide enough support to IoT systems. Various IoT based transmission protocols are extensively applied in the field of agriculture. Some of the highly familiar wireless protocols are Wi-Fi based on IEEE 802.11 standard, Cellular mobile transmission standards such as 2G, 3G and 4G, Wi-max, RFID, Bluetooth, Zigbee, Lora-Wan and reduced rate WPAN (Wireless Personal Area Networks).

4.4 Data Storage and Processing Units

To achieve better evaluation in the forthcoming years, farmers need to save the data regarding crops and utilize such data in various seasons to increase the yield. Data-driven agriculture requires the gathering of massive, intricate and geographical information that needs storage and further processing. The intricacy in the data ranges from methodical (structured) to unmethodical (unstructured) information that could be an image, text, audio or a video. Similarly, the range of data could be market-based, live telecast, enterprise, historical or sensor data.

The emergence of a cloud computing-based IoT environment enables us to save the massive quantity of data gathered from various sensors in the cloud space(Pavón-Pulido et al., 2017). This also contains application hosting which is demanding to establish services and to control the IoT end to end architecture. Currently, emerging technologies in the IoT such as fog or edge computing is proposed which works with gateways and IoT devices to accomplish calculations and evaluations to decrease the latency for demanding applications, resulting in the decrease of costs and advance the quality of service (QoS) (Chen et al., 2018), (Premsankar et al., 2018).

Various agriculture MIS (Management Information Systems) are advanced to control different forms of data (Yan-E, 2011). Some of the examples are Cropx, Farmobile, Onfarm systems, KAA, Easyfarm, Farmx, Farmlogs, etc. The significance of these environments is to accomplish the storage and control of data and data analytics.

5. BLOCKCHAIN TECHNOLOGY FOR SMART AGRICULTURE

The IoT technology has been progressing as an entirely developed technology that can be utilized in every intelligent application today and it manifests itself as a reliable entity for the forthcoming internet generations. Similar to the IoT technology, Blockchain technology is also evolving as a viable solution where every node present in the Blockchain contains a distributed ledger that improves data transparency and security (Bhadoria et al., 2020). Because of this capability of carrying out intelligent contracts and consents, illicit users cannot access the data using defective contracts in case of a Blockchain network (Bhadoria & Agasti, 2019). To enhance the efficiency of the applications in real-time, IoT technology can be integrated with the Blockchain technology (Bhadoria & Nimbalkar, 2020).

The integration of IoT and Blockchain technologies reconstructs the food and agriculture sector and benefits farmers to producers as well as merchants. Through an easy and clear approach, Blockchain technology helps agriculture to implement a continuous procedure to revolutionize the usage of several resources such as water, fertilizers, labour and many more. Few advantages of incorporating the Blockchain in the field of agriculture are explained here (Production, 2019) (Koshy et al., 2018).

5.1 Improved Food Quality Control

Blockchain technology assists farmers to abolish unproductive methods and guarantees the best circumstance for quality control. For instance, one of the major challenges faced by the farmers present across the world is adverse weather conditions namely badly dispensed rainfall, fluctuating weather. IoT devices enable farmers to supervise various components that influence the growth of plants namely pests, quality of the soil and farming. The values of these components get updated frequently and can be visualized on smart mobile phones in real-time by connecting IoT devices to a Blockchain ledger. Because of this portability offered by IoT and Blockchain technology incorporation, farmers can verify the components and if in case they find something erroneous, instantly they will be alerted to do modifications. The application of Blockchain technology also furnishes the potential to identify the nature of the problem quite instantly during the cases of food safety epidemic.

5.2 Increased Transparency in the Supply Chain

The application of Blockchain technology enables the customers to understand about the freshness of the food, where it is produced, who cultivated the food etc., Improvements in the clarity of the food supply chain will certainly have a huge impact in decreasing the hoax, false labelling and eliminates mediators thereby promising the food makers to get good profits for their valuable work and also provide customers about the knowledge on what they pay for. Similarly, improvements in providing clarity to farmers regarding the demand and supply

will help them take complete control over the food crop using a mobile application installed on a smartphone through which they can record, update the current situation of the plants and supervise the overall farming process and learn about the current status of their food products, learn about impending requirements and also make appropriate modifications as per the need.

5.3 Effective Accessibility to Farmers

Modern-day technology allows many farmers to utilize a mix of various software applications, spreadsheets and annotations to log the data and control their operations. But, forwarding this data to various other service providers is complex and needs various exertions to do so. Blockchain technology enables farmers to save their entire data at one central location so that anyone who needs access to that data can comfortably access them thereby streamlining the overall operation that preserves energy as well as time. Utilizing one centralized application for monitoring purposes rather than various applications/methods provides transparency in the operations and eliminates the risk of information loss.

5.4 Reasonable Price for the Farmers' Goods

Nowadays, farmers face a huge challenge in getting rewarded for their food products. Sometimes, it takes many weeks to collect the entire money for their sold products. A notable portion of their earnings gets lost because of the conventional payment mechanism. Intelligent contract jobs that make use of Blockchain technology automatically prompt payments once a particular delivery has been completed based on an earlier stated fulfilment condition by the consumer thus discarding oppressive transaction charges. This technique allows the farmers to get instant payments once they deliver their products and eliminates the time taken for the conventional payment mechanism. Farmers consistently encounter troubles in selling their goods in the market for a profitable price where the mediators gain more with fewer efforts in many situations. These kinds of hassles are resolved by smart contracts that directly connect the farmers with the retail owners through which the farmer gains equitable profit.

6. CASE STUDIES

IoT technology imparts an appropriate understanding of the technology through which the farmers could take punctual decisions about their plants to increase productivity and profit. This section presents various case studies regarding the customization of IoT technology to suit the local requirements specifically adjusting to the irrigation situations of Indian farmers in small and medium scale to enhance the yield of crops and monitoring the diseases and pests are presented. Three case studies are presented, the first one state about providing cultivation advice to the groundnut farmers, the second states about the early indication of a disease for castor crop and the last one states about the effective utilization of water.

6.1 Case Study I - Providing Cultivation Advice to the Groundnut Producers

A novel project had been presented by the Andhra Pradesh Government in India named "Harmonized Information of Agriculture, Revenue and Irrigation for a Transformation Agenda" (Koshy et al., 2018) and is applied to merge three important divisions of agriculture such as revenue, irrigation, and agriculture. Simply, this project is stated as HARITA assures stability, productivity and punctuality in the process of decision making. This project mainly aims to introduce the latest technologies more specifically sensor-based technologies to collect real-time data of irrigation and agriculture to institute highly productive systems for unified water management and personified agricultural expansion solutions.

Followed by the HARITA project, an experimental application of this project called HARITA-PRIYA (an accurate technology for agriculture) was developed, to discover the microclimatic conditions from the crop fields through Wireless Sensor Networks (WSN) that disseminates personified and geographical specific advice to the farmers.

To facilitate a good understanding, farmers were sent agricultural advice through messages (SMS) in their native language Telugu, specifically to alert them about the pest or disease as an early warning and to schedule the best irrigation conditions for groundnut as per the microclimatic data collected in the farmer's agricultural land through WSN technology. A total of 74 IOT nodes (WSN) that contains sensors and 6 number of WSN gateways were set-up in 5 different villages along with One Krishi Vigyan Kendra (KVK) in Anantapur District of AP in the agricultural lands of farmers, that involved in the production of groundnut crop in the period of 2015 Kharif. This model escorted around 450 acres of cultivable land for monitoring the disease and pest and around 710 farmers from the respective villages were enrolled and provided appropriate advice during the 2015 Kharif period.

The wireless sensor nodes collect five environmental parameters such as relative humidity, temperature, the moisture content in the soil, temperature of the soil and wetness in the leaves in the microclimatic season in real-time and at the level of plant canopy and further forward that information consistently to a distant server through a wireless sensor gateway equipped with internet connectivity, installed in the crop field. In every village, various wireless sensor nodes that support WSN architecture were linked wirelessly to a central wireless sensor gateway. The number of WSN nodes installed in every village varies between 5 and 20 depending on the level of the field where groundnut cultivation takes place. In the server end, decision support advisory models were implemented to access the crop field data and to warn about the diseases and pests at an early stage itself. Depending on the alert messages produced by this model, the Municipal Agriculture Office (MAO) forwards personified advice about the crops to the farmers through messages (SMS) in Telugu.

It is noted that 41 early warning indications about the Leaf Spot disease epidemic during the Kharif season between July and October 2015 supported the Agriculture department of Andhra Pradesh state to forward on-time advice alerts to the groundnut farmers present in those villages. The pilot implementation model of HARITA, the HARITA-PRIYA model further supported the agriculture officers to outreach a large number of farmers with personified advice. On an average, it is noted then, every farmer in those villages had received 18 SMS advice in the above said Kharif season while comparing to a just 2 to 3 SMS alerts notified to the farmers by the

Agriculture officers before implementing this system. Overall, the proposed model had produced around 3500 SMS advice to the enrolled farmers as on date hence assuring good communication among the farmers and the agricultural department.

The recognized villages were installed with various wireless sensor (WSN) nodes each spaced at about 200m apart. As per the evaluations on the collected data and the alerts produced by the wireless sensor nodes, it is noted that not many variations were found during microclimatic conditions because of the narrow sowing window installed in the rainfall received areas and hence, this method can be considered for the forthcoming years. The number of wireless sensor nodes can be decreased to denote the important crops alone considering the decision-making policies that were already in place or have been under development by the agricultural experts. These advice alerts produced by the proposed model can also be supplied to the neighbouring villages to make the agriculture sector economically viable by the application of novel technologies.

6.2. Case Study II - Evolving a Disease Early Warning Model for the Castor Crop

To evolve a disease early warning model, wireless sensor network-based methodology has been implemented in alliance with the Indian Institute of Oil Seeds and Research (IIOR), Hyderabad (Koshy et al., 2018) to identify the disease called "gray-mold" prevalently seen in the castor crop. The chief aim of developing this model is to propose a powerful disease advising system that is capable of advising farmers about the likely disease epidemic while testing. Four different places in the state of Telangana where the major cultivation of castor crop was identified. In those places, 12 wireless sensors (WSN) nodes and 24 canopy sensor units were installed.

The sensing devices which were installed in the proximity of crop canopy gathers data such as relative humidity, temperature, and wetness of the leaves. The rate at which the disease can spread is calculated during several stages of the plant growth while cultivating the crop. Further, this data is associated with the microclimatic data collected from the installed sensors to perform the calculations of Percentage Disease Incidence (PDI). The calculated PDI can be utilized to build a disease early warning system based on decision policies along with the localized conditions to provide adequate time for the farmer to carry out preventive measures.

In the periods of 2017 Kharif and Rabi, crop field tests were carried out and were decoded to extend these evaluations in the 2018 Kharif and Rabi periods. These tests were carried out in four different locations covering three different districts in the state of Telangana to form a broad early warning system where the irrigation of castor is prevalent. Every field location was installed with three wireless sensor nodes and six pairs of sensors. Among these field locations, two fields belong to the farmers of recognized villages and the other two were research fields located in Palem and Hyderabad. All these four places were dissociated by an average distance of about 100 km to lodge various weather conditions and soil characters. Out of Six sensor pairs, three pairs were installed inside a poly-house located in Hyderabad to establish a controlled atmosphere to monitor the diseases. Once the crop season began, the disease was instituted to the plants in the poly house. The developments of those plants were assessed along with the data of the sensors to obtain the PDI computations. These tests were carried out in four locations alone and the data observed in these locations were evaluated for further analysis. Further works to bolster the proposed model are currently in progress and the efficiency of this model in the open field conditions will be assessed. Also, an idea of enforcing decision policies to furnish necessary advice to the farmers in these survey areas is underway. During the 2018 season, this study was planned to continue and after further evaluations, the system will be finalized.

6.3 **Case Study III - Water Consumption at the Connected Avocado Farm**

To make one pound of avocados, farmers require about 70 gallons of water whereas in California, which is severely affected by drought generates about 95% of avocados to be grown in the US. An avocado farmer from California named Kurt Bantle determined to undergo trials utilizing IoT technology in his field to check whether utilization of water can be preserved to grow his 900 avocado trees to save water and cost (Study, n.d.).

Hence, he segregated his entire farm to 22 irrigation blocks and installed two soil measuring devices in every block. The data collected from the soil moisture sensing devices which are placed near the avocado trees were forwarded to cloud space, and if an avocado tree requires water, it will automatically turn ON the sprinklers to fetch the right soil moisture for every tree. Once the right moisture levels are attained, the sprinklers will be switched OFF. These trees which are linked via IoT technology will be supervised continuously during day and night.

This system produced astonishing results. Before implementing this IoT technology on his farm, he has to spend annual charges of about $47,336 to water 900 avocado trees. After implementing IoT technology, his annual charges were reduced by about 75% and he had to pay $11,834 alone. He also recovered the investment in hardware within six months.

CONCLUSION

This chapter provides a description of IoT in agriculture. Many fields have been addressed in depth concerning relation to the application of IoT in agriculture. IoT technology can be used to improve farm, livestock, operational performance and productivity. While IoT is expected to bring many benefits to the agriculture sector, several issues remain to be addressed to make it affordable for small and medium-sized farmers. Safety and cost are the main concerns. It is expected that the adoption rate of IoT in agriculture will increase accordingly as competition rises in the agricultural sector and favourable policies are being introduced. If the past is an indicator of the future, however, farmers can keep on finding better ways of growing crops through innovation.

REFERENCES

B22B-01 : Improving Nitrogen and Water Management in Crop Production on a National Scale (Invited). (2020). *December 2018, 346794.*

Affairs, S. (2020). *Department of Economic and Social Affairs World population projected to reach 9 . 8 billion in 2050, and 11.* Academic Press.

Al-fuqaha, A., Member, S., Guizani, M., Mohammadi, M., & Member, S. (2015). *Internet of Things : A Survey on Enabling.* Academic Press.

Ayaz, M., Ammad-Uddin, M., Baig, I., & Aggoune, E. H. M. (2018). Wireless sensor's civil applications, prototypes, and future integration possibilities: A review. *IEEE Sensors Journal, 18*(1), 4–30. doi:10.1109/JSEN.2017.2766364

Ayaz, M., Ammad-Uddin, M., Sharif, Z., Mansour, A., & Aggoune, E. H. M. (2019). Internet-of-Things (IoT)-based smart agriculture: Toward making the fields talk. *IEEE Access: Practical Innovations, Open Solutions, 7,* 129551–129583. doi:10.1109/ACCESS.2019.2932609

Bhadoria, R. S., & Agasti, V. (2019). The Paradigms of Blockchain Technology: Myths, Facts & Future. *International Journal of Information Systems and Social Change, 10*(2), 1–14. doi:10.4018/IJISSC.2019040101

Bhadoria, R. S., Arora, Y., & Gautam, K. (2020). Blockchain Hands-on for Developing Genesis Block. In S. Kim & G. Deka (Eds.), *Advanced Applications of Blockchain Technology. Studies in Big Data.* doi:10.1007/978-981-13-8775-3_13

Bhadoria, R. S., Nimbalkar, A., & Saxena, N. (2020). On the Role of Blockchain Technology in the Internet of Things. In S. Kim & G. Deka (Eds.), *Advanced Applications of Blockchain Technology. Studies in Big Data*. doi:10.1007/978-981-13-8775-3_6

Blockchain, H., & Safety, F. (2020). *How Blockchain and IoT Tech will Guarantee Food Safety*. Academic Press.

Bruinsma, J. (2017). World agriculture: Towards 2015/2030: An FAO Study. *World Agriculture: Towards 2015/2030: An FAO Study*. doi:10.4324/9781315083858

Cambra, C., Sendra, S., Lloret, J., & Garcia, L. (2017). An IoT service-oriented system for agriculture monitoring. *IEEE International Conference on Communications, May*. 10.1109/ICC.2017.7996640

Chen, X., Shi, Q., Yang, L., & Xu, J. (2018). ThriftyEdge: Resource-Efficient Edge Computing for Intelligent IoT Applications. *IEEE Network, 32*(1), 61–65. doi:10.1109/MNET.2018.1700145

COGECA. C. (2018). EU Code of conduct on agricultural data sharing by contractual agreement. *Copa Cogeca*, 1–11. https://cema-agri.org/sites/default/files/publications/EU_Code_2018_web_version.pdf

Dolci, R. (2017). IoT Solutions for Precision Farming and Food Manufacturing: Artificial Intelligence Applications in Digital Food. *Proceedings - International Computer Software and Applications Conference, 2*, 384–385. 10.1109/COMPSAC.2017.157

Elijah, O., Rahman, T. A., Orikumhi, I., Leow, C. Y., & Hindia, M. N. (2018). An Overview of Internet of Things (IoT) and Data Analytics in Agriculture: Benefits and Challenges. *IEEE Internet of Things Journal, 5*(5), 3758–3773. doi:10.1109/JIOT.2018.2844296

Feng, X., Yan, F., & Liu, X. (2019). Study of Wireless Communication Technologies on Internet of Things for Precision Agriculture. *Wireless Personal Communications, 108*(3), 1785–1802. doi:10.100711277-019-06496-7

Gatsis, K., & Pappas, G. J. (2017). Poster abstract: Wireless control for the IoT: Power, spectrum, and security challenges. *Proceedings - 2017 IEEE/ACM 2nd International Conference on Internet-of-Things Design and Implementation, IoTDI 2017 (Part of CPS Week), 1*, 341–342. 10.1145/3054977.3057313

Giacomo, R., & David, G. (2017). Unmanned Aerial Systems (UAS) in Agriculture: Regulations and Good Practices. In E-Agriculture in Action: Drones for Agriculture. Academic Press.

Grofit, S. (2020). *Climate monitoring device Add to Cart.* Academic Press.

Ibrahim, H., Mostafa, N., Halawa, H., Elsalamouny, M., Daoud, R., Amer, H., Adel, Y., Shaarawi, A., Khattab, A., & ElSayed, H. (2019). A layered IoT architecture for greenhouse monitoring and remote control. *SN Applied Sciences, 1*(3), 1–12. doi:10.100742452-019-0227-8

Kaewmard, N., & Saiyod, S. (2014). Sensor data collection and irrigation control on vegetable crop using smart phone and wireless sensor networks for smart farm. *ICWiSe 2014 - 2014 IEEE Conference on Wireless Sensors*, 106–112. 10.1109/ICWISE.2014.7042670

Khanna, A., & Kaur, S. (2019). Evolution of Internet of Things (IoT) and its significant impact in the field of Precision Agriculture. *Computers and Electronics in Agriculture, 157*(January), 218–231. doi:10.1016/j.compag.2018.12.039

King, T., Cole, M., Farber, J. M., Eisenbrand, G., Zabaras, D., Fox, E. M., & Hill, J. P. (2017). Food safety for food security: Relationship between global megatrends and developments in food safety. *Trends in Food Science & Technology, 68*, 160–175. doi:10.1016/j.tifs.2017.08.014

Koshy, S. S., Sunnam, V. S., Rajgarhia, P., Chinnusamy, K., Ravulapalli, D. P., & Chunduri, S. (2018). Application of the internet of things (IoT) for smart farming: A case study on groundnut and castor pest and disease forewarning. *CSI Transactions on ICT, 6*(3–4), 311–318. doi:10.100740012-018-0213-0

Lee, I., & Lee, K. (2015). The Internet of Things (IoT): Applications, investments, and challenges for enterprises. *Business Horizons, 58*(4), 431–440. doi:10.1016/j.bushor.2015.03.008

Li, S., Simonian, A., & Chin, B. A. (2010). Sensors for agriculture and the food industry. *The Electrochemical Society Interface, 19*(4), 41–46. doi:10.1149/2.F05104if

Lin, J., Yu, W., Zhang, N., Yang, X., Zhang, H., & Zhao, W. (2017). A Survey on Internet of Things: Architecture, Enabling Technologies, Security and Privacy, and Applications. *IEEE Internet of Things Journal, 4*(5), 1125–1142. doi:10.1109/JIOT.2017.2683200

Madakam, S., Ramaswamy, R., & Tripathi, S. (2015). Internet of Things (IoT): A Literature Review. *Journal of Computer and Communications, 03*(05), 164–173. doi:10.4236/jcc.2015.35021

Monitor, D. T. (2017). *Agriculture : Focus on IoT aspects Agriculture : Focus on IoT aspects.* Academic Press.

Nandyala, C. S., & Kim, H. K. (2016). Green IoT Agriculture and Healthcare Application (GAHA). *International Journal of Smart Home, 10*(4), 289–300. doi:10.14257/ijsh.2016.10.4.26

Navulur, S., Sastry, A. S. C. S., & Prasad, M. N. G. (2017). *Agricultural Management through Wireless Sensors and Internet of Things.* doi:10.11591/ijece.v7i6.pp3492-3499

Pavón-Pulido, N., López-Riquelme, J. A., Torres, R., Morais, R., & Pastor, J. A. (2017). New trends in precision agriculture: A novel cloud-based system for enabling data storage and agricultural task planning and automation. *Precision Agriculture, 18*(6), 1038–1068. doi:10.100711119-017-9532-7

Premsankar, G., Di Francesco, M., & Taleb, T. (2018). Edge Computing for the Internet of Things: A Case Study. *IEEE Internet of Things Journal, 5*(2), 1275–1284. doi:10.1109/JIOT.2018.2805263

Production, F. (2019). *Blockchain in Agriculture – Improving Agricultural Techniques.* Academic Press.

Sfar, A. R., Chtourou, Z., & Challal, Y. (2017). A systemic and cognitive vision for IoT security: A case study of military live simulation and security challenges. *2017 International Conference on Smart, Monitored and Controlled Cities, SM2C 2017,* 101–105. 10.1109/SM2C.2017.8071828

Shi, X., An, X., Zhao, Q., Liu, H., Xia, L., Sun, X., & Guo, Y. (2019). State-of-the-art internet of things in protected agriculture. *Sensors (Switzerland), 19*(8), 1833. Advance online publication. doi:10.339019081833 PMID:30999637

Sisinni, E., Saifullah, A., Han, S., Jennehag, U., & Gidlund, M. (2018). Industrial internet of things: Challenges, opportunities, and directions. *IEEE Transactions on Industrial Informatics, 14*(11), 4724–4734. doi:10.1109/TII.2018.2852491

Stokes, P. (2018). IoT applications in agriculture: the potential of smart farming on the current stage. *Data Driven Investor,* 1–8. https://medium.com/datadriveninvestor/iot-applications-in-agriculture-the-potential-of-smart-farming-on-the-current-stage-275066f946d8

Study, C. (n.d.). *Spirent IoT*. https://www.spirent.com/blogs/wireless/2016/june/cutting-costs-with-iot-connected-avocados

Talavera, J. M., Tobón, L. E., Gómez, J. A., Culman, M. A., Aranda, J. M., Parra, D. T., Quiroz, L. A., Hoyos, A., & Garreta, L. E. (2017). Review of IoT applications in agro-industrial and environmental fields. *Computers and Electronics in Agriculture*, *142*(September), 283–297. doi:10.1016/j.compag.2017.09.015

Un. (2009). Food Production Must Double By 2050 To Meet Demand From World'S Growing Population, Innovative Strategies Needed To Combat Hunger, Experts Tell Second Committee. *Second Committee, Panel Discussion (AM) GA/EF/3242, 64*, 2–5. https://www.un.org/News/Press/docs/2009/gaef3242.doc.htm

Yan-E, D. (2011). Design of intelligent agriculture management information system based on IoT. *Proceedings - 4th International Conference on Intelligent Computation Technology and Automation, ICICTA 2011, 1*, 1045–1049. 10.1109/ICICTA.2011.262

Zhang, Y., Chen, Q., Liu, G., Shen, W., & Wang, G. (2016). Environment Parameters Control Based on Wireless Sensor Network in Livestock Buildings. *International Journal of Distributed Sensor Networks*, *2016*(5), 9079748. Advance online publication. doi:10.1155/2016/9079748

APPENDIX A

IoT Devices for Smart Agriculture

Wireless sensors are the most important and play a key role in the collection of crop conditions and other details among all the equipment available today for smart agriculture. Wireless sensors can be used independently wherever possible, incorporated further with almost all parts, depending on the relevant requirements and advanced agricultural tools and heavy machinery. Table 1 lists several sensors, their possible uses and the environment to be used (Ayaz et al., 2019).

Table 1. Some notable sensors along with their possible uses in IoT based agriculture

S. No	Sensor	Possible Uses	The Environment Where They Can Be Deployed
1	Ag Premium Weather	Temperature Location/Tracking Wind	Equipment Weather
2	AQM-65	Pollution/Co2	Weather
3	B-102	Location/Tracking	Equipment
4	CI-340	Moisture Pollution/Co2	Plant
5	DEERE 2630	Yield Moisture	Equipment
6	DEX70	Fruit/Stem Size	Plant
7	FI-MM	Fruit/Stem size	Plant
8	Loup 8000i	Yield Moisture	Equipment
9	Met Station One	Wind	Weather
10	MP406	Temperature Moisture	Soil
11	Piccolo ATX	Location/Tracking	Equipment
12	POGO Portable	Temperature Moisture Water	Soil
13	PYCNO	Temperature Moisture Water	Soil Weather
14	SD-6P	Fruit/Stem Size	Plant
15	SenseH2TM	Location/Tracking Wind	Plant
16	SF-4/5	Fruit/Stem Size	Plant
17	Sol Chip Com (SCC)	Pollution/Co2 Water	Weather
18	Wind Sentry 03002	Location/Tracking	Weather
19	XH-M214	Moisture	Soil
20	YieldTrakk	Yield Moisture Location/Tracking	Equipment

APPENDIX -B

IoT Cloud Platforms

IoT cloud applications pave facilities across remote cloud servers such as real-time data collection, visualization, data analytics, decision-making, system management, etc... The agricultural and farming sector is slowly becoming popular with numerous cloud service providers. Here you can find a notable open-source (Kaa and ThingSpeak) and other popular cloud platforms. Kaa and ThingSpeak are open sources and free, well suited for custom applications.

1. ThingSpeak

ThingSpeak is an open, Public Cloud-based IoT data platform. It helps you to analyze and display the data in MATLAB without buying a Mathworks license. IT enables you to collect and store cloud sensor data and create IoT applications. Works with Arduino, Particle Photon and Electron, ESP8266 Wifi System, BeagleBone Black, Raspberry Pi, Mobile, and Web Apps, Facebook, Twilio, and MATLAB to send ThingSpeak the sensor info. The ThingSpeak focuses primarily on sensor logging, location tracking, triggers, warnings, and analysis.

2. KAA

KAA is an open-source multi-purpose IoT framework for the development of smart, wired, and end-to-end IoT applications (Apache License 2.0). It enables data exchange, data processing, visualization and IoT cloud services among the attached devices. The main tasks of KAA are collecting device specifications, performing device provisioning, configuring, facilitating cross-system communication and allowing distributed firmware updates. It provides back-end functionality to run large-scale IoT solutions that include data protection, accuracy, interoperability, and data management using SDK embedded in the chip or computer of the developer. KAA SDK includes a small memory footprint of at least 10 KB of RAM and 40 KB of ROM. SDK collects data endpoints, offers configuration profiles and allows for endpoint messaging. Two NoSQL database options such as Cassandra, Hadoop and MongoDB allow data storage.

3. Mainflux

MainFlux is a cloud-based IoT platform that is an open-source, modern, scalable, stable and patent-free. It is built entirely with the programming language Go. It provides a strong forum for IoT technologies, applications and product development. MainFlux has strong capabilities for handling large-scale installations and large-scale transactions. The configuration of the back-end cloud infrastructure and APIs offers simple application access with no changes to save time for end-users and offers fast data visualizations and analytical tools on dashboards. This framework, unlike other IoT platforms, supports all protocols — MQTT, WebSockets, CoAP, and REST API.

4. Open Remote

As an open-source IoT middleware solution, OpenRemote allows users to integrate any system-protocol and design using available tools such as iOS, Android or web browsers. Using the cloud service offered by OpenRemote, a user can design software for designing fully customized applications that can use a range of protocols from Wi-Fi to ZigBee to integrate. OpenRemote costs designers nothing, while skilled designers are billed in the V150e375 range per usage.

5. Ploty

Plotly is a popular cloud service provider for the visualization of public data. Plotly offers tools for the collection, visualization and analytics of individual, technical and business data to ordinary or IoT applications. File formats Excel, CSV, and XML is used to upload data to the cloud servers. Plotly implements the Python, R, MATLAB, and Julia based APIs. The visualization is provided by graphics libraries such as ggplot2, matplotlib, MATLAB chart conversion. Among other file formats HDF5, SAS, SPSS, MS Access and ZIP are used to temporarily store the data before uploading to the cloud. This provides facilities for exporting vectors Pdf, svg and eps. An additional pillar of huge popularity behind Plotly is LDAP and directory integration. 3D map visualization assisted by Node.JS enables user data to be interpreted appropriately from hardware devices such as Arduino, Raspberry Pi and Electric Imp.

6. Thinger.io

Thinger.io offers a flexible cloud base for connecting devices. Using their REST API, you can deal with them easily by running the admin console or integrating them into your project logic. It supports all sorts of hacker boards like Raspberry Pi, Intel Edison, ESP8266. Thinger can be integrated with IFTT, and it offers data on a beautiful dashboard in real-time.

Chapter 6
The Internet of Things and Blockchain Technologies Adaptive Trade Systems in the Virtual World:
By Creating Virtual Accomplices Worldwide

Vardan Mkrttchian
HHH University, Australia

ABSTRACT

This chapter presents artificial and natural intelligence technologies. As part of the digital economy of the virtual world program, it is envisaged to increase the efficiency of electronic commerce and entrepreneurship; a similar task has been set by the leadership of the People's Republic of China. At present, thinking in the virtual world and China is radically transforming, along with methodological approaches to the development of trade policy and its tools in the digital economy. It is these circumstances that determine the relevance of the study, the results of which are presented in this chapter. Development of the fundamental foundations for improving the efficiency of electronic commerce and entrepreneurship in virtual world and China based on the virtual exchange of intellectual knowledge using blockchain technology and implementation multi-chain open source platform is the goal. An acceleration of scientific and technological progress in all areas of knowledge raises the task for ensuring the continuous growth of professional skills throughout the whole life.

DOI: 10.4018/978-1-7998-5876-8.ch006

INTRODUCTION IN VIRTUAL WORD AND TRADITIONAL TRADING PROCESS

This chapter is presented author idea use Artificial and Natural Intelligence Technologies. As part of the Digital Economy of the Virtual World program, it is envisaged to increase the efficiency of electronic commerce and entrepreneurship; a similar task has been set by the leadership of the People's Republic of China. At present, thinking in the Virtual World and China is radically transforming, methodological approaches to the development of trade policy and its tools in the digital economy. It is these circumstances that determine the relevance of the study, the results of which are presented in this chapter. Goal research: development of the fundamental foundations for improving the efficiency of electronic commerce and entrepreneurship in Virtual World and China based on the virtual exchange of intellectual knowledge using Blockchain technology and Implementation Multi chain Open Source Platform.

An acceleration of scientific and technological progress in all areas of knowledge raises the task for ensuring the continuous growth of professional skills throughout the whole life. In the traditional trading process, there are several more steps from concluding a contract to delivering an importer. It is difficult, the relevant institutions must carry out a large amount of data exchange, and this work should be. Banking business days, accompanied by a large number of manual reviews and paper documents, as a result of which Efficiency and security are reduced, and there are risks such as letter of credit fraud and soft conditions of the letter of credit. This has led to a gradual reduction in the use of letters of credit. A smart contract is a kind of goal for distribution and testing in an information way.

Over the past few years, information technologies have been able to create a unique environment that can provide resources for the development of global digital commerce, which allows for remote communication with the population on trade issues. This phenomenon has become especially relevant in conditions of forced self-isolation of citizens. Confirmation of this fact is the effect of the corona virus COVID-19. In terms of COVID-19, the population had the greatest demand for products and system solutions for organizing assistance providing video broadcasting, storage and data transfer.

Modern information technologies have allowed the seller and the buyer to quickly interact together at a remote distance from each other in real time. E-mail, instant messengers, Wi-Fi and software and hardware for the development of popular trading applications and technologies have become a significant leader in the market for popular services.

Among the main factors that will ensure positive dynamics in the development of global digital commerce, experts note the proliferation of wearable electronics for commercial use and virtual reality technologies.

This chapter discusses the prospects of Blockchain technology to facilitate the analysis and collection of Big Data using AI and IoT devices used by the People's Republic of China in the modern world by creating Virtual Accomplices' worldwide.

Object of Study

Virtual reality (VR) is a promising tool that can create complex events in the real world (past and present), provoked by traumatic stimuli and controlled by specialists.

VR technology has come a long way from the first experiments in the 50s of the XX century to the modern helmets of virtual reality in the 20s of the XXI century. Two main approaches to the formation of VR systems are known: a virtual room and wearable devices. Wearable VR devices include head-mounted indicators and virtual reality goggles. Currently, the market for virtual devices is formed by the following players by manufacturers: Epson BT-200, Google Glass, Oculus Rift, HTC Vive, Microsoft Hololens, Lumus dk-32, Samsung GearVR, Facebook, Sony, Nokia, etc. Publication and patent the activity of these companies allows us to distinguish four groups of manufacturers, characterized as centers of growth of new knowledge in the field of VR, sustainable research centers, dynamically developing R&D divisions and research engineers. The leading countries in this field are researchers from the USA (46% of the intellectual property market), China (34% of the intellectual property market), Japan (19% of the intellectual property market) and South Korea (13% of the intellectual property market). The market of virtual technologies and simulators in the field of global virtual trade as a whole is widely represented.

Smart contracts allow the absence of third parties. Conduct a trusted transaction. These transactions are track able and irreversible. Thanks to the smart contract technology, the credit intermediary function of the traditional bank is transferred to the smart contract for execution through the smart contract. The verification function, using a computer program to quickly judge the terms of the trading contract, and the next step is to monitor the trading process. As in a typical smart contract trading process between an importer and an exporter Creating a commercial contract based on smart contracts in a blockchain network, importers to financial institutions By providing a deposit, a financial institution registers a guarantee payment in real time to the blockchain network. After the deposit is paid, the exporter will send goods, and the conveyor will send the goods. Downloaded to the blockchain network when a smart contract, transport document and commercial sale are reached. Subject to the same conditions of payment, a financial instruction is issued to the financial institution, and the financial institution may calculate the payment for the importer.

Using, thanks to effective blockchain technology, eliminates labor efficiency and low latency, can achieve high-frequency trading around the clock, through smart contracts to eliminate the human factor.

Subject of Study

The People's Republic of China in the modern world by creating Virtual Accomplices' worldwide the blockchain form is mainly divided into a public blockchain alliance. The blockchain consortium is a completely private blockchain (fully private) three, a public blockchain refers to any person in the world, anyone can read it. Anyone can send a transaction, and the transaction can be confirmed, anyone can participate in it. A blockchain process, an alliance blockchain means that its coordinated process is controlled by pre-selected nodes. Blockchain, a completely private blockchain, refers to a zone whose write rights are only in the Joint chapter hands of the Blockchain organization. Among them, the choice of alliance chain technologies is more suitable for creating information technologies for belt and road trade. For the needs of the exhibition, alliance chain nodes are pre-selected, and the pre-selection method can be effective. Eliminate bad, untrusted nodes to protect the blockchain from things like 51% Impact of point attack. In addition, the chain of alliances is not fully decentralized, and its consensus model. To control the alliance, this will contribute to the modernization and expansion of the consensus mechanism in the future. It also facilitates control of the system by the lead organization.

BACKGROUND IN VIRTUAL WORD AND TRADITIONAL TRADING PROCESS

In an environment where technology is a catalyst for new financial ideas, blockchain technology can be integrated into an existing financial system without cost. Currently, the Internet of things and artificial intelligence have become the main form of modern Internet finance, so the future blockchain will certainly develop in the direction of "blockchain + IoT blockchain + artificial intelligence". As the IoT grows geometrically, the cost of computing resources, storage and broadband for centralized services will become inaccessible to operating companies, and blockchain technology can provide direct data transfer for the IoT without the need to create and manage IoT. Secondly, it is necessary to solve the problem of protecting the privacy of the Internet of things. Because the centralized IoT service architecture stores and transmits all information and signals through the central processing unit, excessive data concentration leads to large-scale privacy leaks after information theft. According to blockchain technology, while client data is not controlled by one cloud Service

Company, no one can steal data by encrypting the data transfer process, which makes client privacy more secure. Thirdly, it is creating a new business model for the Internet of things. In accordance with the current IoT architecture, clients cannot perform network transactions using another IoT and can conduct financial transactions on only one network or on a trusted network. This limitation significantly reduces the commercial value of the Internet of things. Blockchain technology eliminates trust transactions for direct transactions, for example, a system of "autonomous centralized remote control between centers" jointly developed by IBM and Samsung. The system uses a distributed network to ensure that IoT devices accessing the system can directly communicate and implement complex business logic.

With the continuous improvement of artificial intelligence technology, its application in the financial sector is becoming more and more extensive, including such important activities as account opening, analysis and trading. Therefore, the safety and reliability of artificial intelligence is attracting more attention. Blockchain can be artificially friendly through the following aspects: Firstly, blockchain technology can improve the reputation of artificial intelligence. Blockchain technology can rely on smart contract forms to ensure that during the transaction process, the system automatically creates electronic contracts and leaves irreparable traces. Secondly, the blockchain sharing mechanism will make artificial intelligence more friendly. Any transaction is carried out on the blockchain and must be confirmed by both sides of the transaction, so only two intelligent machines can confirm the transaction at a time. If a party cannot confirm for any reason, the transaction will be automatically canceled. Thirdly, blockchain technology will provide more accurate information for artificial intelligence. The blockchain system can use its own voting mechanism for the scientific classification of information on the Internet: the first level is spam, the second level is informational recommendations, and the third level is informational consent. The blockchain only sends consistent information to artificial intelligence through a rating system to evaluate and improve its accuracy. Fourth, blockchain technology will improve the security mechanism of artificial intelligence. For example, devices can register in a blockchain, perform various hierarchical evaluations using device registration information, provide different functions for different devices, and prevent smart devices from being misused to better exercise common ownership and device usage rights (Wenbin, 2015). The progress of human society and the development of the economy have benefited from the use and creation of tools since ancient times, and various tools have been continuously created. The initial driving force is undeniable from science and technology. In a market economy there will be a periodic cyclical overabundance, and even people's way of life. And the fundamental changes brought about by ideology are the result of large-scale industrial applications of science and technology. " Since the beginning of the 21st century, it has been based on the rapid development and maturity of information technologies such as the Internet and mobile Internet and cloud computing big data, which Ali, Tencent, JD, Baidu, Amazon, Facebook, Apple, Microsoft and Huawei created. A large number of great world-class enterprises have reached many well-known successful entrepreneurs, significantly increasing the efficiency and viability of socio-economic operations. However, the development of science and technology will never stop. Various new technologies are currently undergoing explosive birth and development. The business logic of applying scientific and technical industrialization is also undergoing fundamental changes, that is, from centralized information interaction. If you combine new technologies, such as artificial intelligence, the Internet of things, big data, cloud computing and blockchain, all together in one innovative project form the most effective form of economic activity. In the future, we will enter the era of the true digital economy, and the realization of the digital economy is the result of the merger of these new technologies. Social structural changes will at least completely change the behavior of business people. I think that I am afraid that these new technologies will be "organized and integrated" in various business scenarios. There is an opinion on the market that even "a predictable future = (artificial intelligence + Internet of things + big data) × blockchain". This formula shows that the three main technologies in brackets are "data", that is, deep data mining, massive data collection and transmission in real time and data mining, while a "block chain" provides data protection and trust him. The mechanisms and means of repaying value transactions allow you to safely use the value data required by the three technologies in brackets in the business environment. The right side of this formula actually expresses the product of "Blockchain Technology" and "Virtual Market".

MAIN FOCUS OF THE ARTICLE

Issues, Controversies, Problems

On the right side of the above formula, artificial intelligence is at the forefront because technology essentially embodies a kind of "ability", that is, an ability that allows intelligent machines (computer intelligent systems) to learn and model human thinking. At the same time, the results of the training model of the engine and the working model can be stored on the blockchain, which ensures that the model is not hacked, and the risk of malicious attacks by the commercial applications is further reduced (Li & Ren, 2016). Artificial intelligence technology can provide a glimpse of the future with massive historical data and real-time observations, while the Internet of Things will provide a large amount of real-time data as well as big data to provide sufficient and efficient "fuel" for artificial intelligence.

The data generated by various system sensors will naturally have some real-time data owners, but some data is temporarily unnecessary, so the data owner can desensitize this part of the temporarily unwanted data. Take it and share it with other data developers or developers, so that it can solve the problem of data loss and generate significant income, to offset the cost of the data creation process, and will also generate partial wins. For project founders, having enough data to train AI or ML models will be an endless challenge. Objectively, only large centralized technology companies with a large number of users will be able to get large data sets. However, in decentralized mode, it's very convenient to add more datasets to the artificial intelligence community, which means that IoT devices will make the data sets needed to teach artificial intelligence a big role in real-world business scenarios. Currently, there are many excellent technical research groups involved in collecting training data and the most practical research algorithms and applying these algorithms to the blockchain. Another question: how can we use a large number of unoccupied computing powers distributed in the market to launch AI or ML computing models? The answer is that blockchain technology can make the data market more equitable and efficient. The biggest injustice in the current market environment is that people tend to ignore the minority, but the most necessary thing in machine learning is the minority. Data, data belonging to a minority, will become more valuable, as I wrote in my previous article entitled "Mathematics is the cornerstone of blockchain + AI technology, and mathematics can interpret the value of all business practice." It is mentioned that if you want to increase the accuracy of the machine learning model from 90% to 99%, then you need not the data that has already been studied, but the data that several people should have that are different from the previous ones. For example, the commercial and technical logic, followed by the Ketai Structural Hole Technology Intelligent Eco-Network Investment and Structural Tunnel Financing System, is "(Artificial Intelligence + Internet of Things + Big Data) × Blockchain, which will be artificial intelligence (Such technologies like cognitive computing, intelligent management (IoT), big data and blockchain are combined with the participation of people in the division of labor on connected devices, jointly generated by management data and the operations that these devices can perform to create the first Innovative Intelligent System that "thinks" and is used for commercial purposes in the venture capital market We strongly believe that multicenter, de-mediation, self-organization and data exchange and network synergy are reliable The "intelligent ecosystem system" will be reconstructed from the existing traditional industry in accordance with this new business and technical logic. And this is what the future era of the digital economy needs (Li & Ren, 2016).

Solutions and Recommendations

1. Consensus Mechanism and Performance

A consensus protocol is used to achieve accessibility and consistency in distributed systems. This is a key technology in the blockchain, the main indicators of which include: Typical agreements include BFT consensus presented by PBFT, Nakamoto consensus presented by PoW / PoS, and the new hybrid consensus. Currently, the biggest challenge in consensus agreements is how to strike a balance between safety and efficiency.

Based on the premise of security, there are four ways to increase productivity:

1. Improving the hardware and computing capabilities, from CPU, GPU, FPGA to ASIC, mining equipment is constantly updated, and the general level of computer processing power is also rapidly developing. According to OpenAl analysis, since 2012, the task of teaching artificial intelligence, the computing power used is growing exponentially, and its current speed doubles every 3.5 months (compared with Moore's law, which doubles every 18 months). If computing power goes beyond a certain critical point, the blockchain performance issue may no longer be a problem;
2. The improvement of the consensus agreement system has not changed. Representative methods include reducing the generation interval of blocks, increasing the size of a block, adopting a two-layer chain structure, introducing a lightning-fast network, changing the basic structure of a block + chain, and reducing blocks.
3. Data, a advanced algorithms
4. New data structures, such as the use of directed acyclic graph (DAG) data structures, typical projects have 10TA and ByteBall;
5. New consistent protocols, such as the Thunder Ella algorithm for the PoW mechanism proposed by the researchers, the Algorand protocol and the Ouroboros algorithm for the PoS mechanism, PoS consensus based on the Sleepy model and Proof of Space.

2. Cross Chain

Currently, there are various chains: public, alliance and private. A public chain serves the public, an alliance chain is limited to one alliance, and a private chain serves only one private organization. From a private chain, an alliance chain to a public chain is a decentralization process, and from a public chain an alliance chain to a private chain, this is a centralization process.

During these transformations, various blockchain products will appear for private networks, alliance networks, and government networks. Then, when business interactions between different organizations, how to interact between different chains and chains becomes a big problem. There are currently three cross-chain technologies:

Notary Schemes Side Chains / Relays Hash Lock Technology

Cross-chain technology is the center of the next technological development of the blockchain. In addition, the current private network has a problem with the game, which is who, joins, and each other wants them to join their own blockchain system. Although BaaS (Backend as a Service) can reuse the underlying technology platform, the key is the exchange of data between different business systems and users, as well as collaboration between business systems. If there is no connection between the various systems, it is not possible to reuse core resources such as customers, assets and data.

There a two possible ways to solve this problem:

1. The government or standardization organizations promote the standardization and standardization of blockchain technology and improve the interaction between different systems;
2. The government is creating a public service platform. For example, the HKTFP supported by the Hong Kong Monetary Authority is typical. The advantage of this model is that a platform built on the basis of public interests can better resolve disputes between the subject of construction and the management mechanism, as well as open users and scenarios. And public services to achieve the integration of resources, but also easy for government regulation, improve regulatory efficiency.

3. Control Mechanisms

Since the blockchain itself is a natural voting system that contains all the logic necessary to change the validation assembly or update its own rules, and the voting results can be automated, the chain voting mechanism naturally becomes a blockchain ecosystem. The preferred control mechanism currently has a number of chain voting mechanisms, such as EOS, NEO, Lisk, and other systems in the Proof of Equity (DPOS) mechanism, through chain voting to determine who controls the super node that the network is running on or by agreement. Options are voted to determine Essence gas restriction or vote on protocol updates such as Toes.

Disadvantages of the current voting mechanism in the chain:

1. Low participation in the vote, which leads to two problems. Firstly, the results of the vote reflect only a small number of people's opinions and it is difficult to obtain universal recognition, and secondly, an attacker can vote at low cost.
2. There may be a chapbook-style minority chain management that is detrimental to the interests of ordinary users.

In addition, relying entirely on chain management, he still cannot solve the problem of the main agent of the blockchain ecosystem, and also needs the support of chain supervision, such as legal oversight and a reputation mechanism.

Governments have now begun to take action. For example, the National Network Bureau recently announced the "Regulation on the Management of Information Services of the Blockchain (draft for comments)" and publicly sought public opinion. Of course, this is building a system level. From a technical point of view, how to improve the chain management mechanism is the next step in the study of blockchain technology.

4. Identity Management

Blockchain makes self-sovereign identity possible. By itself, it can be used as a decentralized public key infrastructure (PKI) to make public key authorities more useful and secure. Blockchain can be thought of as a decentralized certification authority that maps support for authentication to a public key.

Smart contracts can also add complex logic, implement cancellation and recovery, and reduce the burden on key management for end users. These technologies push identity ownership from centralized services to end-to-end services between people and make identity itself manageable. This is called autonomy. This approach distracts the data and calculations and transfers them to each individual, which is less economical for hackers because it takes a lot of effort to attack many people one by one.

In the alliance chain, different nodes must be assigned different permissions and they satisfy a certain control. To do this, it is necessary to create a safe and effective mechanism for authentication and identity management.

An authentication mechanism based on biometrics technology or an effective combination of biometrics and cryptography can be used;

An efficient and practical password scheme based on identifiers / attributes can also be used to achieve detailed access control / rights management for nodes / users.

5. Privacy Protection

In a public chain, it is necessary to protect confidential information, such as transaction data, address, identity, etc., and at the same time allow the accounting node to verify the legality of the transaction, and for the alliance chain, when building a privacy protection scheme, it is necessary to take into account the control / tracking of authorization.

Protection of transaction identification and content confidentiality can be achieved with cryptographic primitives and schemes, such as effective knowledge with zero knowledge, commitment and indistinguishable evidence. For example: Zkash uses zk-SNARK to implement a privacy mechanism.

A privacy mechanism based on a cryptographic scheme such as a ring signature, a group signature, and a privacy protection mechanism based on a hierarchical certificate mechanism is also optional. For example:

Montero uses a ring signature scheme to implement privacy protection mechanisms. Hyper ledger Fabric uses a hierarchical certificate mechanism to implement privacy protection mechanisms.

Protecting the confidentiality of transactional contents can also be achieved with an efficient holomorphic encryption scheme or a secure multi-part computing scheme. For example:

Ripple introduces privacy protection for trading channels, introducing a secure multi-user computing solution.

A simple coin protection mechanism can also be used to provide simple privacy protection.

6. Digital Wallet

Currently, digital wallets are trying to move from pure wallet services to environmental portals of digital assets, hoping to gain more market share and develop richer asset management services, mainly in the areas of asset management, asset trading, information aggregation, DApp distribution, etc. .

Asset management can be divided into production of value added, value added management, asset management, asset collection, etc. Asset transactions mainly include a decentralized exchange of digital assets and the exchange of legal currencies, information aggregation - this is mainly information exchange and aggregation of project information, DApp distribution is similar. In a small software store.

Although the entry points and development paths of different wallets are different, and each has its own strengths, the functions of different value-added wallets slightly overlap, because the long-term goals of each other are gradually converging. With the continuous development of the digital asset industry and the continuous improvement of the environment, the digital wallet scene function will become more and more important.

There a three aspects to its future development:

1.   ensure the security, openness and convenience of the wallet;
2.   Creation of a digital asset management platform based on the demand for added value of assets, providing users with rich financial products and increasing the conversion rate of users;
3.   The third is to open the connection between digital assets and the real world, enrich the scenarios of digital assets and create ecology of digital assets.

Security is fundamental. Software technologies can use keyless cryptographic algorithms (a standard white box scheme or create new white box cryptographic algorithms) and code obfuscation methods to allow an adversary to extract basic cryptographic algorithms and key information, or use passwords, an authentication factor encryption algorithm such as personality and biometrics, encrypts and stores the key.

The hardware aspect can be based on the TEE (Trusted Execution Environment) or SE (Security Environment) security module and a technical solution that helps to configure the terminal device, which is one of the important additional directions for protecting a digital wallet.

7. Smart Contracts and Self-organizing Business Models

Smart contracts have the advantages of transparency, reliability, automatic execution and mandatory compliance. Once it is deployed in the blockchain, the code and data of the program are open and transparent, cannot be faked and must be executed in accordance with predefined logic to obtain the expected results, and the execution of the contract will be recorded.

It should be said that blockchain technology and its commercial application mutually reinforce each other. Self-organizing business applications built on smart contracts can help add value to blockchain technology and expand the scope of the encryption economics model.

Although from a technical point of view, a smart contract is just part of the code, it essentially carries a lot of business logic, and even a smart contract is a business model with unlimited imagination. Conversely, the implementation of a self-organizing business model also requires the delicate development of smart contracts, and also requires the support of technical measures, such as improving productivity, increasing security and protecting privacy. In other words, this is both the creation of a business model, and the development of a technical system.

The security of smart contracts is crucial. Due to the openness of smart contracts, their code and content can be obtained using open methods that allow hackers to analyze contracts and attack vulnerabilities. Once the attack is successful, this will result in significant losses. Consequently, there is an urgent need for sophisticated smart contract detection technology to detect, detect, and eliminate vulnerabilities before the contract is chained.

There were many smart contract detection tools or online testing sites, but these tests are still based on experience and there is nothing to be done about unknown contract vulnerabilities.

The formal check method is a possible solution for determining exactly whether a program can work in accordance with the developer's expectations by creating an appropriate model. However, formal verification of smart contracts is difficult, and no suitable solution has been found at this time, and further research is needed.

When applying smart contracts, on the one hand, it is necessary to clarify the possibility of using smart contracts from the legal level, on the other hand, since smart contracts have natural certainty and do not have the flexibility and selectivity of ordinary contracts, therefore, in specific scenarios, in order to establish an intervention mechanism that allows code to pause or stop execution.

FUTURE RESEARCH DIRECTIONS

- **Integration with other technologies:** It is often said that cloud computing, big data, artificial intelligence, blockchain technology, etc. In essence, they are the embodiment of "algorithm + data", and there are no other priorities. Since the essence is the same, mutual integration is inevitable.

For example, an asset securitization scenario requires ongoing disclosure of information from multiple business systems, and also requires a large-scale distributed file storage.

Blockchain technology can ensure the consistency of distributed ledgers on all sides of a transaction by signing a transaction, a consistent algorithm and cross-chain technology to ensure that a transaction is executed in real time and automatically complete real-time information disclosure to ensure accounting. Accounting and accounting are consistent, which greatly improves credit rating of traded products and significantly reduces the cost, which allows information users to receive global information ju about the activities of the enterprise in real time and through it, and receiving global information means information. Mass growth, the best way to store and retrieve the value of information, is becoming the key to the chain.

Therefore, the integration of blockchain technology with distributed file systems, big data analysis, cloud computing, artificial intelligence and other technologies is an important direction for future development.

CONCLUSION

In the presented chapter, the following tasks were solved: the analysis of goods and services of Russia and China was carried out; outline the main policy guidelines and its impact on globalization and regional integration; disclosing the prospects for the development of blockchain technologies in international trade and its impact on the global financial industry; the role of blockchain technology in the development of the global economy is substantiated.

The following research areas were disclosed:

1. The development of international cooperation based on innovative intelligent technologies
   a. Prerequisites for international cooperation on the example of "Belts and Roads". The historical need of the project "One belt – one way"
   b. China's banking industry indicators in the belt and road
   c. Blockchain Technology - the strongest push in international multilateral financial and trade cooperation
   d. Cross-border capital flows: transactional efficiency, risk management, checking the creditworthiness of counterparties
2. Creating conditions for mutually beneficial trade relations in the process of digitalization of national economic systems
   a. Application of blockchain technology in international trade in the context of the "Belt and Road" initiative
   b. Vision of the Alliance Belt and Road Blockchain
   c. Blockchain technology can be combined with more technical means
3. Development of reflective adaptive software for applying Blockchain technology, big data analysis and virtual exchange of intellectual knowledge.

Were disclosed the future direction of blockchain technology: consensus mechanism and performance, cross chain, control mechanism, identity management, privacy protection, digital wallet, smart contracts and self-organizing business models.

REFERENCES

Li, Z., & Ren, X. (2016). Analysis of the impact of blockchain on the Internet finance and its prospects. *Technical Economics and Management Studies, 10*, 75–78.

Technology illuminates the future - when blockchain technology and adaptive security technology enter social management and economic life. (n.d.). Retrieved October 02, 2019, from http://blog.sina.com.cn/s/blog_67804b9a0102z2gn.html

The fusion of artificial intelligence and blockchain technology represents the future of the digital economy. (n.d.). Retrieved May 14, 2019, from http://www.sohu.com/a/313838766_99985608?qq-pf-to=pcqq.c2c

Wenbin, U. (2015). Principles, models and proposals of banking trading blockchain. *Hebei University Journal, 6*, 159–160.

ADDITIONAL READING

Alguliyev, R. M., Aliguliyev, R. M., & Sukhostat, L. V. (2020). Efficient algorithm for big data clustering on single machine. *CAAI Trans Intell Technol, 5*(1), 9–14. doi:10.1049/trit.2019.0048

Antonopoulos, A. M. (2014). *Mastering bitcoin: unlocking digital crypto-currencies*. O'Reilly Media Inc.

Ash, J. S., Berg, M., & Coiera, E. (2004). Some unintended consequences of information technology in health care: The nature of patient care information system-related errors. *Journal of the American Medical Informatics Association, 11*(2), 104–112. doi:10.1197/jamia.M1471 PMID:14633936

Chang, X., & Han, F. (2016). *Block chain: From digital currency to credit society*. China Citic Press.

Conoscenti, M., Vetr, A., & Martin, J. C. D. (2016) Blockchain for the internet of things: a systematic literature review. In: *Proceedings of the IEEE/ACS 13th international conference of computer systems and applications (AICCSA)*, IEEE, Agadir, Morocco 10.1109/AICCSA.2016.7945805

Devi, D., Namasudra, S., & Kadry, S. (2020). A boosting-aided adaptive cluster-based undersampling approach for treatment of class imbalance problem. *International Journal of Data Warehousing and Mining, 16*(3), 60–86. doi:10.4018/IJDWM.2020070104

Haber, S., & Stornetta, W. S. (1991). How to time-stamp a digital document. *Journal of Cryptology*, *3*(2), 99–111. doi:10.1007/BF00196791

Ho, D. C. K., Au, K. F., & Newton, E. (2002). Empirical research on supply chain management: A critical review and recommendations. *International Journal of Production Research*, *40*(17), 4415–4430. doi:10.1080/00207540210157204

Huang, G. Q., Lau, J. S. K., & Mak, K. L. (2003). The impacts of sharing production information on supply chain dynamics: A review of the literature. *International Journal of Production Research*, *41*(7), 1483–1517. doi:10.1080/0020754031000069625

Hwang, J., Choi, M., Lee, T., Jeon, S., Kim, S., Park, S., & Park, S. (2017). Energy prosumer business model using blockchain system to ensure transparency and safety. *Energy Procedia*, *141*, 194–198. doi:10.1016/j.egypro.2017.11.037

Kshetri, N. (2017). Cybersecurity in India: Regulations, governance, institutional capacity and market mechanisms. *Asian Research Policy*, *8*(1), 64–76.

Li, S., Wang, G., & Yang, J. (2019). Survey on cloud model based similarity measure of uncertain concepts. *CAAI Trans Intell Technol*, *4*(4), 223–230. doi:10.1049/trit.2019.0021

Lin, Q., Yan, H., Huang, Z., Chen, W., Shen, J., & Tang, Y. (2018). An ID-based linearly homomorphic signature scheme and its application in Blockchain. *IEEE Access: Practical Innovations, Open Solutions*, *6*, 20632–20640. doi:10.1109/ACCESS.2018.2809426

Ming, Z., Jun, C., Yuqing, W., Yuanfei, L., Yongqi, Y., & Jinyue, D. (2017). The primarily research for multi module cooperative autonomous mode of energy internet under blockchain framework. *Zhongguo Dianji Gongcheng Xuebao*, *37*(13), 3672–3681.

Namasudra, S. (2017). *An improved attribute-based encryption technique towards the data security in cloud computing*. Concurr Comput Pract Exer., doi:10.1002/cpe.4364

Namasudra, S. (2018). Taxonomy of DNA-based security models. In S. Namasudra & G. C. Deka (Eds.), *Advances of dna computing in cryptography* (pp. 53–68). Springer. doi:10.1201/9781351011419-3

Namasudra, S. (2018). Cloud computing: A new era. *J Fundam Appl Sci*, *10*(2), 113–135.

Namasudra, S., Chakraborty, R., Majumder, A., & Moparthi, N. R. (2020). *Securing multimedia by using DNA based encryption in the cloud computing environment.* ACM T Multi Comput Commun Appl.

Namasudra, S., & Deka, G. C. (2018). *Advances of DNA computing in cryptography.* Taylor & Francis. doi:10.1201/9781351011419

Namasudra, S., & Deka, G. C. (2018). Introduction of DNA computing in cryptography. In S. Namasudra & D. C. Deka (Eds.), *Advances of dna computing in cryptography* (pp. 27–34). Springer. doi:10.1201/9781351011419-1

Namasudra, S., Deka, G. C., & Bali, R. (2018). Applications and future trends of DNA computing. In S. Namasudra & G. C. Deka (Eds.), *Advances of DNA computing in cryptography* (pp. 181–192). Taylor & Francis. doi:10.1201/9781351011419-9

Namasudra, S., Devi, D., Choudhary, S., Patan, R., & Kallam, S. (2018). Security, privacy, trust, and anonymity. In S. Namasudra & G. C. Deka (Eds.), *Advances of DNA computing in cryptography* (pp. 153–166). Taylor & Francis. doi:10.1201/9781351011419-7

Namasudra, S., Devi, D., Kadry, S., Sundarasekar, R., & Shanthini, A. (2020). Towards DNA based data security in the cloud computing environment. *Computer Communications, 151*, 539–547. doi:10.1016/j.comcom.2019.12.041

Namasudra, S., & Roy, P. (2016). Secure and efficient data access control in cloud computing environment: A survey. *Multiagent Grid Sys Int J, 12*(2), 69–90. doi:10.3233/MGS-160244

Namasudra, S., & Roy, P. (2017). Time saving protocol for data accessing in cloud computing. *IET Communications, 11*(10), 1558–1565. doi:10.1049/iet-com.2016.0777

Namasudra, S., & Roy, P. (2018). PpBAC: Popularity based access control model for cloud computing. *Journal of Organizational and End User Computing, 30*(4), 14–31. doi:10.4018/JOEUC.2018100102

Namasudra, S., Roy, P., Vijayakumar, P., Audithan, S., & Balusamy, B. (2017). Time efficient secure DNA based access control model for cloud computing environment. *Future Generation Computer Systems, 73*, 90–105. doi:10.1016/j.future.2017.01.017

Sarkar, M., Saha, K., Namasudra, S., & Roy, P. (2015). An efficient and time saving web service based android application. *SSRG Int J Comput Sci Eng, 2*(8), 18–21.

Swan, M. (2015). *Blockchain: blueprint for a new economy.* O'Reilly Media.

Williams, A. (2016). *IBM to open first blockchain innovation centre in Singapore, to create applications and grow new markets in finance and trade*. The Straits Times Singapore Press Holdings Ltsd. Co.

Wood, G. (2014). *Ethereum: a secure decentralised generalised transaction ledger*. Ethereum Project Yellow Paper.

Xia, Q. I., Sifah, E. B., Asamoah, K. O., Gao, J., Du, X., & Guizani, M. (2017). MeDShare: Trust-less medical data sharing among cloud service providers via blockchain. *IEEE Access: Practical Innovations, Open Solutions*, *5*, 14757–14767. doi:10.1109/ACCESS.2017.2730843

Xue, T., Hongbin, S., & Qinglai, G. (2016). Electricity transactions and congestion management based on blockchain in energy internet. *Power Syst Technol*, *40*(12), 3630–3638.

Zhao, X., Li, R., & Zuo, X. (2019). Advances on QoS-aware web service selection and composition with nature-inspired computing. *CAAI Trans Intell Technol*, *4*(3), 159–174. doi:10.1049/trit.2019.0018

Zheng, Z., Xie, S., Dai, H. N., & Wang, H. (2016). Blockchain challenges and opportunities: A survey. *International Journal of Web and Grid Services*, *14*(4), 314–335.

KEY TERMS AND DEFINITIONS

Blockchain: A continuous sequential chain of blocks (linked list) containing information built according to certain rules.

Digital Economy: Is an economic activity focused on digital and electronic technologies. This includes electronic business and commerce, as well as the goods and services they produce. This definition covers all business, cultural, economic, and social operations performed on the Internet and using digital communication technologies.

EDI (Electronic Data Interchange): A series of standards and conventions for the transfer of structured digital information between organizations, based on certain regulations and formats of transmitted messages.

Electronic Commerce: Financial transactions and transactions carried out through the Internet and private communication networks, during which purchases and sales of goods and services are made, as well as money transfers.

Intellectual Capital: Knowledge, skills and production experience of specific people and intangible assets, including patents, databases, software, trademarks, etc. that are productively used to maximize profits and other economic and technical results.

Chapter 7
An Analytical Study on Machine Learning Techniques

Law Kumar Singh

iD https://orcid.org/0000-0002-7073-6852

Sharda University, India

Pooja

Sharda University, India

Hitendra Garg

GLA University, India

Munish Khanna

Hindustan College of Science and Technology, India

Robin Singh Bhadoria

iD https://orcid.org/0000-0002-6314-4736

Birla Institute of Applied Sciences (BIAS), Bhimtal, India

ABSTRACT

The last few months have produced a remarkable expansion in research and deep study in the field of machine learning. Machine learning is a technique in which the set of the methods are used by the computers to make prediction, improve prediction and behavior prediction based on dataset. The learning techniques can be classified as supervised and unsupervised learning. The focus is on supervised machine learning that covers all the predictions problem for which we had the dataset in which the outcome is already known. Some of the algorithm like naive bayes, linear regression, SVM, k-nearest neighbor, especially neural network have gain growth in this area. The classifiers of machine learning are completely unconstrained with the assumptions of statistical and for that they are adapted by complex data. The authors have demonstrated the application of machine learning techniques and its ethical issues.

DOI: 10.4018/978-1-7998-5876-8.ch007

1. INTRODUCTION

Machine learning is the branch of artificial intelligence that analyzes and responds to the data on the basis of similar pattern collection called clusters, which helps in analyzing and responding to the data. It is like a blank human mind that understands any image by its physical structure or the data it has from its past experience (Smola and Vishwanathan, 2008).

Key features of machine learning

- It converts the data into information where the data can be in the form of image, videos, texts, CSV etc
- It is a problem-solving tool.
  ex: n-queens, 8-queens, traveling salesman, etc
- It is the combination of computer science, engineering, and statistics, where computer science means it performs the programming work; engineering means applying different types of applications and statistics means the application of mathematical computations.
- It interprets data and acts on it, means it takes the data and analyzes that data, learns that data, and based on that learning, it performs actions.
- It optimizes the performance criteria using past information.

For example, in the finance sector, with the help of past data and algorithms given to a machine, it detects the difference between legal and fraudulent activities, if in case any illegal transaction takes place the machine can detect it easily.

In the e-commerce sector: by calculating the previous record, a machine gets to know customer's interest and sellers conditions, and by using a mathematical algorithm, it gives results having maximum profits for sellers.

2. TYPES OF MACHINE LEARNING

Figure 1 shows the detailed block diagram of the type of Machine Learning.

- Supervised Learning
- Unsupervised Learning
- Semi-Supervised Learning
- Reinforcement Learning

Figure 1. Types of machine learning

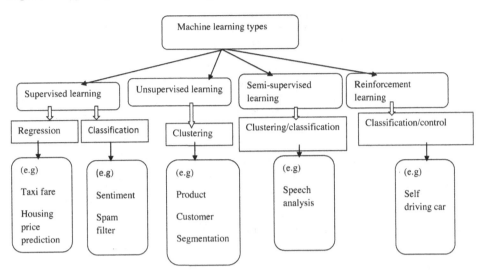

2.1 Supervised Learning

Supervised learning also is known to be associative learning in which the model has been trained in the presence of the teachers and supervisor. It uses to pair each of the input vectors with target vectors, which represents the desired outputs, where the input vectors are closely related to the target vectors that show the expected outputs. In this type of training method, we provide inputs for the models, and this gives an output vector (Pearl and Stevers, 2012). These output vectors are compared within the target values. If we find these target values are differed by the actual values, then the model results in a type of error, the synaptic weight adjustment has to be calculated on the basis of error values for matching actual values with target values. This training method performs non-linear mapping in the pattern classification networks, pattern associated network & multilayer neural networks, as shown in Figure 2.

Figure 2. Model of the machine learning algorithm

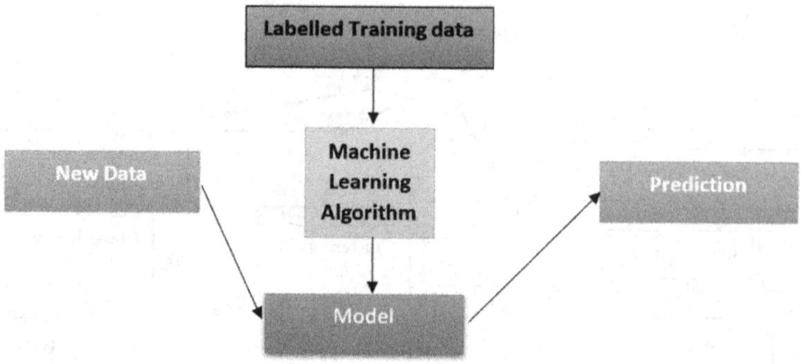

Some of the algorithm used in supervised learning

- Naive Bayes
- Neural Networks
- Linear Regression
- Support Vector Machine (SVM)
- K-Nearest Neighbor
- Decision Tree

2.1.1 Naive Bays

It is a type of Bayesian network model in machine learning, where variable class(C) is the root that has to be predicted & these attribute variables are leaves. This is a naive bays model because it resumes the attribute, which is conditionally different from each other. This algorithm, which is a type of machine learning algorithm, is used for classification problems. Naive Bayes is primarily used for text classification, which could involve high-dimensional training data sets. There are so many examples where the naive Bayes algorithm is used like spam filtration, sentimental analysis, and classifying news articles. This algorithm is also called 'naive' because it makes the assumption that the occurrence of a certain feature is independent of the other features.

2.1.2 Neural Network

A neural network is a highly interconnected network of a large number of processing elements called neurons. Its architecture is motivated by the brain; a neural network can be massively parallel and therefore said to be exhibit parallel distributed processing. The neural network can be taught to perform a complex task and are intrinsically fault-tolerant. In a neural network, neurons are interconnected to the synopsis, which provides input from other neurons, which intern provides output and input to other neurons. There are two types of neural networks:

- **Artificial neural network:** An artificial neural network is the fastest in processing information; they operate a sequential mode that is one instruction after others in a conventional computer. It has an input layer, hidden layer, and output layer, as in Figure 3.

Figure 3. Data extraction in an artificial neural network

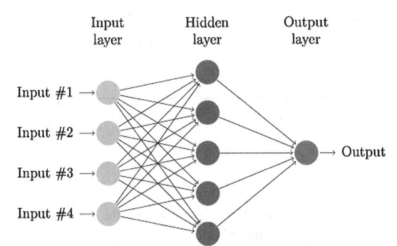

2.1.3 Linear Regression

Linear Regression is the type of machine learning algorithm which depends upon the supervised learning, where it performs all the regression tasks. Regression models depend on the independent variable(s) where the target prediction is made. This is usually performed for calculating the relationship between the variable and the forecasting. There are different types of regression models that are based on – the type of relationships among dependent and independent variable(s). Linear regression performs tasks for predicting the dependent variable values (y), which depends on the given independent variables (x). So, in this regression technique, we find out the linear relationship between x (input) &and y(output).

Figure 4. Graph for linear regression

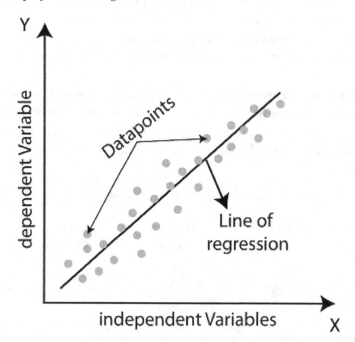

$$\hat{Y} = bX + a$$

Where b=slope=rate of the predicate for y scores for the per unit increase in x. Y-intercept =level of the 'y' when 'x' is 0

2.1.4 Support Vector Machine (SVM)

It is a type of Supervised learning which uses the regression and the classification both as in Figure 5. We can also use the support vector machine as support vector networks in machine learning. SVM has supervised learning models that associated learning by the algorithm. When we talk about classification, support vector machine is classified into various vectors machine that can be categorized into three types:

- **Relevance vector machine (RVM)** – A support vector machine having identical functional form is known as a relevance vector machine; it provides the probabilistic classification so that it is entirely equivalent.
- **Least square support vector machine (LS-SVM)** - Least square support vector machine is having versions of least squares which is related to the set of supervised learning

- **Structured support vector machine (S-SVM)** – Structured support vector machine is used to generalized the classifiers of support vector machine-like SVM classifier

Figure 5. Support vector machine classifier

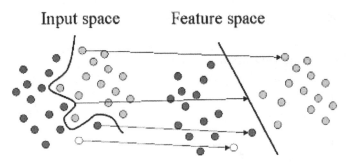

2.1.5. K- Nearest Neighbor Algorithm

The k-nearest neighbor algorithm is basically used in the process of classification and regression; this algorithm is completely non-parametric.In both of the cases, classification and regression, the input variable are always having training examples of k-closest, which is deeply extracted from featured space, and in this case, the output is dependent on the K-NN values for classification and regression as in Figure 6.

Figure 6. KNN (K-nearest neighbors)

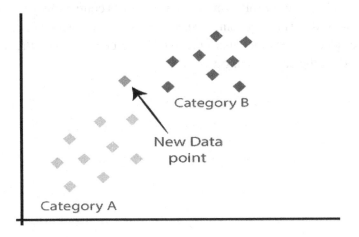

It is used in Euclidean distances for finding the distance metric of a continuous variable, and it uses text classification for discrete variables, we can also use other different metrics such as Hamming distance, i.e., overlaps metric. The basic drawback of this majority voting algorithm is the skewing of class distribution, which occurs during classification. We can improve the classification accuracy of K-NN very slightly if the learning of distance metric is done within different specialized algorithms like large margin nearest neighbor and neighborhood component analysis

Figure 7. Non-parametric k-nearest neighbor classifier

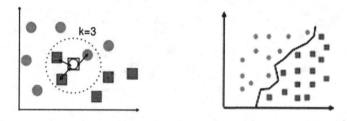

In Figure 7 there are two basic parameter selections in the K-NN algorithm they are The Nearest Neighbor Classifier and The Weighted Nearest Neighbor.

2.1.6 Decision Tree Algorithm

The process of decision tree algorithm is to describe the input and output, i.e., what the input is? Or what is the corresponding output from the training data? A decision tree is one of the types of supervised machine learning algorithms where the input data is split or break up by following some parameters continuously, as in Figure 8. This tree can be described by using two entities such as decision nodes and leaves; here, leave nodes means the final outcome or the decision, and the meaning of decision node is the data which gets splits.

Figure 8. Process of the decision tree in machine learning

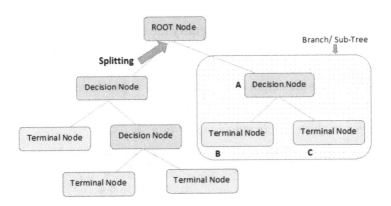

2.2 Unsupervised Learning

In this type of learning, the output units are trained to respond to the entire cluster pattern from the given inputs, and the self-organized pattern is employed (Zheng and Liu, 2007). Here, in this case, the vector inputs of the same type have been grouped without using the training data set for specifying how can typical members of each group look or for which the group members belong. In the training period, the neural networks gain their patterns, which is obtained from the input and arranges all those patterns to the categories. When the new inputs of the pattern are applied, the neural network gives a new output response resulting in the class to that a group member belongs. Grouping could be performed on the basis of color, shapes, and remaining all the other properties of an object. It is a type of machine learning method by which a model is fit to observations.

Different types of algorithms used in Unsupervised Learning are given below:

- Hidden Markov Model(HMM)
- K-mean Clustering

2.2.1 Hidden Markov Model (HMM)

The hidden markov model contains the set of states which consists of transition probability along with probability distributions. HMM is the type of model, which is the new extension of the markov model, and these states of the model do not need any correspondence for observable states. The process, which gives a sequencing of observable symbols as output, is known to be HMM.

2.2.2 K-mean Clustering

In this type of clustering, the clusters identify the data object without knowing the level of the class. Here the clusters do not have the pre-knowledge of the given attributes of the dataset. K-mean clustering is completed only by using the grouping of input data because the output is not predefined, as in Figure 9.

Figure 9. K-mean clustering in machine learning

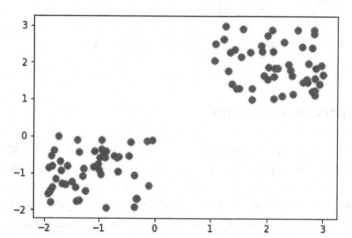

2.2.3 Semi-supervised Learning

It is a type of machine learning approach which connects a very small quantity of the labeled data with a large quantity of unlabeled data during the training period. This type of learning lies between unsupervised learning (which did not have any labeled training set data) &supervised learning (which consists of an only labeled training set of data).

2.2.4 Reinforcement LEARNING

This is the type of learning in which the area of science, the rewards and punishments are given on the basis of the behavior (Sutton and Barto, 1998). The reinforcement algorithm is implemented by taking a general optimal control approach, which is co-related to dynamic programs. This work has been observed, and these rewards for learning the optimal policy of the environment.

2.3 Application of Machine Learning

Machine learning has various applications in terms of automation, as in Figure 10 (Kononenko and Matjaž, 1997).

Figure 10. Application of machine learning

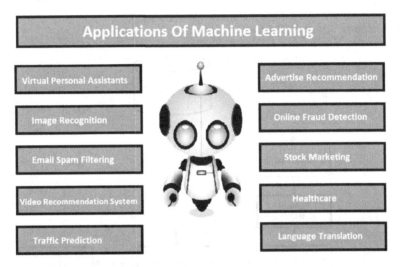

2.3.1 Virtual Personal Assistants

Virtual assistants use the natural language processing or NLP for relating and matching user's texts or voice inputs to the executable commands. This type of process recurrently learns by using an artificial intelligence technique, which includes machine learning (ML) (Kepuska & Bohouta,2018)to make the virtual assistant to be started by the use of voice; the wake words may be used. It depends on the command and question. Virtual, the personal assistant, uses the software agent, which performs tasks and services for the individual.

2.3.2 Image Recognition

Image recognition is the method of a system and the software for the recognition of an object, people, place, and all the actions of the images. Image recognition always uses machine vision technologies within artificial intelligence, and it trains the algorithm for recognizing images by using camera systems. All the human being is able to recognize and distinguish different feature of all objects. It happens because our brain has been previously trained by using similar sets of the image, which results in the developing capabilities to differentiate among things effortlessly in image recognition. Numerical values are put in the array set and look for a pattern that is in the digital images. It can be in the form of a still, videos, graphics, or can be even live, for identifying and differencing key feature of all the images. The computer vision use image processing algorithm for analyzing and understanding visual from a single image or the sequences of the image.

Figure 11. Email spam Filtration

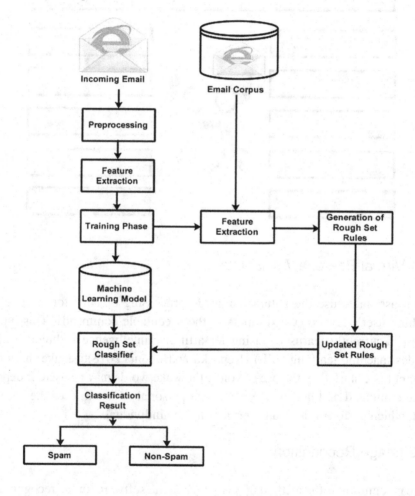

Biometric identification is one of the most important area of computer vision. In which we capture the biometric of person.After that apply the preprocessing technique and filtering technique for enhance the capture image.we extract the features of enhanced image and for further processing in therms of recognition machine learning technique is also helpful(Singh, L. K. et al., 2020c)

2.3.3 Email Spam Filtration

The machine learning model is used by the Google email spam filtration, and it is now so much trained and become advanced such that it now has the power of detecting and filtering out spam (by using phishing emails) with almost 99.8 percentage of accuracy. Figure 11 shows the process of email spam filtration.

2.3.4 Video Recommendation System

A video recommendation system is one of the best effective and widespread applications of machine learning business technology. With the help of this application, anyone can apply recommenders systems in this scenario where there are multiple users who are able to interact with multiple items. We can find the large scale video recommendation system in retail, videos on demands, or music streaming. Machine learning algorithms in the recommender system is typically classified into two categories; content-based method and collaborative filtering method, the modern recommender joins both the approaches. The content-based method is dependent on the similarity of the attributes of the items, and the collaborative method finds similarity in the interactions. Factorization, which is based on the matrix method, is applied to decrease dimensionality in the interaction matrix and approximate it by using two & more small matrix with K latent component.

2.3.5 Traffic Prediction

Machine learning algorithms are used for traffic prediction, calculation, and navigations systems. This application of machine learning helps us in the prediction of website traffic also. With these technologies of machine learning, we can minimize the chances or the probability of accidents on the road; by predicting the speed of transport on the road.

2.3.6 Advertise Recommendation

The advertising recommendation machine learning system permits us to repeat the mind of the experienced buyer in which software would make the same optimization for buyers. Additionally, the system understands with time and generates the result with much accuracy and helps in working for new campaigns, implementation of correlation, which teaches us for the detection of the human brain. Advertise machine learning helps in predicting and boosting the performance of advertising, allows the advertisement to draw the correlations; finally, machine learning also helps in becoming the team of media-buyers smarter and intelligent; machine learning can decrease the cost of advertising recommendation and also implements the reports better.

2.3.7 Online Fraud Detection

Machine learning supports online fraud detection, as it can manage more detailed issues like fake claims, duplicate claims, and overstating repair costs. Machine learning also helps in creating solutions for anti-fraud for medical claims and healthcare, fraud prevention solution in e-commerce, fraud detection in banking and credit card payments, preventing loan application fraud, and machine learning for anti-money laundering.

Figure 12 shows the fraud detection algorithm in which hidden patterns are recognized well, but it uses more complex data algorithms in which large data sets can be iterated and analyses the patterns in data. The algorithm implements the machine for the result of different situations in which they could not be programmed explicitly.

Figure 12. the process of online fraud detection

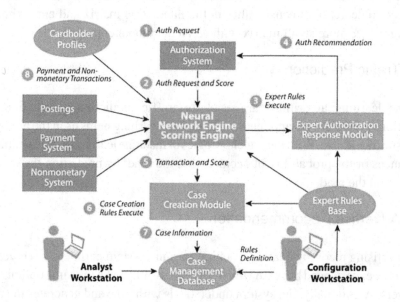

2.3.8 Stock Marketing

It is well known that machine learning is becoming very trending in every area of digital processing regarding the performance of future securities, this algorithms of machine learning completely give allowance in computers for using the available information to predict the future results (Reza et al., 2011). It helps in predicting the future price of stocks as well as the movement of indices too. If we talk about the detailed view of the stock market, we can say that the stock markets are commonly driven from ''human-emotions'' so if the algorithm can easily capable of analyzing human emotions and reactions accurately, then it is surely capable of predicting the accurate stocks too.

2.3.9 Health Care

The roles and values of machine learning techniques in the healthcare sector are very promising (Simon et al., 2017). Machine learning in healthcare is capable of processing large datasets, which is limitless, i.e., beyond the scope of the capabilities of humans. It is totally reliable for converting the data, which is analyzed into clinical insights, and that provides the planning to aid physicians and providing care. It generates a better outcome and results and helps in lowering the cost of care.

Figure 13. Uses of Machine learning in health care

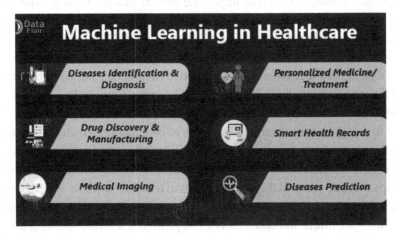

2.3.9.1 Application of Healthcare in Glaucoma Diagnosis

This is the application of a machine learning algorithm in the healthcare sector, where we diagnose glaucoma in OCT (optical coherence tomography) images and fundus images. Glaucoma is the second leading eye disease that causes blindness by gradually harming the optical nerve and which results in the visual field loss in the human eye. It usually occurs at the age of 42 and above and predominantly affects the inner macular retinal layers. In glaucoma, intraocular pressure increases and may cause progressive loss of ganglion cells (Omodaka et al.,2019). If it is not detected at an early stage, it may lead to complete blindness. Hence, to detect glaucoma at an early age, OCT techniques can be applied. The patient with open-angle glaucoma depends on three-dimensional optical coherence tomography (OCT) data & color fundus images. By using machine learning technology, we can extract for some specific features which help in the diagnosis of glaucomatous and non-glaucomatous eyes. In this process, we select the OCT image or fundus image of some glaucomatous and healthy eyes, thereafter feature extraction of the layers is performed in which each and every layer of the computations using multiplications and the mathematical operation for extracting features are implemented.Detection of glaucoma using machine learning techniques,we can also suppose retinal fundus image for extracting some important features.We can apply these features on machine learning modal to training and testing purpose (Singh, L. K. et al.,2020a,2020b).

2.3.10 Commercial Application of Machine Learning

As a novel prominent application of the machine learning, machine learning chips have been recently comes into play. Many big giants like Google, IBM Microsoft and Amazon are working on it to improvise and its practical usage. The machine learning chip market is segmented neuromorphic chips, Graphics Processing Unit (GPU) chips, Flash based chips, Field Programmable Gate Array (FPGA) chip. These chips can be practically applied into multidisciplinary industries like Robotics Industry, Consumer Electronics, and Automotive Healthcare. The countries who have adopted these chips cover U.S., France, U.K., Germany, Canada, India, Australia etc.

Assessment of the opportunities in the machine learning chip market plays a vital role to recognize the advantageous areas of investment, which are the technical insights for major market players, suppliers, distributors and other stakeholders.

Many research reports have been recently published on forecast of applications of these chips, market-share in the coming years in terms of applications and areas, its multi-faceted opportunities and performances in multiple domains, and moreover to felicitate manufacturers and consumers . The profound information intends to offer the most related beneficial domains in the global market place. In-depth analysis is performed in these reports where geographical based analysis is also being performed to hold existing chances and also to catch upcoming opportunities even before they approach the actual location.

Some research studies have also been published to broadly explain the applications of machine learning in various industries. These reports explore possible growth opportunities across the globe, market share with each nation, along with regional development of this industry. The report displays key statistics and the priceless resource of supervision for companies and individuals (executive officials, potential investors) interested in the market. They also limelight on latest advancements, product description, manufacturing capacities, sources of raw material, and profound business strategies.

According to the most recent research is a new business area which will raise the revenue the relevant industry by multifolds, some research reports predicts that global demand for the machine learning as a service (MLaaS) market is set to witness a healthy CAGR of 44.53% in the forecast period. This rise in the market value can be attributed due to the advancement in data science and artificial intelligence and an increasing need to understand the desires and needs of the customers.

Machine learning as a Service (MLaaS) industry may look after multiple domains like Component (Software Tools, Services), Application (Marketing & Advertising, Fraud Detection & Risk Analytics, Predictive Maintenance, Augmented Reality, Network Analytics & Automated Traffic Management. Others), Organization Size (Small & Medium Enterprises, Large Enterprises), End User (Education, Banking & Financial Services, Insurance, Automation & Transportation, Healthcare, Defense, Retail and E-Commerce, Media & Entertainment, Telecom, Government, Aerospace).

2.4 Ethical Aspects of Machine Learning

To understand all the importance, the actuality, and the total power of machine learning, we had to take the ethical aspects of the technology of machine learning too. There are many running examples which give the ethical aspects of machine learning in the present scenario (kumar et al., 2016). There are ethical aspects in this type of learning for that the organization should select this technology over other technologies, and these are mentioned below.

2.4.1 Ability for Performing Automated Visualization of the Data

Large size data is generated by the common peoples and trades on a daily basis by the visualization of the denotable relationship of the data (Alemu et al., 2014). Trades cannot make alone the best decision, but it can build up confidence. Machine learning gives many numbers of tools that provide rich snippets of the given data set, which could be used for both the unstructured and structured data sets.

By helping the user-friendly automatic data visualizing platform in this technology of machine learning, trading can gain the health of the new insight into the efforts to enhance the process of productivity.

2.4.2 Automation at Its Best

Automation is the biggest ethical aspect of machine learning, it is used for the automation of repeating tasks, and that is why it enhances the productivity of the organization

(Niranjan and Shin, 2008). Large numbers of the organization are already working on the machine learning for paperwork and email automation. In financial sectors, for example, a large number of repetitive, heavy data and predictable tasks should be required for performance, and because of it, the sectors use a different type of machine learning solution for the excellent benefits. Machine learning makes the task faster, much insightful, and accurate. There are some of the aspects which may be addressed by machine learning, like solving financial queries using chatbots. It makes predictions, arranging expenses, simplifying invoicing, & automating bank reconciliation.

2.4.3 Engagement of Customer as Never Before

For any type of business, in which there is the most important way for customer meetings, which promotes best honesty and buildup long-term and long-lasting customer relationship by a trigger with meaningful conversation within its target customers where Machine learning play a important role in the allowing businesses & brand for spark very important conversations in the process of customer engagement. This technology of machine learning finds or specific phrases, word, sentence, idiom, and content format by which they resonated with some of the audience members. They could think of the interest that successfully uses machine learning for personalized suggestions for their users. This uses the technologies for sources that content in that the users will be interested in; it is based on the object that they have been already pinned.

2.4.4 Ability to Take Efficiency Up to the Next Level When Merged With the IoT

When merged with IoT, machine learning supports human beings to the next higher level and also gaining popularity by generating more and more intelligent devices. IoT has been designated in strategically significant areas where there are a lot of companies already exist and working on it, and newcomers have launched a pilot project for gauges of the importance of an IoT in the content of the business operation. In order to gain success, who are offering IoT consulting services and platforms, it is required to clearly determine the area that will change with the help of the implementation of IoT strategies. Many of these trades had been failed to address it. In this type of scenario, this type of learning technology is the best, which is used to attaining the highest level of efficiency. By combining machine learning with the help of IoT, it could boost the efficiency of the whole production process IOT (Meidan et al.,2017).

2.4.5 Ability for Changing the Mortgage Market

This is the genuine thing that fostering is one of the most positivity credits scores, which normally takes some disciplined & having many of the financial planning and has a lot of customers (Stephens, 2015). whenever we talk about the lender, In creditworthiness the customer credit scoring is one of the largest measures which contains lots number of factors that includes payments histories, summation debt, length of the history of credit, etc. but in spite of all this would not be great, if they find any sampled and best measurement using the machine learning then lenders could obtain many comprehensive consumers images just in recent ways as well as they would predict either the customers are from the fewer spenders or having high spender on the basis of understanding his or her tipping points of the spending while part from all this mortgage lending and financial institution always uses the similar technique to other different kinds of customers loan.

2.4.6 Accurate Analysis of Data

For both logically and traditionally, data analysis has always been incremented on trial and error methods with an approach in which working with a huge amount of heterogeneous datasets would become very impractical. After many instances, machine learning has come out with better and superior solutions for all these problems by providing effective alternative offers (Berg and Hagersten,2004). Analyzing massive volumes of data sets along with the use of fast and effective developed algorithms, they also manage with the driving data, and at the same instance, the model to process the real-time data set. A machine learning algorithm is capable of generating accurate outcomes and result from analysis.

2.4.7 Business Intelligence on Its Top or Best

The features of machine learning teach that when there is a merging of large datasets with analytical work, machine learning is capable of generating a high level of business intelligence and helps in various different industries to strategic initiations, except all retailing of economic services to medical and much more. Machine learning technique has the most efficient technologies for boosting the operations of the business; it contributes in a significant amount for critical decision making required for business intelligence support. Being one of the most critical and crucial technologies of trends (Reshi and Khan, 2019).

REFERENCES

Aghababaeyan, Khan, & Siddiqui. (2011). Forecasting the Tehran Stock Market by artificial neural network. *International Journal of Advanced Computer Science and Applications*, 13-17.

An, G., Omodaka, K., Hashimoto, K., Tsuda, S., Shiga, Y., Takada, N., Kikawa, T., Yokota, H., Akiba, M., & Nakazawa, T. (2019). Glaucoma diagnosis with machine learning based on optical coherence tomography and color fundus images. *Journal of Healthcare Engineering*, *2019*, 2019. doi:10.1155/2019/4061313 PMID:30911364

Berg, E., & Hagersten, E. (2004, March). StatCache: a probabilistic approach to efficient and accurate data locality analysis. In *IEEE International Symposium on-ISPASS Performance Analysis of Systems and Software*, 2004 (pp. 20-27). IEEE. 10.1109/ISPASS.2004.1291352

Kepuska, V., & Bohouta, G. (2018, January). Next-generation of virtual personal assistants (microsoft cortana, apple siri, amazon alexa and google home). In *2018 IEEE 8th Annual Computing and Communication Workshop and Conference (CCWC)* (pp. 99-103). IEEE.

Kononenko, I., Bratko, I., & Kukar, M. (1997). Application of machine learning to medical diagnosis. *Machine Learning and Data Mining: Methods and Applications*, *389*, 408.

Kumar, N., Kharkwal, N., Kohli, R., & Choudhary, S. (2016, February). Ethical aspects and future of artificial intelligence. In *2016 International Conference on Innovation and Challenges in Cyber Security (ICICCS-INBUSH)* (pp. 111-114). IEEE. 10.1109/ICICCS.2016.7542339

Liu, H., & Setiono, R. (1997). Feature selection via discretization. *IEEE Transactions on Knowledge and Data Engineering*, 9(4), 642–645. doi:10.1109/69.617056

Mathews, S., Golden, S., Demski, R., Pronovost, P., & Ishii, L. (2017). Advancing health care quality and safety through action learning. *Leadership in Health Services*, *30*(2), 148–158. doi:10.1108/LHS-10-2016-0051 PMID:28514917

Meidan, Y., Bohadana, M., Shabtai, A., Guarnizo, J. D., Ochoa, M., Tippenhauer, N. O., & Elovici, Y. (2017, April). ProfilIoT: a machine learning approach for IoT device identification based on network traffic analysis. In *Proceedings of the symposium on applied computing* (pp. 506-509). 10.1145/3019612.3019878

Pearl, L., & Steyvers, M. (2012). Detecting authorship deception: A supervised machine learning approach using author writeprints. *Literary and Linguistic Computing*, *27*(2), 183–196. doi:10.1093/llc/fqs003

Reshi, Y. S., & Khan, R. A. (2014). Creating business intelligence through machine learning: An Effective business decision making tool. In Information and Knowledge Management (Vol. 4, No. 1, pp. 65-75). Academic Press.

Singh, L. K., & Garg, H. P. (2020b). Automated Glaucoma Type Identification Using Machine Learning or Deep Learning Techniques. In Advancement of Machine Intelligence in Interactive Medical Image Analysis (pp. 241-263). Springer.

Singh, L. K., Khanna, M., & Garg, H. (2020c). Multimodal Biometric Based on Fusion of Ridge Features with Minutiae Features and Face Features. *International Journal of Information System Modeling and Design*, *11*(1), 37–57. doi:10.4018/IJISMD.2020010103

Singh, L. K., Pooja, & Garg, H. (2020a). Detection of Glaucoma in Retinal Images Based on Multiobjective Approach. *International Journal of Applied Evolutionary Computation*, *11*(2), 15–27. doi:10.4018/IJAEC.2020040102

Smola, A., & Vishwanathan, S. V. N. (2008). Introduction to machine learning. Cambridge University.

Stephens, M. (2007). Mortgage market deregulation and its consequences. *Housing Studies*, *22*(2), 201–220. doi:10.1080/02673030601132797

Sutton, R. (1998). *S. and Barto, Andrew G. Reinforcement Learning: An Introduction*. MIT.

Sutton, R. S., & Barto, A. G. (1998). *Introduction to reinforcement learning* (Vol. 135). MIT Press.

Zhao, Z., & Liu, H. (2007, June). Spectral feature selection for supervised and unsupervised learning. In *Proceedings of the 24th international conference on Machine learning* (pp. 1151-1157). 10.1145/1273496.1273641

Chapter 8

A Blockchain–Based Federated Learning:
Concepts and Applications

Ankit Khushal Barai
Department of CSE, Indian Institute of
Information Technology, Nagpur, India

Robin Singh Bhadoria
 https://orcid.org/0000-0002-6314-4736
Department of Computer Science and

Engineering, Hindustan College of
Science and Technology, India

Jyotshana Bagwari
Department of CSE, Uttarakhand
Technical University, India

Ivan Perl
ITMO University, Russia

ABSTRACT

Conventional machine learning (ML) needs centralized training data to be present on a given machine or datacenter. The healthcare, finance, and other institutions where data sharing is prohibited require an approach for training ML models in secured architecture. Recently, techniques such as federated learning (FL), MIT Media Lab's Split Neural networks, blockchain, aim to address privacy and regulation of data. However, there are difference between the design principles of FL and the requirements of Institutions like healthcare, finance, etc., which needs blockchain-orchestrated FL having the following features: clients with their local data can define access policies to their data and define how updated weights are to be encrypted between the workers and the aggregator using blockchain technology and also prepares audit trail logs undertaken within network and it keeps actual list of participants hidden. This is expected to remove barriers in a range of sectors including healthcare, finance, security, logistics, governance, operations, and manufacturing.

DOI: 10.4018/978-1-7998-5876-8.ch008

1. INTRODUCTION

Supervised deep learning (LeCun et al., 2015) algorithms offer very good performance for a variety of image classification tasks. The typical approach for these tasks comprises 3 steps

1. Centralize a large data repository.
2. Acquire ground truth annotations (labels) for these data, and
3. Employ the ground truth annotations to train Deep Learning (DL) networks for classification.

However, this methodology poses significant practical challenges. In particular, data privacy and security concerns pose difficulties in creating large central data repositories for training. Two years back, Google proposed a de-centralized `federated learning' (Yang et al., 2019) technique to train deep learning models across multiple data sources without sharing sensitive information.

Even though federated learning has significant advantages over centralized learning, there are multiple disadvantages with Federated Learning.

1. All participating clients have the same final model. This is unfair to clients that contribute more data. For example, a client might claim to have good data, but might only want the final model. This can be seen at worst as DL model theft and at best as free-rider.
2. Clients might introduce back-doors (through bad and/or carefully crafted adversarial data) to corrupt the final model (Bagdasaryan et al., 2018).

Recently, MIT proposed a new approach to federated learning called Split Neural Networks SpiltNN, which can address the above issues. In SplitNN, the final deep learning model isn't shared with all clients - there is no single final deep learning model. Each client computes its own model, but still shares some "wisdom" derived from other contributing clients. With SplitNN, each client trains a partial deep learning network up to a specific layer known as the cut layer. The rest of the layers are computed by each client.

Blockchain is the technology addressing the issue of privacy, enforcing trust in uncontrolled environments like in Healthcare, Financial etc. Industries. We are reviewing the works in this Blockchain and Federated learning can be combined to get the best of both the technologies to address the underlying issues. Blockchain is a sequential data structure that contains data stored in blocks linked to each other using hashing. There is no limit in the size of the chain and hence the chain can grow larger as new blocks are added to it. Any change in Block b_i would require change in all blocks following b_i which adds the security to the Blockchain. It is nearly impossible to change this many blocks without getting it noticed by other stakeholders. This distributed ledger is duplicated across all nodes i.e. All nodes have a copy of the ledger. Initially, Blockchain was used for cryptocurrencies but soon, it started finding application in number of domains which requires trust. Blockchain is a computerized, decentralized record that tracks all transaction that happen over a shared system. It is an interlinked and persistently extending list of records put away safely over various interconnected frameworks.

The challenges addressed by the convergence of Federated learning and Blockchain are:

1. Privacy Problem: How entities will train model without disclosing data.
    a. Influence problem: 3rd parties can influence the way an AI model behaves
2. Economic Problem: How to incentivized 3rd parties correctly to contribute to knowledge of AI models.
3. Transparency Problem: Is AI model behavior available to all parties.
4. Latency Problem: Centralized AI is inappropriate for use-cases where AI needs to interact in real time with the real world

2. FEDERATED LEARNING

2.1. Problem Formulation

The accepted combined learning issue includes learning a solitary, worldwide factual model from information put away on tens to possibly a huge number of remote gadgets. We plan to gain proficiency with this model under the limitation that gadget produced information is put away and handled locally, with just infrequent updates being shared intermittently with server. Specifically, the objective is normally to limit the accompanying target work as given in Equation 1 and 2:

$$\min F(w), \text{ where } F\left(w\right) := \sum_{k=1}^{m} p_k F_k\left(w\right) \tag{1}$$

Here m is the total number of devices, Fk is the local objective function for the kth device, and pk specifies the relative impact of each device with

$$pk^3 0 \text{ and } \sum_{k=1}^{m} p_k = 1. \tag{2}$$

Federated learning includes training machine learning (Alpaydin et al., 2020) or Deep learning models over distributed devices or like mobile phones or distributed places like hospitals, while keeping data contained within the distributed devices. Training in varied and possibly huge networks introduces new challenges that necessitate a important exit from typical methods for large-scale machine learning. This chapter covers the novel features and challenges of federated learning and offers a comprehensive summary of present methods, and sketch numerous guidelines of upcoming effort that are pertinent to a varied range of research groups. Cell phones, wearable gadgets, and independent vehicles are only a couple of the cutting-edge distributed systems creating an abundance of information every day. Because of the developing computational intensity of these devices. Federated learning can utilize this computational capacity to train models locally and then share trained model weights with the server thus preserving data privacy.

The requirements of Federated learning are:

1. Privacy is needed (FL not the whole solution)
2. Bandwidth or power consumption are concerns
3. High cost of data transfer
4. Your model improves with more data

The key features of Federated learning are:

1. Performance improves with more data.
2. Models can be meaningfully combined.
3. Nodes can take part in training also not only during the inference.

As the capacity and computational abilities of the gadgets inside distributed systems develop, it is possible to use improved neighborhood assets on every gadget. This has prompted a developing enthusiasm for federated learning, which investigates preparing measurable models straightforwardly on remote devices. We examine some use-cases of federated learning here:

1. Mobile phones: Federated models can be built to give personalized AI models like, for example, next-word anticipation, face detection. Also, client experience must not affect, so Federated learning can possibly train when plugged in charging and not in use without decreasing the customer experience or releasing private data.
2. Organizations: Associations or organizations can likewise be seen as 'gadgets' with regards to federated learning. For instance, clinics are associations that contain a huge number of patient information for prescient medicinal services.

3. Internet of things: For instance, a ñeet of autonomous vehicles may require a modern model of trafðc, construction, or person on foot conduct to securely work. Federated learning techniques can assist with preparing models that can adjust to changes in these frameworks while keeping up client security.

2.2. Federated Learning Process

The steps involved in Federated learning are briefly described as follows:
    Repeat steps (1) to (8) many times

1. A network of nodes shares models rather than training data with the server
2. The server has an untrained model

Figure 1. Server has an untrained model

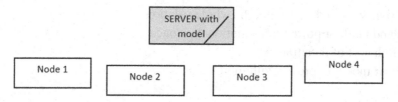

3. It sends a copy of that model to the nodes

Figure 2. Server sends a copy of that model to the nodes

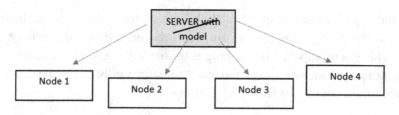

4. The nodes now also have the untrained model

Figure 3. All nodes now also have the untrained model

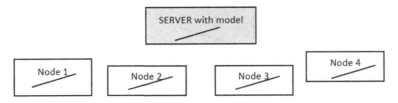

5.   The nodes have data on which to train their model

Figure 4. The nodes have data on which to train their model

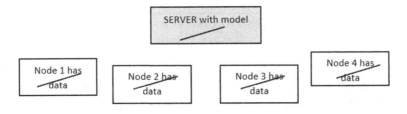

6.   Each node trains the model to fit the data they have

Figure 5. Each node trains the model to fit the data they have

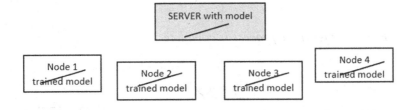

7.   Each node sends a copy of its trained model back to the server

Figure 6. Each node sends a copy of its trained model back to the server

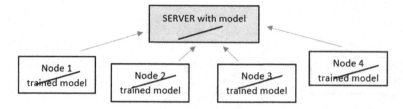

8.   The server combines these models by taking an average

Figure 7. The server combines these models by taking an average have

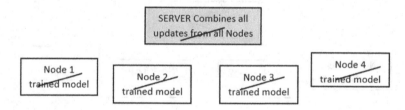

9.   The server now has a model that captures the patterns in the training data on all the nodes
10.   But at no point did the nodes share their training data which increases privacy and saves on bandwidth.

Figure 8. Federated learning process is complete

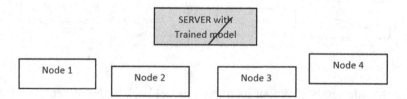

2.3. Challenges to Federated learning

2.3.1. Communication Expense

Communication is a serious tailback in federated systems, which, joined with confidentiality anxieties over transfer of raw data, requires that data produced on each device persist local. Message sending time can be greater than local computation time. It is very essential in federated networks to have communication efficient approaches (Bonawitz et al., 2019) that repeatedly send small messages and updates instead of sending the complete dataset.

Some of the solutions are:

1. The number of message cycles can be reduced.
2. The size of message in each cycle can be reduced.

2.3.2. Heterogeneity of System

The Computational capacity of devices in distributed systems varies in terms of CPU, memory, connectivity, and power. Furthermore, the network size and systems-related limitations on every gadget commonly bring about just a little division of the gadgets being dynamic without a moment's delay, e.g., several dynamic gadgets in a million-gadget organize. Every gadget may likewise be temperamental, and it isn't phenomenal for a functioning gadget to drop out at a given cycle because of network or vitality limitations (Konecny et al., 2016).

These framework level attributes drastically intensify difficulties, for example, stray relief and adaptation to internal failure. federated learning techniques that are created and broke down must in this manner:

1. visualize a low measure of involvement,
2. endure diverse hardware, and
3. be robust to faults in the system

2.3.3. Statistical Heterogeneity

The quantity of information across gadgets may differ signiðcantly, and there might be a fundamental structure present that catches the relationship among gadgets and their related disseminations. (Geyer et al., 2017) The independent and identically distributed (I.I.D.) assumptions in distributed systems, improves the probability of strays, and may include unpredictability (Bonawitz et al., 2017).

2.3.4. Privacy Concern

There is no need to share raw data with the central server, the raw data is with local devices only. Local devices download the initial model and whenever the device is free, raw data is used to train on that model and the updates weights are then sent as single update to the cloud where they are immediately averaged with updates from other devices. In this way, without sharing any raw data, the model gets trained and learned features in form of updates are shared with the central server (Truex et al., 2019) (Nasr et al., 2018). Advanced analysis of privacy concerns for federated settings is found here (Gupta et al., 2018).

3. SPLIT NEURAL NETWORKS

Split learning is a novel technology developed by MIT Media lab's Camera culture group that allows to train ML models without sharing any raw data. Federated learning also allows to train ML models without sharing raw data but Federated learning has some disadvantages like:

- All clients have same final model, this is unfair to clients which contributes maximum of data.
- Adversarial Backdoor attacks are possible when willingly crafted non useful data is used for training by a client which can decrease the model performance.

In Split learning, instead of downloading complete model to client's machine, some part of model is downloaded to client (Vepakomma et al., 2018). In CNN's some initial layer of the model are downloaded up to a specific layer called cut layer. Client runs forward pass of model with raw data up to cut layer and then send these activations to server where remaining layer of model are used with these activations of cut layer as input and similarly, during backpropagation of gradients, the gradients are also sent back from the server to the cut layer for updating the weights.

There are few variations of SplitNN, one in which is called Folded-SplitNN in which some intermediate layers are there in server while labels are also in the client's local machine. These are shown in Figure 9. SplitNN overcomes the disadvantage of Federated learning as:

- All clients have no same model but some intelligence is shared between models of all clients.
- Adversarial backdoor attacks are not feasible because it will affect the malicious user itself the most.

Figure 9. Variations in SplitNN architecture

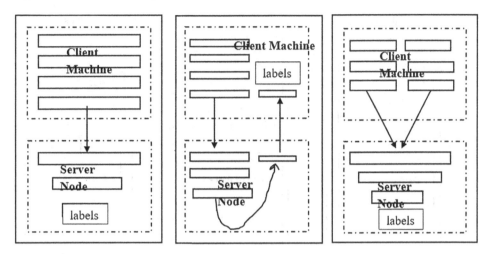

4. BLOCKCHAIN

Blockchain Technology was created as the fundamental innovation behind the cryptographic money called bitcoin. The consequence of the 2008 subprime emergency decreased trust in the current budgetary framework. This is the point at which an individual or a gathering of individuals called Satoshi Nakamoto composed a white paper containing the 'bitcoin technology' which utilized an appropriated record also, consensus working to register calculations. (Zheng et al., 2018) The bitcoin convention was composed to disintermediate customary monetary Institutions as a method for encouraging direct P2P transaction. Since the introduction of the Web, there have been endeavors to make virtual monetary standards, yet those endeavors bombed due to the 'twofold spend' issue, in particular the hazard that a computerized resource, for example, a money can be burned through twice (Lin et al., 2017).The present answer for take out the double spend issue is through the presentation of 'go-betweens of trust, for example, banks. In any case, the utilization of blockchain innovation makes it conceivable to take care of the principal issue of twofold spending without the requirement for such middle people of trust, consequently encouraging the transaction of benefits for example, virtual monetary standards over the Web safely (Crosby et al., 2016). This idea can be reached out to non-money related zones and that is the guarantee of blockchain innovation. Chaining of blocks in Blockchain is shown in Figure 10.

Figure 10. Chain of blocks in Blockchain

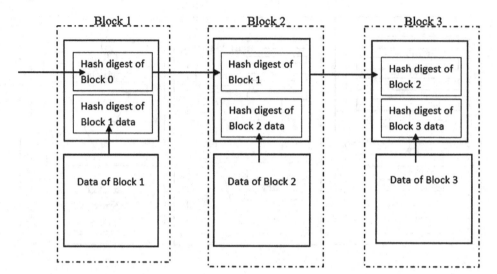

Blockchain is a sequential data structure that contains data stored in blocks linked to each other using hashing. There is no limit in the size of the chain and hence the chain can grow larger as new blocks are added to it. Any change in Block b_i would require change in all blocks following b_i which adds the security to the Blockchain. It is nearly impossible to change this many blocks without getting it noticed by other stakeholders. This distributed ledger is duplicated across all nodes i.e. All nodes have a copy of the ledger. Initially, Blockchain was used for cryptocurrencies but soon, it started finding application in number of domains which requires trust (Tastanattakol et al., 2018). Blockchain is a computerized, decentralized (distributed) record that tracks all transaction that happen over a shared system. It is an interlinked and persistently extending list of records put away safely over various interconnected frameworks. This makes blockchain innovation flexible since the system has no single purpose of helplessness. Moreover, each block is interestingly associated with the past blocks through an advanced hashing which implies that making a change to a block without disturbing the past records in the chain is unimaginable, in this manner rendering the data carefully designed. The key development in blockchain innovation is that it permits its member to transfer resources over the Web without the requirement for an integrated unknown user (Kim et al., 2018).

4.1. How Blockchain Works?

4.1.1. Data From Transactions

Transactions are stored in form of blocks. A number of transactions are collected over time to be added as a new block to blockchain, there is metadata also to be stored for each block.

4.1.2. Chaining the Blocks (With a Hash)

Block 1 contains the completed transaction that collected up to 1 MB, let's say it included first 12 transactions then the next 1 MB of transactions are put in block 2 and similarly for further blocks.

In order to connect these blocks together, a signature is used. For example, if signature of block 1 is 'X2' then this signature becomes part of data of block 2. Similarly, signature of block i is put as part of data of block i+1. To get a unique signature for a block, we have different hashing functions like SHA-256 which takes in data and produces output of fixed data size.

Even if malicious user changed the signature residing as data in block 2, the signature of that block will change meaning that 2nd block's signature would then don't match to signature inside contents of block 3. This means that if malicious user tries to change block i then all blocks needs to be altered that are after the given block which is nearly impossible due to computational expense and time required for calculating the signature, within that duration some new block will get added to the network and hence any such malicious attempt gets noticed.

4.1.3. Signature (Hash)

A cryptographic hash work consistently gives a similar output for a similar input, yet consistently an alternate yield for various info. This cryptographic hash is utilized by the Bitcoin blockchain to give the privacy to their signatures. There is an enormous assortment of hash capacities, yet the hashing capacity that is utilized by the Bitcoin blockchain is the SHA-256 hashing function.

4.1.4. Nonce for Mining

Mining a block not simply requires calculating the signature using hash functions like SHA-256 but it needs to yield a signature with some constraints for example, the signature must begin with a fixed number of zeroes. Since the transactions information and metadata (block number, timestamp, and so forth) need to remain the manner in which they are, a little explicit bit of information is added to each block that has no reason with the exception of being changed over and again so as to locate a qualified signature. This bit of information is known as the nonce of a block.

4.1.5. How Does This Make the Blockchain Immutable?

Let's say an attacker has modified a block of transaction and is presently attempting to figure new signatures for the resulting hinders so as to have the remainder of the system acknowledge his change. The issue for him is, the remainder of the system is additionally ascertaining new signatures for new blocks. The attacker should ascertain new signatures for these blocks too as they are being added as far as possible of the chain. All things considered, he needs to keep the entirety of the blocks connected, including the new ones continually being included. Except if the attacker has more computational power than the remainder of the system joined, he will never find the remainder of the system finding signatures. Huge number of clients are mining on the Bitcoin blockchain, and in this way it very well may be expected that a malicious attacker will never have more computational power than the remainder of the system joined, which means the system will never acknowledge any changes on the blockchain, making the blockchain immutable.

4.1.6. Governance of Blockchain

The longest chain is only considered to be valid. Blockchain

4.2. Features

1. Decentralized: The blockchain is not in control of any central authority.
2. Transparent: Any node can validate the transactions and transactions are publicly visible.
3. Immutable: Once entered in blockchain, that block can never be deleted.
4. Secure: Even if attacker hacked into one of the computers on the network and altered information there, the network would remain unaffected. As blockchain is distributed.

4.3. Public vs. Private Blockchain

A blockchain system can either be open or private in view of who is approved to take an interest. The basic contrast between an open and private blockchain is that one works in a distributed open condition where there are no limitations on the quantity of individuals joining the system, while the different works inside the limits characterized by a controlling substance. A straightforward similarity is the distinction between the Web and the intranet. While the characteristic innovation for organized PCs continues as before, there is a major contrast between the elements and utility related with a shut organize, (for example, a home system) and an open organize, (for example, the Web). Truly, this distinction plays out dependent on how 'nodes' are boosted to stay a piece of the organize. The key thought here is that in an open blockchain, the consensus component is based around remunerating every individual member to stay a piece of the system. In a private blockchain, the requirement for making this motivation doesn't exist. The democratized idea of a genuine straightforward public ledger probably won't be of utility to an association or an undertaking system as the gatherings are known, and a level of understanding exists about which individuals can take an interest in the system and on what sort of transaction. The general consensus is that while open blockchains function admirably for specific applications for example, cryptographic money-based transaction (bitcoin), the bigger use of blockchain innovation as an undertaking arrangement would just be conceivable with the expanded administrative control related with a private blockchain environment. Note that the innovation is still incipient. Subsequently, its various applications are advancing consistently and iteratively. The subject of open versus private blockchain systems may inevitably get tended to by a biological system where various private blockchains associate with each other over an openly conveyed organize. The response to the question may not be a basic decision between the paired choices accessible; it might just lie in a common environment where both open and private blockchains work cooperatively in much the same way private systems (secured by firewalls) collaborate with the Web.

5. BLOCKCHAIN IN FEDERATED LEARNING

In this section, we consider important points for analysis of blockchain in federated learning.

5.1. Challenges to Federated Learning and Blockchain as Its Solution

1. How to train models without a centralized authority?
2. How to use trained models without trusting a central party?
3. How to validate and enforce trust among the different parties in the lifecycle of a deep learning model
4. How to build incentives for data scientists training, testing and building models?
5. How to build incentives for parties contributing datasets?

6. How to discourage bad behaviors in the network?

The solution is token based blockchain smart contracts as shown in Figure 11.

Figure 11. Blockchain based AI architecture

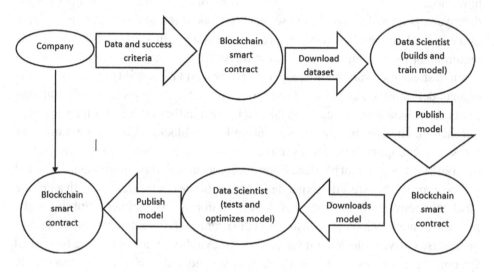

Figure 12. Comparison of resources consumed per client when training CIFAR-10 over VGG
Source: (Vepakomma et al., 2018)

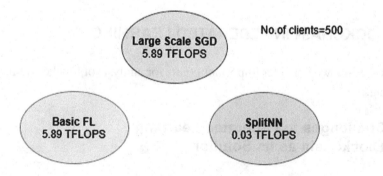

5.2. Multiparty Data Retrieval

Since a large portion of the information is delicate and the measure of information is huge, it is an asset serious and dangerous task to put information on the blockchain

(Zhu et al., 2018). Hence, blockchain is used to recover information, while the genuine information is put away locally by its proprietors. Every data sharing access is likewise put away in the blockchain as a transaction.

5.3. Data Sharing Policy

Existing strategies use encryption for information security. In any case, in information sharing situations, it is as yet dangerous for information holders to share the first information because of different assaults towards the encryption. An increasingly secure strategy is using Smart contracts to share the appropriate responses towards the solicitations, which can give the requesters legitimate data and ensure protection of information holders.

5.4. Analysis of Security

Figure 13. Comparison of Bandwidth consumed per client when training CIFAR-10 over VGG
Source: (Vepakomma et al., 2018)

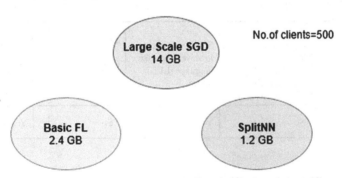

Figure 12 and 13 shows the efficiency of performance of FL and SplitNN over Large scale SGD (Stochastic Gradient Descent). The utilization of permissioned blockchain builds up a protected tool for different groups without shared trust. We coordinate federated learning into the smart contract of permissioned blockchain to address the previously mentioned security dangers. Table 1 gives comparison of various Public and private blockchain platforms.

1. Accomplishing differential protection: Different advances, utilizing the training strategies for ascertaining residuals, are just mapping tasks that are information independent and won't reveal any private data.

2. Evacuating concentrated trust: No central trusted authority.
3. Ensuring the nature of shared information
4. Secure information: Permissioned blockchain utilizes elliptic curve cryptography to ensure security of information.

Table 1. Core characteristics of four example blockchain platforms

	Bitcoin	Ethereum	Hyperledger Fabric	Corda
Cryptocurrency	Bitcoin (BTC)	Ethereum (ETH)	No built-in currency	No built-in currency
Access policy	Public	Public	Private	Private
Validation policy	Permission less	Permission less	Permissioned	Permissioned
Consensus protocol	Proof of work	Proof of work	Voting-based algorithm (Apache Kafka)	Validity consensus, Uniqueness consensus
Transaction processing time (average)	~ 10 minutes	~ 15 minutes	Almost instantaneous	Almost instantaneous
Max transaction rate	~ 7 TPS	~ 20 TPS	3500+ TPS	~ 170 TPS
Smart contract language	Bitcoin Script, high-level languages compilable to Bitcoin native transactions	Solidity, Serpent, lowlevel Lisp-like language (LLL), Mutan	Go	JVM programming languages like Kotlin, Java
Turing completeness	No	Yes	Yes	Yes

6. CONCLUSION AND FUTURE RESEARCH WORK DIRECTIONS

This chapter shows how Blockchain technology and decentralized AI can be combined together to solve bigger issue in application of AI into Information sensitive domains like Financial Industries, Hospitals data, which joins federated learning into permissioned blockchain. This chapter also showed that how Blockchain based smart contracts can enforce data privacy by logging in every data access as a transaction onto the immutable ledger. With help of Integration of federated learning into the smart contracts of permissioned blockchain, it increases efficiency of information sharing plan. This blend of federated learning and Blockchain is very helpful in Industrial IoT. Some of the basic issues includes How to efŏciently ensure information protection by applying blockchain strategy is as yet an open issue, how to improve the utility of information models mapped from raw information. In addition, the limited resource of devices imposes new difficulties. This topic has seen significant improvements in the recent days. Big technology companies are deploying Federated learning solutions in production and are able to address privacy and data challenges.

It is found that federated learning comes with exceptional opportunities and challenges for researchers. Federated learning allows datasets which are distributed to enable modeling and research using distributed data which may be too private to be shared. Future scope of research includes developing new federated datasets and advance currently available datasets. Researchers also need to tackle the fairness-related challenge. There is need of research to tackle newer sources of bias based on considerations such as device type, location and local dataset size. To examine the grade to which these numerous sampling restraints affect the fairness of the resulting model. Studies are needed to check the limitations of other parts of FL, like model compression. There has been good amount of research in conventional ML to train fair classifiers, like constrained optimization and distributional-robust optimization. Researchers also need to work out additional assumptions if any under which this will be applicable.

REFERENCES

Alpaydin, E. (2020). *Introduction to machine learning*. MIT Press.

Bagdasaryan, E., Veit, A., Hua, Y., Estrin, D., & Shmatikov, V. (2018). *How to backdoor federated learning.* arXiv preprint arXiv:1807.00459

Bonawitz, K., Eichner, H., Grieskamp, W., Huba, D., Ingerman, A., Ivanov, V., . . . Van Overveldt, T. (2019). *Towards federated learning at scale: System design.* arXiv preprint arXiv:1902.01046

Bonawitz, K., Ivanov, V., Kreuter, B., Marcedone, A., McMahan, H. B., Patel, S., ... Seth, K. (2017, October). Practical secure aggregation for privacy-preserving machine learning. In *Proceedings of the 2017 ACM SIGSAC Conference on Computer and Communications Security* (pp. 1175-1191). 10.1145/3133956.3133982

Crosby, M., Pattanayak, P., Verma, S., & Kalyanaraman, V. (2016). Blockchain technology: Beyond bitcoin. *Applied Innovation, 2*(6-10), 71.

Geyer, R. C., Klein, T., & Nabi, M. (2017). *Differentially private federated learning: A client level perspective.* arXiv preprint arXiv:1712.07557

Gupta, O., & Raskar, R. (2018). Distributed learning of deep neural network over multiple agents. *Journal of Network and Computer Applications, 116*, 1–8. doi:10.1016/j.jnca.2018.05.003

Kim, H., Park, J., Bennis, M., & Kim, S. L. (2018). *On-device federated learning via blockchain and its latency analysis.* arXiv preprint arXiv:1808.03949

Konečný, J., McMahan, H. B., Yu, F. X., Richtárik, P., Suresh, A. T., & Bacon, D. (2016). *Federated learning: Strategies for improving communication efficiency.* arXiv preprint arXiv:1610.05492

LeCun, Y., Bengio, Y., & Hinton, G. (2015). Deep learning. *Nature, 521*(7553), 436-444.

Lin, I. C., & Liao, T. C. (2017). A survey of blockchain security issues and challenges. *International Journal of Network Security, 19*(5), 653–659.

Nasr, M., Shokri, R., & Houmansadr, A. (2018). *Comprehensive privacy analysis of deep learning: Stand-alone and federated learning under passive and active white-box inference attacks.* arXiv preprint arXiv:1812.00910

Tasatanattakool, P., & Techapanupreeda, C. (2018, January). Blockchain: Challenges and applications. In *2018 International Conference on Information Networking (ICOIN)* (pp. 473-475). IEEE. 10.1109/ICOIN.2018.8343163

Truex, S., Baracaldo, N., Anwar, A., Steinke, T., Ludwig, H., Zhang, R., & Zhou, Y. (2019, November). A hybrid approach to privacy-preserving federated learning. In *Proceedings of the 12th ACM Workshop on Artificial Intelligence and Security* (pp. 1-11). 10.1145/3338501.3357370

Vepakomma, P., Gupta, O., Swedish, T., & Raskar, R. (2018). *Split learning for health: Distributed deep learning without sharing raw patient data.* arXiv preprint arXiv:1812.00564

Weng, J., Weng, J., Zhang, J., Li, M., Zhang, Y., & Luo, W. (2019). Deepchain: Auditable and privacy-preserving deep learning with blockchain-based incentive. *IEEE Transactions on Dependable and Secure Computing*, 1. doi:10.1109/TDSC.2019.2952332

Yang, Q., Liu, Y., Chen, T., & Tong, Y. (2019). Federated machine learning: Concept and applications. *ACM Transactions on Intelligent Systems and Technology, 10*(2), 1–19. doi:10.1145/3298981

Zheng, Z., Xie, S., Dai, H. N., Chen, X., & Wang, H. (2018). Blockchain challenges and opportunities: A survey. *International Journal of Web and Grid Services*, *14*(4), 352–375. doi:10.1504/IJWGS.2018.095647

Zhu, X., Li, H., & Yu, Y. (2018, December). Blockchain-based privacy preserving deep learning. In *International Conference on Information Security and Cryptology* (pp. 370-383). Springer.

KEY TERMS AND DEFINITIONS

Blockchain: Blockchain is the technology addressing the issue of privacy, enforcing trust in uncontrolled environments like in Healthcare, Financial etc. Industries. We are reviewing the works in this Blockchain and Federated learning can be combined to get the best of both the technologies to address the underlying issues. Blockchain is a sequential data structure that contains data stored in blocks linked to each other using hashing.

Federated Learning: Federated learning is a technology to enable distributed client devices to train AI models without sharing the data.

Machine Learning: It is a subset of Artificial Intelligence in which Machines learns from the data rather than being programmed explicitly.

Split Neural Network (SplitNN): Split learning is a novel technology developed by MIT Media lab's Camera culture group that allows to train ML models without sharing any raw data and overcomes the drawbacks of Federated learning.

Chapter 9
Prospects of Machine Learning With Blockchain in Healthcare and Agriculture

Pushpa Singh
iD https://orcid.org/0000-0001-9796-3978
Delhi Technical Campus, Greater Noida, India

Narendra Singh
iD https://orcid.org/0000-0002-6760-8550
G. L. Bajaj Institute of Management and Research, India

Ganesh Chandra Deka
iD https://orcid.org/0000-0002-7176-1590
Ministry of Skill Development and Entrepreneurship, Guwahati, India

ABSTRACT

Presently, machine learning (ML) techniques have gained considerable attention, with growing interest in various areas and applications. Healthcare, agriculture, and bioinformatics are the most identified areas to study with the help of ML. This chapter introduces about the basic principle of ML such as data, model, basic mathematical details of ML, and types of learning. The important aspect of ML is "how to teach a machine." This chapter focuses on the types of learning: supervised, unsupervised, semi-supervised, and reinforcement learning. Some commonly used ML algorithms such as decision tree (DT), k-nearest neighbor (KNN), support vector machine (SVM), naïve Bayes, k-mean, q-learning, etc. are briefly discussed for understanding. Finally, the author offers the application of ML with blockchain that is reforming the traditional healthcare and agricultural sector to a more reliable means.

DOI: 10.4018/978-1-7998-5876-8.ch009

1. INTRODUCTION

Currently ML is one of the prominent techniques that are being applied in an extensive range of applications to solve a variety of complex problems. ML is a branch of Artificial Intelligence (AI) that offers computer systems the ability to automatically learn without explicitly programmed. The massive volumes of data are the base of ML concept and capable to design an expert system. These data are growing at an exponential rate due to a large number of connected devices and applications. ML enables us to tackle the difficult and challenging tasks that are also complex to resolve with traditional programs. ML is the training of computer algorithms that learn, expand and evolve automatically through knowledge and observation. Healthcare, Agriculture, human brain, Bioinformatics etc. are the most identified areas to study with the support of ML. The field of ML revolves around the basic principle:

- Collecting the data
- Preprocessing of data
- Learn the model with training data and algorithm
- Test the model for accuracy.

'Learning' in ML refers to the determination of model parameters using the given training dataset. There are four categories of ML: Supervised, Unsupervised, Semi-supervised and Reinforcement Learning that is used to sustain competitiveness in various fields and industries.

The basic principle of ML includes: data, computer algorithm and mathematics. With the knowledge of mathematics one can easily understand the ML. So, it is important to understand the mathematical concepts that are specifically applied in ML. ML comprises linear algebra, multivariate calculus, matrix decompositions, optimization, probability and statistics (Deisenroth, Faisal, & Ong, 2020). The existing initiative of integrating the AI with Blockchain and IoTs are reshaping the world. This will create a new opportunity in a big range of domains, like smart health, agriculture, retail, green energy, supply chain management, smart city and also personalized end-user applications. The Blockchain holds the potential, mainly when integrated with AI. With Blockchain technology, patients can attach to other hospitals, diagnostic center and accumulate their medical data automatically (Yoon, 2019). These medical data may also help the patient for disease prediction and treatment suggestion when refined by ML.

The main contributions of this chapter are to present an overview of basic concept of mathematics applied in ML. Author will cover the major types of ML algorithms; explain the benefits and applications of each of them.

The rest of the chapter is structured in different parts. Section 2 deliberates about the terminology used in ML. Mathematical Background of ML has been presented in section 3. Types of ML and its application have been discussed in section 4. Applications of ML and Blockchain have been given in section 5. Future work directions are represented in section 6. Section 7 concludes the overall chapter.

2. BACKGROUND AND TERMINOLOGY USED IN MACHINE LEARNING

In ML, computers use massive sets of data and apply ML algorithms for training, testing and predictions. The two definitions of ML have been most popular. According to Arthur Samuel *"ML is a core branch of AI that aims to give computers the ability to learn without being explicitly programmed"*.

However, Tom Mitchell provides a more modern definition: *"A computer program is said to learn from experience E with respect to some class of tasks T and performance measure P, if its performance at tasks in T, as measured by P, improves with experience E."* The term is briefly explained with example robot driving learning problem (Mitchell, 1997).

- **Task T:** The formal definition of the word "task," means of achieving the capability to achieve the task not the process of learning. For example, if a robot is able to walk, then walking is called as a task. One can program the robot to learn to walk. Some popular ML "task" is classification, regression, clustering etc. For example: In case of the robot driving learning problem, driving on public six-lane highways by using vision sensors.
- **Performance measure (P):** To assess the capabilities of a ML algorithm, it is necessary to design a computable measure of its performance. Typically the, P is specific to the task T being carried out by the system and represented in term of accuracy, precision, etc.

For example: In case of the robot driving learning problem, increasing accuracy in average distance traveled before an error.

- **Experience (E):** The experiences that are being used to increase performance of the task. For example: In case of robot driving learning problem, a classification of images and navigation commands recorded(data set) by perceiving a human driver.

2.1 Data, Model and Algorithm

ML is called as the design of algorithms that automatically extract precious information from data. There are three main concepts that are applied as a core of ML: data, model, and learning (Deisenroth, Faisal, & Ong, 2020) as shown in figure 1.

Figure 1. Core of ML

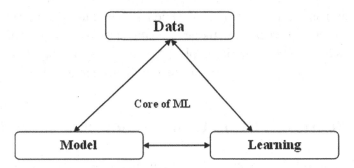

ML is, fundamentally data driven. Data can be any raw fact, text, audio, image, or video that is not being interpreted and analyzed. Data is the most important part of ML. Model training is not possible without data. Data is used for training of the model, validation and testing of the model. A model is believed to learn from the data. Model entails algorithm that effort to learn latent pattern and relationships from data. The ultimate aim of model is to find better models that generalize well to yet unseen data. Learning can be defined as a method of automatically discover the patterns and structure in data by improving the parameters of the model.

- **ML Algorithm:** Various machines learning algorithm are available for model building that is discussed in the next section. ML algorithms are a program that entails math and logic. Algorithms modify themselves to perform well as when they are exposed to more data.
- **Training data set:** A subset to train a model. Training data is the most important data to learn the machines and make the predictions. More than 70% of the total data is used to train the ML model.

Example: Consider the physical characteristics (input feature) of each tissue, like 'mean radius', 'mean texture', 'mean perimeter', 'mean area' etc. in breast_cancer. csv that is freely available in the data folder of datasets in sklearn library (Pedregosa et al., 2011) along with the 'malignant' and 'benign' that tissue (target output class).

Feed 70% of this data to the ML algorithm (classification) and it learns a model of the correlation between an average tissues's characteristic, and its quality.

- **Testing data set:** A subset to test the trained model. The test data is used to check how well the machine can predict new results, based on the basis of training.

Example: The characteristics of the tissue which you have taken as a test data (rest 30% data) and feed it to the ML techniques. It will use the model which was calculated earlier to predict if the tissue is 'malignant' or 'benign'. The algorithm may be DT, KNN, SVM etc. If all sample data used for testing, predict same output as an actual target class. Then testing accuracy is considered as 100%.

3. MATHEMATICAL FOUNDATION OF MACHINE LEARNING

Mathematics provides a strong base to computer science. AI is the branch of computer science concerned with making computers act like humans. ML and deep learning both are the subsets of AI. This has been observed that ML rely on necessary mathematical concept like linear algebra, statistics and probability, calculus, entropy etc. as represented in figure 2. Linear algebra is critical to understanding the concept of ML. Statistics and calculus also requires prior knowledge of linear algebra. These mathematical concepts and principles are used for model building, validation, and acceptance confidence.

Figure 2. Mathematical Concept used in ML

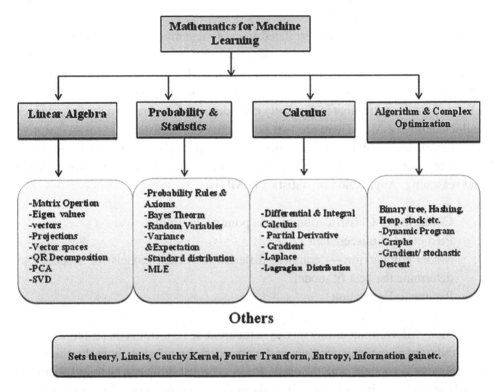

3.1 Linear Algebra

Linear algebra is a core mathematical principle used in ML. Its concepts are important for understanding the basic concept of ML and especially Deep Learning algorithm In order to understand and use tools of ML one has to have a firm background in linear algebra and optimization theory (Gallier & Quaintance, 2019). Linear Algebra is valuable for compact representation of linear transformations on data transformations on data. This offers dimensionality reduction techniques such as Principal component analysis (PCA). There are following application of linear algebra in ML:

1. Loss functions
2. Regularization
3. Covariance Matrix
4. Support Vector Machine Classification

3.2 Statistics and Probability

Probability and statistics are interrelated areas of mathematics and used to investigate the comparative occurrence of events. The basic difference between probability and statistics is that *Probability* deals with predicting the likelihood of future events, while *Statistics* includes the analysis of the frequency of past events. Statistics are a field of mathematics that is generally considered to be a prerequisite for a deeper understanding of ML. There are two perspectives of statistics: first is descriptive statistics that consist mean, medium, variance etc., and another perspective is inferential statistics. "Infer" means to derive or deduce something from evidence and reasoning. Application of statistics in ML is:

1. Clustering or Classification of data points into groups.
2. Prediction of unseen data
3. Model comparison — compare different statistical models for a dataset to determine the best fit model.
4. Parameter Estimation

Various ML techniques rely on Bayes theorem. It's a formula that establishes the probability of an event depending on the preceding knowledge about the situations that might be associated with the event. Reverse probabilities can be found out using the Bayes theorem if the conditional probability is known to us. Bayes theorem is also used to predict the probability of the target class label when a set of attributes is given. Some of the essential statistical and probability theory needed for ML is shown in figure 2.

3.3 Calculus

Multivariate calculus is another important field that assists in understanding the relationships between input and output variables. Matrix calculus is used to understand the training of deep neural networks (Parr & Howard, 2018). Calculus is important to optimize an artificial neural network (ANN) in form of gradient descent where error term is reduced. ML uses integral calculus in defining the probability of events, for instance, in finding the posterior in a Bayesian model, or bounding the error in a sequential decision according to the Neyman-Pearson lemma. Integral Calculus, Partial Derivatives, Vector-Values Functions, Gradient, Laplacian and Lagragian distribution are some essential topics included in ML.

Figure 3. Types of ML

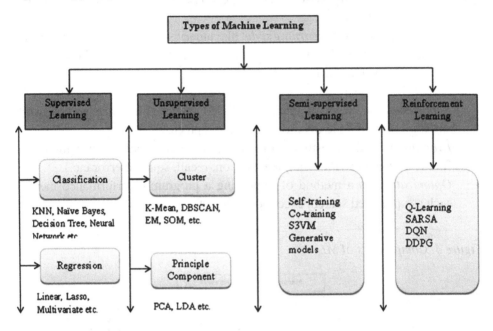

3.4 Algorithms and Complex Optimizations

This is significant to understand the computational efficiency and scalability of ML algorithm for exploiting sparsity in datasets. The ML algorithm is based on voluminous data and complex set of instruction. Hence, optimization is used to improve the program's performance for execution speed. Optimization methods have a significative influence on various fields of ML. The stochastic optimization method can also be applied to Markov Chain Monte Carlo (MCMC) sampling to improve efficiency (Sun et al., 2019).

4. TYPES OF MACHINE LEARNING (ML)

The ultimate aim of ML algorithms is to generalize beyond the training samples, i.e. effectively infers data. Algorithm in ML is used in two different perspectives. In one perspective ML algorithm used to make predictions based on input data also referred as 'predictor'. In the second perspective, ML algorithm adjusts some internal parameters of the predictor so that it performs well on future hidden input data. There are many different types of ML algorithm that can be divided into four types: Supervised, Unsupervised, Semi-supervised and Reinforcement Learning as shown in figure 3.

This division is based on '*learning style*' like supervised learning or unsupervised or combination of both. Each type of ML algorithms comprises the following components as shown in figure 4.

- *Representation*: a set of classifiers based on tree, instance and network structure (for example tree, hyper plane, graph etc.).
- *Evaluation*: goals to estimate the performance or accuracy of a model on future unseen data (for example precision, recall, squared error etc.).
- *Optimization*: is a method of improving a program's performance metrics such as optimized search, execution speed etc.

Figure 4. Components of ML

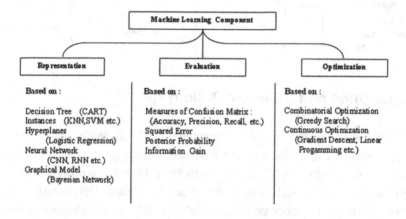

4.1 Supervised Learning

Supervised learning data is based on labeled data. One can also say that the target class label is already given corresponding to input feature vector. Supervised learning is learning with the help of a teacher. The training data act like a teacher that teaches the model about the correct class label for a specific input feature so that it can make accurate decisions when later presented with new data. Once the model is trained, it is tested with testing set of data and finds the accuracy of the model. The overall working is depicted in figure 5. Data preprocessing is used to transform the raw data into a suitable and efficient format. Data preprocessing consists: data cleaning, data transformation and data reduction (Han, Pie & Kamber,

2011). Classification accuracy is the ratio of the number of correct predictions to the total number of input samples.

$$Accuracy = \frac{\text{No. of correct prediction}}{\text{Total No. of prediction}}$$

Accuracy is best fit only when there is equal number of samples related to each class. KNN, Decision tree, SVM, Logistic Regression, Neural Network, Naïve Bayes etc., are some well- known algorithm of supervised learning.

Figure 5. Process of Supervised Learning

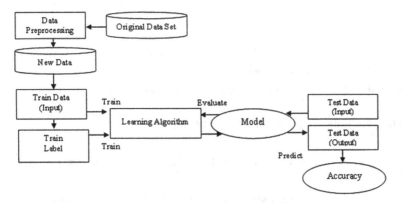

4.1.1 Decision Tree

A decision tree is a tree based structure. Each internal node represents a "test" on an attribute, each branch denotes the outcome of the test, and each leaf node denotes a class label. Iterative Dichotomizer (ID3), C5.0 and Classification *And Regression Trees* (CART) are some well-known algorithm based on decision tree. Decision tree can be used to solve both classification and regression problem.

Important concept: Entropy and Information Gain.

Entropy: It is used to measure the impurity or randomness of a dataset as shown in figure 6.

$$Entropy = \sum_i -p_i \log_2 p_i \tag{1}$$

In (1), p_i is the probability of class i, calculate it as the proportion of class i in the set.

Figure 6. Impurity Representation

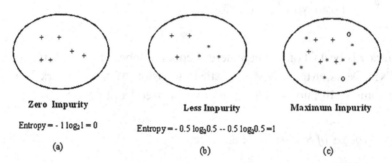

Zero Impurity | Less Impurity | Maximum Impurity

Entropy = - 1 $\log_2$1 = 0 | Entropy = - 0.5 $\log_2$0.5 -- 0.5 $\log_2$0.5 = 1

(a) | (b) | (c)

Information Gain: is used to select best feature which acts as a root node first use each descriptive feature and divided the dataset along the values of these descriptive features and then compute the entropy of the dataset as given in (2).

IG (feature) = Entropy (Dataset)- Entropy (feature)   (2)

Advantage: No need to normalize the data. Decision tree can be implemented without the scaling.

Disadvantage: Require more memory and time to compute mathematical calculation

Application: Telehealth services (Chern, 2019), Healthcare (Khan, Zardar, & Bhatti, 2018), waste management (Dubey et. al., 2020).

4.1.2 k-Nearest Neighbors (KNN)

KNN is a simple and non-parametric technique that is used for classification and regression. KNN stores all existing cases and categorizes new cases built on their similarity measure. Similarity measure computes that how much two objects are alike on the basis of distance function (Euclidean, Manhattan etc.). Large distance means there are low degree of similarity and small distance implies a high degree of similarity between two objects. The similarity measure within the range [0, 1]. The nearest neighbor represents to the single or multidimensional feature vector that is used to define the sample on the similarity measure. The similarity measures can be the Euclidean distance of the feature vector (Singh & Agrawal, 2018).

Important Concept: Distance function like Euclidean, Manhattan, Minkowski, Cosine Index etc. (Prasatha et. al, 2017). Various distance function between two points (x1, y1) and (x2,y2) as shown in figure 7 has shown by (3a,3b and 3c)

$$D_{manhatton} = |x_1 - x_2| + |y_1 - y_2| \tag{3a}$$

$$D_{euclidean} = \sqrt{\left(x_1 - x_2\right)^2 + \left(y_1 - y_2\right)^2} \tag{3b}$$

$$D_{minkowski} = \left(\left|x_1 - x_2\right|^p + \left|y_1 - y_2\right|^p\right)^{1/p} \tag{3c}$$

Figure 7. Distance representation

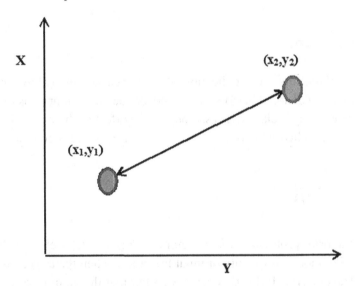

Advantage: Very simple implementation. Robust with regard to the search space; *Disadvantage:* KNN is not suitable for the large dimensional data.

Application: GDP economic forecasting (Priambodo et. al, 2019), loyalty prediction (Singh & Agrawal, 2018), customer retention (Singh & Agrawal, 2019), big data (Saadatfa et al., 2020) and waste Management (Dubey, 2020).

Figure 8. SVM Classifier

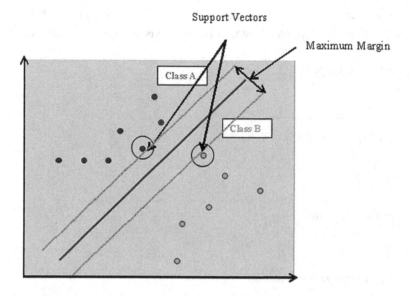

4.1.3 Naïve Bayes

Naive Bayes classifiers are a collection of classification algorithms constructed on Bayes' theorem denoted in (4) with the independence assumptions between the predictors. Naïve Bayes classifiers assume that the effect of the value of a predictor (P) on a particular class label (C) is independent of the other predictors' values.

$$P(C \mid I) = \frac{P(I \mid C)P(C)}{P(I)} \tag{4}$$

P (I) is the prior probability of predictor and P (C) is prior class probability. P (I |C) is the likelihood probability of input feature (I) when the target class label is specified. The posterior P (C | I) is the probability that the input feature I, is in the class output label (C).

Important Concept: Bayes theorem and Probability

Advantage: It has a higher speed for large numbers of training and queries.

Disadvantage: Need to calculate the prior probability

Application: Typical applications include filtering spam (Rusland et al., 2017), classifying documents (Adetunji, 2018), sentiment analysis (Hasan, 2018) etc.

4.1.4 Support Vector Machine (SVM)

SVM is a set of supervised ML methods that offers classification, prediction, regression and outlier detection. It is effective in high dimensional spaces. There are two classes in an x-y plane with points overlapping each other. A straight line can be drawn that can be flawlessly distinct them and also maximizes the minimum margin between two classes. This maximum-margin separator is referred by a subgroup of the data points that is frequently termed as "support vectors". In figure 8, support vectors are indicated by the circles nearby them.

Advantage: SVM is best suited when there is perfect margin of separation between classes and also memory efficient.

Disadvantage: SVM is not appropriate for big data sets.

Applications: healthcare, medicine (Sidey-Gibbons & Sidey-Gibbons, 2019), handwritten recognition (Hamid & Sjarif, 2017), Bioinformatics, face detection etc.

4.1.5 Neural Network

A neural network is a network of neurons connected in diverse layers like input layer, hidden layer and output layer. Each neuron takes an input, applies an activation function and provides the output that passes to the next layer. Each neuron in the input layer, use a linear transfer function or identity function and neurons in the hidden layer and output layer generally used non-linear function such as sigmoidal, tangent etc. Usually the networks are defined as feed-forward where each neuron feeds its output to all the neuron (or units) in the next layer. There is no feedback to the former layer. Weights are applied to the signals passing from one unit to another, and must tune during the training phase to adjust a neural network.

Figure 9. Common Model of ANN

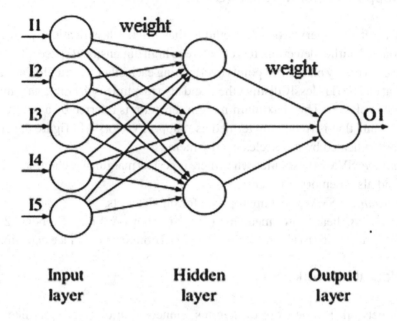

Input
layer

Hidden
layer

Output
layer

Figure 9 represented a common model of artificial neural network (ANN) and the net input can be computed as (5):

$I_{in} = I_1.w_1 + I_2.w_2 + I_3.w_3 ... I_m.w_m$

i.e., Net input

$$I_{in} = \sum_{i=1}^{n} I_i W_i \tag{5}$$

The output can be computed by applying the activation function of the net input as shown in (6).

$Y = f(I_{in}) \tag{6}$

Important concept:

- Neuron & Network Topology.
- Adjustments of Weights or Learning rule: Hebbian Learning Rule, Perceptron Learning Rule, Delta Learning Rule, Competitive Learning Rule etc.

- Activation function: performs a mathematical operation on the signal output.

Table 1. Important Activation Function

Activation Function	Formula	Shape
Linear	$f\left(x\right) = cx$	
Sigmoidal	$f(x) = \dfrac{1}{1 + e^{-x}}$	
Tangent	$f(x) = \dfrac{e^x - e^{-x}}{e^x + e^{-x}}$	
ReLu	$f\left(x\right) = \max\left(0, x\right)$	
Softmax	$f_i(x) = \dfrac{e^{x_i}}{\sum_k e^{x_k}}$	

Figure 10. Type of ANN

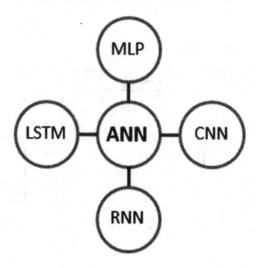

Table 2. Difference between classification and Regression

S.N.	Classification	Regression
1.	Nature of attributes is categorical or discrete in the case of classification.	Nature of the attribute is continuous in the case of Regression.
2.	Ex. If you give student profile to classification then it predicts as 'Pass' or 'Fail' class.	Ex. If you give student profile to Regression then it predicts student's marks in (%).
3.	Popular classification algorithms are DT, KNN, ANN etc.	Popular regression algorithms are linear regression, regression trees, lasso regression and multivariate regression (Bhatia, 2018).

Figure 11. Types of Regression Algorithm

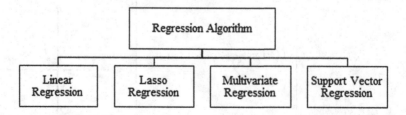

Table 3. Linear Regression vs. Logistic Regression

S.N.	Linear Regression	Logistic Regression
1.	It captures the relationship between a dependent variable and one or more independent variables.	It predicts the probability of an consequence that can have two values only.
2.	Used to solve regression problem.	Used to solve binary classification problem.
3.	The output value is continuous that uses a straight line.	The output value is discrete that uses an s curve or sigmoid function.
4.	Estimate the dependent variable in case of modification in the independent variable.	Calculate the likelihood of an event happening.

These functions transform the summed, weighted input from the node into the activation of the node or output to that input. Some popular activation function are represented in table 1:

Types of ANN: various types like Multilayer Perceptron (MLP), Convolution Neural Network (CNN), Recurrent Neural Network (RNN) and Long Short Term Memory networks (LSTM) as shown in figure 10.

Advantage: ANN can store information on the entire network and has the capability to work with partial information.

Disadvantage: It is computationally very expensive and time consuming to train with traditional CPUs.

Application: Medical Imaging (Lundervold & Lundervold, 2019), disease diagnosis, Drug discovery (Xu, Yao, & Lin, 2018), Genome study (Yin et al., 2019), and Healthcare (Shahid, Rappon, & Berta, 2019).

4.1.6 Classification and Regression

Supervised learning has two variation i.e. classification and regression. The classification is defined to predict categorical or discrete class label output for an occurrence. There are two types of classifiers: Binary classifier and multi-class classifier. Binary classifier is classification with only two classes, for example, On the basis of input feature such as blood glucose value etc., patient is suffering from "hyperglycemia" or "hypoglycemia" is classification (Agrawal, Singh, & Sneha, 2019). Multi-Class classifier defined as classification with more than two discrete classes, for example types of user i.e. Very Loyal, Loyal, Normal, and Recent (Singh & Agrawal, 2018). Various classification applications include:

Figure 12. Unsupervised Learning

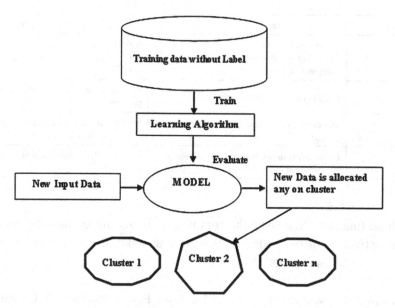

- HealthCare: For Disease Diagnosis and Prediction, drug discovery, treatment suggestion etc.
- Bioinformatics: Gene classification, protein structure prediction (Singh & Singh, 2020) etc.
- Spam mail classification, Natural language Processing (NLP), Face detection, accident prediction etc.

The regression is defined to predict continuous amount of class label output for an occurrence. It provides the response of "How much" and "How many" nodes is diseased. Consider the table 2 for better understanding.

The regression algorithms effort to evaluate the mapping functions from the input variables to numerical or continuous output variables. Consequently, regression prediction problems are usually quantities or sizes. Some of the popular types of regression algorithms are as shown in figure 11.

There are following application of regression algorithm.

1. Lasso regression algorithms are broadly applied in financial networks and economics.
2. Lasso-based regression algorithms are applied in evaluating the risk framework of enterprise.

3. Application of logistic regression in real estate business (ex. predict house price), insurance sector (ex. Customer lifetime value).
4. SVR regression algorithms have been widely applied in the oil and gas industry, image classification, and stock price prediction (Rustam, Z., & Kintandani, 2019).
5. The Multivariate Regression algorithm is widely applied in the retail sector.

The term "Logistic Regression", consists "Regression" in their names only, but not regression algorithms. For better understanding, the difference between logistic regression and linear regression is given in table 3.

4.2 Unsupervised Learning

Learning without a teacher is called as unsupervised learning. This type of learning is entirely based on experience and observation. This type of learning is used to train a machine to govern hidden patterns from unlabeled data in the absence of target variables as shown in figure 12. Two basic concepts used in unsupervised learning are *principal component* and *cluster analysis*. Principle components remove highly correlated features on the basis covariance matrix, eigenvalues and eigenvectors. It uses an orthogonal transformation to alter a set of observations of probably correlated variables into a set of values of linear uncorrelated variables termed principal components. It is used to reduce the similar features or dimensionality. Clustering means finding subgroups or clusters in a dataset that are similar to each other. This is realized by reducing the sum of the squared Euclidean distance between each observation within a cluster. Inter cluster distance should be maximized and intra-cluster distance should be minimized to form a better cluster. K-Mean, Self Organized Model, Expectation Model, PCA and LDA etc. are specific eminent unsupervised learning algorithm.

4.2.1 K-Mean

K-Mean is a simple unsupervised learning process that solves the renowned clustering problem. The method follows a simple technique to categorize a specified data set through a definite number of clusters (assume k clusters) fixed apriori. The basic concept is to state the k centers, one center for each cluster. The algorithm will classify the items into k groups based on their of similarity measure. To calculate a similarity measure, distance functions are used as a measurement.

Important concept: Distance Function

Advantage: Fast, vigorous and simple to understand.

Disadvantage: K-Mean needs apriori specification of the number of cluster centers.

Application: Bioinformatics (Jose et. al, 2017), Networking (Usama et. al, 2019), customer segmentation (Ezenkwu, Ozuomba, & Kalu, 2015).

4.2.2 Self-organizing Map (SOM)

SOM is a kind of Artificial Neural Network (ANN) that is trained by unsupervised learning to yield a low-dimensional, discretized depiction of the input space of the training samples and also used to do dimensionality reduction.

Basic concept:

- Best Matching Unit (BMU)
- Euclidean Distance and/or Consine Distance.

Advantages: SOM has the ability to organize large, complex data sets. Data mapping is easily interpreted.

Disadvantages: Difficult to compute the weight of inputs

Application: Phonetic typewriter, WEBSOM, Classifying World Poverty (Miljković, 2017).

4.2.3 Expectation- Maximization (E-M)

The core of E-M algorithm is to use the existing observed data of the dataset to assessment the missing data and then update the values of the parameters that are missing. This algorithm has two basic steps: expectation and maximization as represented in figure 13.

Expectation step is used observed data in order to approximate the values of the missing data. It is mainly used to update the variables.

Maximization uses the complete data set created in the prior step to update the values of the parameters. It is mainly used to update the hypothesis.

Advantage: It is always guaranteed that likelihood will increase with each iteration.

Disadvantage: It has slow convergence.

Application: Clustering, Computer Vision, Computed Tomography (Leahy, Clackdoyle, & Noo, 2009),

NLP (Wintrode, 2017), quantitative genetics, psychometrics, medical image (Prakash & Kumari, 2018), segmentation (Li et al., 2019).

Figure 13. Expectation-Maximization

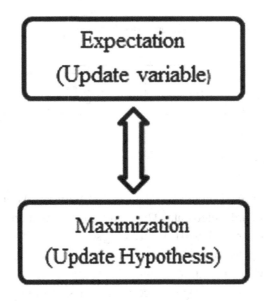

4.2.4 Principal Component Analysis (PCA)

PCA is a dimensionality reduction method for high-dimensional datasets with conserving the original structure and relationships essential to the original dataset hence ML models could still learn from them and be used to make correct predictions.

Basic concept: eigenvalue, covariance, correlation and orthogonal.

Advantage: PCA improves the correlated feature and improve the performance of the algorithm.

Disadvantage: Independent variables become less interpretable and sometime suffer from information loss.

Application: facial recognition (Chen, 2017), computer vision and image compression.

4.3 Semi-supervised Learning

Semi-supervised learning syndicates both labeled and unlabeled data to create a right model. Self-training, Co-training, generative models, Semi Supervised Support Vector Machines (S3VM), and graph based algorithms are several well-known algorithm of semi-supervised learning (Zhu, 2007) as shown in figure 14.

Figure 14. Types of Semi-supervised Learning

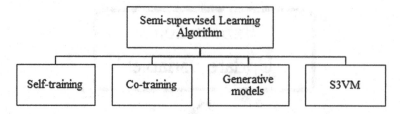

4.3.1 Self-training

A classifier is first trained on labeled data in self-training. After that, classifier is used to categorize all unlabeled data. The unlabeled data that are predicted with the maximum confidence are included in the training set. The classifier is retraining again.

Advantages: Simplest form of semi-supervised learning method.

Disadvantage: Mistakes can re-enforce themselves.

Application: natural language processing, classification, and regression on several services.

4.3.2 Co-Training

Co-Learning is used two different learners with all features of both learners. A data point of one highly confident learner is used to train other learner. Each classifier's high confidant data points are IID samples to the other classifier.

Advantage: Best when one classifier correctly labels a data that the other classifier misclassified.

Disadvantage: If no natural feature split is exist, then need to split features randomly in two parts.

Application: Face Recognition, human action recognition (Liu et al., 2015) etc.

4.4 Reinforcement Learning

Reinforcement learning is built on reward and punishment or feedback system. Learning achieves a task through recurrent trial-and-error interactions with a dynamic environment that maximize a reward for the task without human intervention. There are some key terms that use to describe the reinforcement learning as shown is figure 15.

- *Environment:* Agent operates in physical world called as the environment.
- **State:** Present position of the agent

- **Reward/Punishment:** Agent got positive feedback (reward) and negative feedback (punishment) from the environment.
- **Policy:** A method that is used to map the state of agent to actions.

Figure 15. Reinforcement Learning

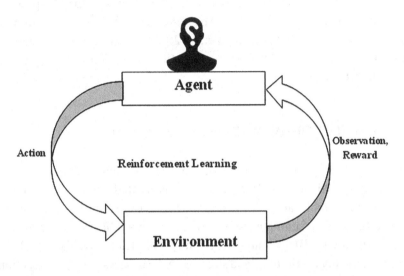

Reinforcement Learning has four algorithm types: Q-Learning, Deep Q Network (DQN), State-Action-Reward-State-Action (SARSA), and Deep Deterministic Policy Gradient (DDPG), represented in figure 16. Q-learning and SARSA is the best known reinforcement learning algorithm.

Figure 16. Types of Reinforcement Learning

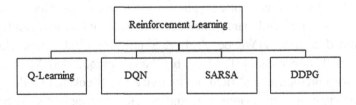

Q-Learning is an off policy Reinforcement learning techniques that search to discover the best action to take specified the current state. 'Off-policy' means that learns from actions that are not available in the present policy, like taking random actions. Hence, there is no need of policy. SARSA is an on-policy technique means it learns the value rely on its present action that is derived from its present policy. Limitation of Q-Learning and SARSA is that both are not able to evaluate values for unseen states.

This limitation is overcome by DQN which use ANN to evaluate Q-values. DQNs is used to handle discrete, low-dimensional action spaces. DDPG algorithm overcomes this problem and handles continuous, high dimensional action space. DDPG is model-free and based on off-policy. The various applications of Reinforcement Learning are Disease Prediction (Singh et. al, 2020), Video Gaming based on DQN (Torrado et. al., 2018), Self-Driving car based on DQN (Vitelli & Nayebi, 2016; Fayjie et. al, 2018) etc.

5. APPLICATION OF ML WITH BLOCKCHAIN

ML models can be applied to anything that consist vast volume of data. Blockchain is not exception in this line. A Blockchain is a distributed, public ledger, recording transactions, immutable and tracking assets. The immutability is assured by a peer-to-peer network of computers. There are many application areas where ML can be combined with Blockchain successfully and efficiently. The Blockchain is designed specifically to stimulate and streamline the process of how transactions are verified. Blockchain offers a transparent transaction system for any type of asset by using decentralized system. When ML and Blockchain unite then the ability of ML accelerates the analysis of an enormous amount of data to different connected part of Blockchain. AI and Blockchain can perform well in healthcare application. The health sector is connected to a different set of block such as patient, doctor, medical health agent which requires safe and reliable data transfer (Singh & Singh, 2020). Block chain can anonymously track medical records and medication taken, and then use AI/ ML to see relationships/patterns between health and medication, location, visits etc. The objective is to offer a platform that integrates Blockchain and AI for: electronic health record management, effective data integration, and consistent computer-aided diagnoses (Wehbe, Zaabi & Svetinovic, 2018). Agriculture 4.0 is an integration of Blockchain, IoT, AI and big data (Clercq, 2018). ML will assist in the better crops prediction and field productivity and Blockchain will ensure that data is distributed in a transparent way and efficient transaction system. A smart contract 'OurSQL' is one of the Blockchain features that can be used as a actual agreement between the seed firm and farmer (Surasak, 2019).

6. FUTURE RESEARCH DIRECTIONS

Current ML algorithms recognize statistical regularities in complex data sets and are regularly used in a wide range of application like Healthcare, Agriculture, Bioinformatics, Stock Market, and targeted advertising. But these applications lack the robustness, accuracy, transparency and generalization (Greenwald, & Oertel, 2017). For accuracy, deep learning as a subfield of ML has been widely used in medical imaging.

ML is still hot at present and will be research hotspot in coming ten years when integrated with Blockchain and IoT. Healthcare and agriculture sector are likely to have access to integrated service platforms based on an emergent set of technology i.e. AI, IoT and Blockchain. ML and IoT data become a basic necessity of healthcare big data analytics, and Blockchain can provide an inventive and effective approach to ensure that all that big data is used and stored properly. Autonomous vehicle technology has seen a rapid progress due to several challenges and difficulty in proving completely functional in seamless, interoperable, and trusted manner. Automation in healthcare, agriculture and vehicles offers future scope areas of AI and ML technology to more explore, research and integration with other parallel technology.

7. CONCLUSION

In this chapter, author discussed about basic principle of ML. ML is based on data, learning algorithm and basic mathematics. Mathematics is at the core of ML because it provides the means of implementation of learning algorithm. Each type of ML algorithm is briefly discussed with advantages, disadvantages and related application areas. ML techniques offer benefits and solve real life problems specifically healthcare and agriculture. ML is accelerating itself many times while integrating with other emergent technology like Blockchain and IoT.

REFERENCES

Adetunji, A. B., Oguntoye, J. P., Fenwa, O. D., & Akande, N. O. (2018). Web Document Classification Using Naïve Bayes. *Journal of Advances in Mathematics and Computer Science*, 1-11.

Agrawal, V., Singh, P., & Sneha, S. (2019, April). Hyperglycemia Prediction Using Machine Learning: A Probabilistic Approach. In *International Conference on Advances in Computing and Data Sciences* (pp. 304-312). Springer. 10.1007/978-981-13-9942-8_29

Bhatia, R. (2018). Regression Algorithms Used In Analytics & Data Mining. *Analytics India Magazine*.

Chen, J., & Jenkins, W. K. (2017, August). Facial recognition with PCA and machine learning methods. In *2017 IEEE 60th International Midwest Symposium on Circuits and Systems (MWSCAS)* (pp. 973-976). IEEE. 10.1109/MWSCAS.2017.8053088

Chern, C. C., Chen, Y. J., & Hsiao, B. (2019). Decision tree–based classifier in providing telehealth service. *BMC Medical Informatics and Decision Making*, *19*(1), 104. doi:10.118612911-019-0825-9 PMID:31146749

De Clercq, M., Vats, A., & Biel, A. (2018). Agriculture 4.0: The Future of Farming Technology. *Proceedings of the World Government Summit*, 11-13.

Deisenroth, M. P., Faisal, A. A., & Ong, C. S. (2020). *Mathematics for machine learning*. Cambridge University Press. doi:10.1017/9781108679930

Dubey, S., Singh, M. K., Singh, P., & Aggarwal, S. (2020). Waste Management of Residential Society using Machine Learning and IoT Approach. *2020 International Conference on Emerging Smart Computing and Informatics (ESCI)*, 293-297, 10.1109/ESCI48226.2020.9167526

Dubey, S., Singh, P., Yadav, P., & Singh, K. K. (2020). Household Waste Management System Using IoT and Machine Learning. *Procedia Computer Science*, *167*, 1950–1959. doi:10.1016/j.procs.2020.03.222

Ezenkwu, C. P., Ozuomba, S., & Kalu, C. (2015). *Application of K-Means algorithm for efficient customer segmentation: a strategy for targeted customer services*. Academic Press.

Fayjie, A. R., Hossain, S., Oualid, D., & Lee, D. J. (2018, June). Driverless car: Autonomous driving using deep reinforcement learning in urban environment. In *2018 15th International Conference on Ubiquitous Robots (UR)* (pp. 896-901). IEEE.

Gallier, J., & Quaintance, J. (2019). *Linear A lgebra for Computer Vision*. Robotics, and Machine Learning.

Greenwald, H. S., & Oertel, C. K. (2017). Future directions in machine learning. *Frontiers in Robotics and AI*, *3*, 79. doi:10.3389/frobt.2016.00079

Hamid, N. A., & Sjarif, N. N. A. (2017). *Handwritten recognition using SVM, KNN and neural network*. arXiv preprint arXiv:1702.00723

Han, J., Pei, J., & Kamber, M. (2011). *Data mining: concepts and techniques*. Elsevier.

Hasan, A., Moin, S., Karim, A., & Shamshirband, S. (2018). Machine learning-based sentiment analysis for twitter accounts. *Mathematical and Computational Applications*, *23*(1), 11. doi:10.3390/mca23010011

Jose, J. T., Zachariah, U., Lijo, V. P., Gnanasigamani, L. J., & Mathew, J. (2017). Case Study on Enhanced K-Means Algorithm for Bioinformatics Data Clustering. *International Journal of Applied Engineering Research*, *12*(24), 15147–15151.

Jung, A. (2018). *Machine learning: Basic principles*. arXiv preprint arXiv:1805.05052

Khan, R. S., Zardar, A. A., & Bhatti, Z. (2018). *Artificial Intelligence based Smart Doctor using Decision Tree Algorithm*. arXiv preprint arXiv:1808.01884

Leahy, R. M., Clackdoyle, R., & Noo, F. (2009). Computed tomography. In *The Essential Guide to Image Processing* (pp. 741–776). Academic Press. doi:10.1016/B978-0-12-374457-9.00026-3

Li, X., Zhong, Z., Wu, J., Yang, Y., Lin, Z., & Liu, H. (2019). Expectation-maximization attention networks for semantic segmentation. In *Proceedings of the IEEE International Conference on Computer Vision* (pp. 9167-9176). IEEE.

Liu, W., Li, Y., Tao, D., & Wang, Y. (2015). A general framework for co-training and its applications. *Neurocomputing*, *167*, 112–121. doi:10.1016/j.neucom.2015.04.087

Lundervold, A. S., & Lundervold, A. (2019). An overview of deep learning in medical imaging focusing on MRI. *Zeitschrift fur Medizinische Physik*, *29*(2), 102–127. doi:10.1016/j.zemedi.2018.11.002 PMID:30553609

Miljković, D. (2017, May). Brief review of self-organizing maps. In *2017 40th International Convention on Information and Communication Technology, Electronics and Microelectronics (MIPRO)* (pp. 1061-1066). IEEE. 10.23919/MIPRO.2017.7973581

Parr, T., & Howard, J. (2018). *The matrix calculus you need for deep learning*. arXiv preprint arXiv:1802.01528

Pedregosa, F., Varoquaux, G., Gramfort, A., Michel, V., Thirion, B., Grisel, O., ... Vanderplas, J. (2011). Scikit-learn: Machine learning in Python. *The Journal of Machine Learning Research, 12*, 2825-2830.

Prakash, R. M., & Kumari, R. S. S. (2018). *Modified Expectation Maximization Method for Automatic Segmentation of MR Brain Images.* Conference: MRBRAINS13, Japan.

Prasatha, V. S., Alfeilate, H. A. A., Hassanate, A. B., Lasassmehe, O., Tarawnehf, A. S., Alhasanatg, M. B., & Salmane, H. S. E. (2017). *Effects of Distance Measure Choice on KNN Classifier Performance-A Review.* arXiv preprint arXiv:1708.04321

Priambodo, B., Rahayu, S., Naf'an, E., Handriani, I., Putra, Z. P., Nseaf, A. K., ... Jumaryadi, Y. (2019, December). Predicting GDP of Indonesia Using K-Nearest Neighbour Regression. *Journal of Physics: Conference Series, 1339*(1), 012040. doi:10.1088/1742-6596/1339/1/012040

Rusland, N. F., Wahid, N., Kasim, S., & Hafit, H. (2017, August). Analysis of Naïve Bayes algorithm for email spam filtering across multiple datasets. *IOP Conference Series. Materials Science and Engineering, 226*(1), 012091. doi:10.1088/1757-899X/226/1/012091

Rustam, Z., & Kintandani, P. (2019). Application of Support Vector Regression in Indonesian Stock Price Prediction with Feature Selection Using Particle Swarm Optimisation. *Modelling and Simulation in Engineering, 2019*, 2019. doi:10.1155/2019/8962717

Saadatfar, H., Khosravi, S., Joloudari, J. H., Mosavi, A., & Shamshirband, S. (2020). A New K-Nearest Neighbors Classifier for Big Data Based on Efficient Data Pruning. *Mathematics, 8*(2), 286. doi:10.3390/math8020286

Shahid, N., Rappon, T., & Berta, W. (2019). Applications of artificial neural networks in health care organizational decision-making: A scoping review. *PLoS One, 14*(2), e0212356. doi:10.1371/journal.pone.0212356 PMID:30779785

Sidey-Gibbons, J. A., & Sidey-Gibbons, C. J. (2019). Machine learning in medicine: A practical introduction. *BMC Medical Research Methodology, 19*(1), 64. doi:10.118612874-019-0681-4 PMID:30890124

Singh, N., Singh, P., Singh, K. K., & Singh, A. (2020a). (in press). Diagnosing of Disease using Machine Learning, accepted for Machine Learning & Internet of medical things in healthcare. *Elsevier Publications*.

Singh, P., & Agrawal, R. (2018). A customer centric best connected channel model for heterogeneous and IoT networks. *Journal of Organizational and End User Computing, 30*(4), 32–50. doi:10.4018/JOEUC.2018100103

Singh, P., & Agrawal, R. (2018). Prospects of Open Source Software for Maximizing the User Expectations in Heterogeneous Network. *International Journal of Open Source Software and Processes, 9*(3), 1–14. doi:10.4018/IJOSSP.2018070101

Singh, P., & Agrawal, V. (2019). A Collaborative Model for Customer Retention on User Service Experience. In *Advances in Computer Communication and Computational Sciences* (pp. 55–64). Springer. doi:10.1007/978-981-13-6861-5_5

Singh, P., & Singh, N. (2020). (in press). Role of Data Mining Techniques in Bioinformatics. *International Journal of Applied Research in Bioinformatics, 11*(6).

Singh, P., & Singh, N. (2020). Blockchain with IoT & AI: A Review of Agriculture and Healthcare. International Journal of Applied Evolutionary Computation, 11(4).

Sun, S., Cao, Z., Zhu, H., & Zhao, J. (2019). A Survey of Optimization Methods from a Machine Learning Perspective. *IEEE Transactions on Cybernetics*. Advance online publication. doi:10.1109/TCYB.2019.2950779 PMID:31751262

Surasak, T., Wattanavichean, N., Preuksakarn, C., & Huang, S. C. H. Thai Agriculture Products Traceability System using Blockchain and Internet of Things. *System, 14*, 15.

Torrado, R. R., Bontrager, P., Togelius, J., Liu, J., & Perez-Liebana, D. (2018, August). Deep reinforcement learning for general video game ai. In *2018 IEEE Conference on Computational Intelligence and Games (CIG)* (pp. 1-8). IEEE. 10.1109/CIG.2018.8490422

Usama, M., Qadir, J., Raza, A., Arif, H., Yau, K. L. A., Elkhatib, Y., Hussain, A., & Al-Fuqaha, A. (2019). Unsupervised machine learning for networking: Techniques, applications and research challenges. *IEEE Access: Practical Innovations, Open Solutions, 7*, 65579–65615. doi:10.1109/ACCESS.2019.2916648

Vitelli, M., & Nayebi, A. (2016). Carma: A deep reinforcement learning approach to autonomous driving. Tech. rep. Stanford University.

Wehbe, Y., Al Zaabi, M., & Svetinovic, D. (2018, November). Blockchain ai framework for healthcare records management: Constrained goal model. In *2018 26th Telecommunications Forum (TELFOR)* (pp. 420-425). IEEE.

Wintrode, J., Bui, N., Stepinski, J., & Reed, C. (2017, June). Online Expectation Maximization for Language Characterization of Streaming Text. In *International Conference on Web Engineering* (pp. 200-208). Springer.

Xu, Y., Yao, H., & Lin, K. (2018). An overview of neural networks for drug discovery and the inputs used. *Expert Opinion on Drug Discovery*, *13*(12), 1091–1102. doi: 10.1080/17460441.2018.1547278 PMID:30449189

Yin, B., Balvert, M., van der Spek, R. A., Dutilh, B. E., Bohte, S., Veldink, J., & Schönhuth, A. (2019). Using the structure of genome data in the design of deep neural networks for predicting amyotrophic lateral sclerosis from genotype. *Bioinformatics (Oxford, England)*, *35*(14), i538–i547. doi:10.1093/bioinformatics/btz369 PMID:31510706

Yoon, H. J. (2019). Blockchain technology and healthcare. *Healthcare Informatics Research*, *25*(2), 59. doi:10.4258/hir.2019.25.2.59 PMID:31131139

Zhu, X. (2007, June). Semi-supervised learning tutorial. In *International Conference on Machine Learning (ICML)* (pp. 1-135). Academic Press.

Chapter 10

Using AI Technology to Support Speaking Skill Development for the Teaching of Chinese as a Foreign Language

Goh Ying Yingsoon
https://orcid.org/0000-0002-6654-2887
Universiti Teknologi MARA, Malaysia

ABSTRACT

The teaching of Chinese as a foreign language can be supported by using AI technology. Traditionally, the non-native learners can only interact with the instructors and depend on them solely for speaking practices. However, with the advancement of AI technology, the learners can use AI technology for interactive speaking skill development. In this study, the learners were instructed to download an application at https://m.wandoujia.com/apps/6790950. The process on the preparation of this AI technology in supporting their speaking skill development can be accessed at https://sites.google.com/site/gohyi141/assignments/projectinteractivespeakingapp. By using this AI technology, the findings showed a tremendous affirmative responses pertaining to the use of this AI technology. Hence, AI technology should be encouraged in active utilization for the teaching of Chinese as a foreign language in particular and for all language speaking skill development in general.

DOI: 10.4018/978-1-7998-5876-8.ch010

1. INTRODUCTION

Artificial intelligence (AI), deep learning, machine learning and neural networks represent incredibly exciting and powerful machine learning-based techniques used to solve many real-world problems (Castrounis, 2017). It is an area of computer science that emphasizes the creation of intelligent machines that work and react like humans. Some of the activities computers with artificial intelligence are designed for include: Speech recognition, Learning, Planning, Problem solving. It is also a branch of computer science that aims to create intelligent machines and it has become an essential part of the technology industry. Research associated with artificial intelligence is hence highly technical and specialized. The core problems of artificial intelligence include programming computers for certain traits such as: Knowledge, Reasoning, Problem solving, Perception, Learning, Planning, and Ability to manipulate and move objects. Knowledge engineering is therefore a core part of AI research. Artificial intelligence must have access to objects, categories, properties and relations between all of them to implement knowledge engineering. AI is an extremely powerful and exciting field. It's only going to become more important and ubiquitous moving forward, and will certainly continue to have very significant impacts on modern society, which of course include language instruction. This opens a new future direction in the society of ICT: the Internet of Things (IoT). Nowadays, the IoT, early defined as Machine-to-Machine (M2M) communications, becomes a key concern of ICT world and research communities (Abdul-Qawy, et al, 2015) and in the area of AI. These and other IoT related technologies significantly affect new ICT and enterprise systems technologies (Lee, and Lee, 2015). In the IoT, different devices and smart objects are included to expand the Internet and become accessible and uniquely identified (Weber, 2015). In the ICT innovations and economy developments, a significant focus has shifted to the IoT related technologies where it is widely considered as one of the most important infrastructures of their promotion and one of the future promise strategies. By approaching the IoT world aiming to understand and participate to its development, the progression of artificial intelligence techniques and applications will certainly be very exciting to anticipate!

The teaching of Chinese as a foreign language can be supported by using AI technology. Traditionally the non-native learners can only interact with the instructors and depend on them solely for speaking practices. However, with the advancement of AI technology, the learners can use AI technology for interactive speaking skill development, such as the use of AI chatbot (Lomas, 2016, Medhi, Menon, Magapu, Subramony & O'Neill, 2017), internet of things (Hoffman, Donna, Novak, & Thomas, 2016; Ng, Irene, Wakenshaw, & Susan, 2017), and etc. It has been well accepted by the users, and the number of loyal followers of AI technology is tremendously increasing (D'Onfro, 2015). AI technology is shaping and changing the world including how language can be learned and practiced (The Wall Street Journal, 2017). With the passion on the advocating of AI technology for language learning, hence, the objective of this study is to verify how AI technology can be utilized in coping the need of interactivity with an intelligent agent in supporting speaking skill development. The main goal of the usage is to maximize speaking opportunities for the non-native learners. It can also be used for oral drillings by dependence-free on the instructor.

2. BACKGROUND AND LITERATURE REVIEW

2.1 Advantage of Using the Technology Over Conventional Methods

Advances in artificial intelligence open to new possibilities and challenges for teaching and learning of language (Popenici & Kerr, 2017). The accuracy of AI is above 90% in terms of speech recognition, written text recognition, and etc. (Tang & Wei, 2019). The utilization of AI technology will hence enhance the teaching and learning of foreign language. However, there are research gaps that justify the new research needed which can inform the design, conduct, and reporting of further research in this area. Many examples of existing efforts to identify and prioritize research gaps are in living use, but research on the application for language learning are still lacking.

AI technology has been used in various aspects for the teaching of Chinese as a foreign language. These include vocabulary instruction (Yu & Xie, 2018), writing, instruction (Zhao, 2018), translation application (Xu, 2018; Yang, 2017), and etc. However, there is a need to explore further on the use of AI for Mandarin learning in which AI can be utilized as a practical educational technology tool in enriching Mandarin instruction (Chen, Sha, He & Wang, 2017).

2.2 Typical Example of AI Technology

The typical example of AI technology can be the use of chatbot (Przegalinska, Ciechanowski, Stroz, Gloor, & Mazurek, 2019). This chatbot is a piece of software that conducts a conversation via auditory or textual methods. In this chapter the focus will be on the use of auditory method. Such programs are often designed to convincingly simulate how a human would behave as a conversational partner. This is vital as to provide conversation opportunities for the learners of foreign language. Chatbots are also used frequently in business to facilitate various processes, particularly those related to customer service and personalization. While for language teaching, since students are the customer to the educational industry, it is also good to provide conversation practice services and personalized oral practice occasions as to strengthen their speaking skill using AI technology.

AI technology can be effective teaching assistant (Maderer, 2016). In a language class, when teaching speaking skill, often the students will find that they didn't have ample of speaking opportunities as the classroom time is normally limiting each student to communicate in the classroom. Additionally, some students might find it quite embarrass to speak in the language that they are learning to the instructor and in front of their classrooms. So, AI technology can be very helpful to provide personal speaking practice and enhancement.

By conversing with a machine in a dialogic fashion, using natural language (Dale, 2016), it opens up speaking drill for language classroom. Students no more tie to the engagement of dialogic exercises sole depending on their instructors. Human-computer interaction with AI technology element actualize the interacting conversationally. Very soon we'll be in a world where some of those conversational partners we'll know to be humans, some we'll know to be bots, and probably some we won't know either way, and may not even care (Dale, 2016) as long as it is able to uphold the effectiveness of speaking skill teaching.

2.3 Understanding of the Users

The understanding of the users is essential. There is always a gulf between the user expectation and the authentic experience of conversational agent (Luger & Sellen, 2016). Therefore, studies have to be continuously carried out by using various methods, inclusive quantitative design, qualitative design and mixed mode. Focus of the study will also have to take into account on how well the conversational agents are able to understand the foreign accents carried by the non-native learners of a foreign language.

Hence, AI technology has the potential towards artificial intelligence-based assessment systems (Luckin, 2017). This will sure to provide a more objective kind of intelligence-based assessment. The subjectivity of the instructor in the assessment of speaking skill can be eliminated. Psychologically, the students might find it more confident and comfortable to talk to an intelligent agent and not a human being (Stuart, 2017). Affectively they are more at ease. Subsequently, they will keen to practice more frequently with AI technology. The utilization of AI technology as to be moved from being a *tool* to being an active *partner*, as active partner for classroom speaking instruction agents (Bankins & Formosa, 2019).

Even there are lots of benefits AI technology can offer, however there are sure some weakness in artificial conversational agents in which there are inabilities in these agents in making them function entirely represented as human (Corti & Gillespie,

2016). For that reason, we still need to carry out studies to verify the effectiveness on the use of AI technology to support speaking instruction particularly to find out if these AI technology agents are able to comprehend non-native learners who bring variety of accents in the foreign language they learn. On top of that, the technical aspects can also not be neglected. The major challenge is with the availability of multiple platforms (Daniel, Cabot, Deruelle & Derras, 2019). This is a practical hindrance that instructors who keen to use AI technology in their language classroom. They have to understand problems that their students will encounter with various platforms they are using. Instructors need to find ways to assist the students to tackle the problems or direct them to seek for assistance from IT department.

2.4 Research Framework of This Study

It is agreeable that AI technology can function well as social conversation agents that played an active role in the language classroom (Augello, Gentile, Weideveld, & Dignum, 2016; Xu, Liu, Guo, Sinha, & Akkiraju, 2017). Nevertheless, the effectiveness and the feasibility of its utilization still need to be verified through thorough studies.

In sum, the research framework of this study is as showed as figure below. The oral output of the user, include the questions asked by the learners will become input for the AI technology system. After processing, the AI technology system would response by giving appropriate output by answering the questions of the learners. These output of the system will then become the input for the user to learn. The user may try to understand the output of the AI system. This is the learning process offered by the AI system as a whole.

Figure 1. Research framework

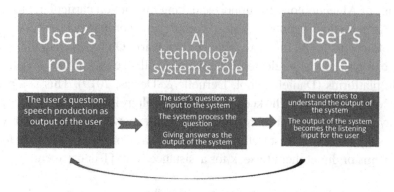

3. MAIN FOCUS OF THE CHAPTER

The issues in the learning of Chinese as a foreign language are mainly on the opportunities to practice speaking skill. The interaction by using the language is very vital. However, the non-native learners may find it difficult to find native learners to practice their Chinese. The learning time during the formal classes limit the opportunities for the learners to practice speaking with their instructors. Therefore, by introducing wandoujia, an AI technology based application, it may cater the need of interaction in Chinese for speaking skill development.

4. RESEARCH METHODS

In this study, the learners were instructed to download an application at https://m.wandoujia.com/apps/6790950. The process on the preparation of this AI technology in supporting their speaking skill development can be accessed at https://sites.google.com/site/gohyi141/assignments/projectinteractivespeakingapp.

The students used this wandoujia, an AI technology based application to prepare for their speaking project. As shown in figure 2, the student would start to ask a question in Chinese, e.g. 你喜欢吃什么?(What do you like to eat?) and the intelligent agent would give response, e.g. 我喜欢吃鱼香肉丝。(I like to eat fish-flavored shredded pork).

For the respondents in this study, they were 76 students from level 1, 65 students from level 2 and 22 students from level 3, with a total of 163 respondents. They were students from MARA University of Technology, Terengganu Campus, taking Mandarin as a foreign language courses.

The students accessed the Wandoujia for 2 weeks to prepare their speaking project. They have to screenshot their conversations using this Wandoujia and sent in their CD in the end of the semester. They would have to answer a self-developed questionnaire. In this questionnaire, is was divided into five sections to measure the five areas pertaining to this study. In each of the section, there were five questions

Figure 2. Screenshot of wandoujia

Table 1. Descriptive statistics of students' responses in the use of Wandoujia to support their learning

Course Level		Interest in the Conversation Process	Ease of Use of the System	Oral Conversation Support	Confidence to Talk	Understanding of the Conversation
LEVEL 1	Mean	4.48	4.23	4.55	4.57	3.93
	N	76	76	76	76	76
	Std. Deviation	.620	.743	.746	.711	.728
LEVEL 2	Mean	4.36	4.43	4.31	4.23	3.07
	N	65	65	65	65	65
	Std. Deviation	.633	.756	.825	.514	.829
LEVEL 3	Mean	4.18	4.49	4.14	4.15	3.05
	N	22	22	22	22	22
	Std. Deviation	.733	.590	.774	.800	.999
Total	Overall Mean	4.21	4.31	4.41	4.37	3.59
	N	163	163	163	163	163
	Std. Deviation	.650	.704	.771	.718	.819

related to the particular areas. Descriptive statistics and inference statistics were analyzed using SPSS version 20.

The student would then video record their conversation with this intelligent agent. After that, they gave their feedback on the effectiveness on the use of this AI technology based application to support their speaking skill development.

5. FINDINGS AND DISCUSSIONS

By using this AI technology, the findings showed a tremendous affirmative responses pertaining to the use of this AI technology. Hence, AI technology should be encouraged in active utilization for the teaching of Chinese as a foreign language in particular and for all language speaking skill development in general.

As a whole, for the three levels of the students, they were very positive in the use of Wandoujia in supporting the speaking development in the areas of interest in the conversation process using the system (mean of level 1: 4.48, mean of level 2: 4.36, and mean of level 3: 4.18), ease of use of the system (mean of level 1: 4.23, mean of level 2: 4.43, and mean of level 3: 4.49), oral conversation support (mean of level 1: 4.55, mean of level 2: 4.31, and mean of level 3: 4.14) and confidence to talk to the intelligent agent of Wandoujia (mean of level 1: 4.57, mean of level 2: 4.23, and mean of level 3: 4.15). however, for the aspect of the understanding of the system, the responses were neutral or less positive (mean of level 1: 3.93, mean of level 2: 3.07, and mean of level 3: 3.05).

Using ANOVA analyses, it was found there were no significant differences for

Table 2. ANOVA analyses of students' responses in the use of Wandoujia to support their learning

		Sum of Squares	df	Mean Square	F	Sig.
Interest in the conversation process	Between Groups	.355	2	.178	.414	.663
	Within Groups	33.032	161	.429		
	Total	33.388	163			
Ease of use of the system	Between Groups	.979	2	.490	.920	.403
	Within Groups	40.971	161	.532		
	Total	41.950	163			
Oral conversation support	Between Groups	2.140	2	1.070	2.133	.125
	Within Groups	38.610	161	.501		
	Total	40.750	163			
Confidence to talk	Between Groups	.309	2	.154	.226	.798
	Within Groups	52.679	161	.684		
	Total	52.988	163			
Understanding of the conversation	Between Groups	.527	2	.264	.699	.500
	Within Groups	29.023	161	.377		
	Total	29.550	163			

all aspects studied. It implied that the students of the three levels were basically having similar perceptions pertaining to the five areas studied.

However, since this is a free AI technology-based application, there are limitations to the use and trials. After using for several times, it will show the message that you have finished the number of trials given per day (as showed in figure 3). Hence,

Figure 3. Screenshot of the application indicating that the user has finished using the limit of use for a day

the students will have to use it again the next day or uninstall the application and re-install again.

The responses to the open answer question also revealed some of the hindrances the users encountered in the use of this application. They were showed in table below. Basically there were two areas of problems encountered by the students, namely technical problems and language problems. Solutions to these problems were explained in Table 3.

Table 3. The hindrances the users encountered in the use of this application

	Problems	Solutions
Technical	• difficulties in installation process. • Getting acquainted with the application. • Running tasks using the application.	• explaining in the classroom time. • individual attention, guidance and assistance. • peer assistance.
Language	• the interface of the application is in Chinese. • cannot understand the input is correct or not especially students who use pinyin, Romanized Mandarin in the learning process. • cannot understand the responses given by the intelligent agent.	• giving general instruction. • showing screenshot of the system and interpreting to the students. • giving personal instruction. • help to check the input. • guide students to check their input by using their text books. • guide students to check the students to check the responses of intelligent agent by using their text books or online translation system.

6. RECOMMENDATIONS AND FUTURE RESEARCH DIRECTIONS

For the aspect of the understanding of the system, the responses were neutral or less positive (mean of level 1: 3.93, mean of level 2: 3.07, and mean of level 3: 3.05). This was due to the language competency limitation especially for those beginner learners. Their understanding by listening is still weak. By only offering Chinese character text of answering still difficult for those beginner learners as their command of Chinese characters are still inadequate. Hence, it is suggested that for the improvement of the system, there should be translated texts of the conversations to ease the users in understanding their input as well as the responses of the intelligent agent (Gao & Zhang, 2018). The improvement, reviewing, evaluation and feedback on the interface design of AI technology is essential for the betterment of the AI technology utilization (Klopfenstein, Delpriori, Malatini, & Bogliolo, 2017; Masche & Le, 2018; Radziwill & Benton, 2017). Another aspect of AI technology that needs to be improved is on its response system. So far the system is able to answer questions posed to the AI speaking agents. However, the AI speaking agent stops at this level, whereby it is able to answer but not able to ask questions. This is the area for future improvement of the system that it will be able to function as human being in which question and answer is port of the conversation process. Solely answer without questioning back is considered odd in normal conversation.

With the perceived language complexity in which various accents carried by the non-native learners as well as technical issues encountered which of course include multiple platforms used (Kavaler, Sirovica, Hellendoorn, Aranovich, & Filkov,

2017; Mayo, 2017), it will sure bring about negative effects in the actual use of AI technology in the language classroom in enhancing speaking skill. Especially, when this AI technology is used in mobile learning mode, the issue of multiple platforms is even obvious. Consequently, supporting actions are required in order to assist the learners to handle their hindrances realistically. It is not wise for the instructors to leave the learners with the AI technology without giving proper guidance and advises.

Artificial intelligence (AI) is increasingly reshaping service by performing various tasks, constituting a major source of innovation, yet threatening human jobs (Huang & Rust, 2018; Acemoglu & Restrepo, 2017). In the passion of introducing AI technology, one has to keep in mind that these conversation agents are not going to replace the role of instructors in the classroom but they are solely playing the role of facilitating tool for oral practicing. There shouldn't be any issue whereby the language instructors will lose their jobs. The proper use of AI technology for language classroom is to make sure that it can provide adaptive personalization oral practice opportunities for all language learners (Chung, Wedel, Rust, & Roland, 2016). The challenge is still on how well prepared and the level of acceptance by the language instructors to make room for the assistance and support of these AI technology (Colby, & Mithas, 2016). Suitable and appropriate strategy in integrating AI technology to support speaking skill needs to be employed (Huang & Rust, 2017).

In order to encourage the active and effective use of AI technology in supporting the speaking skill development, there should be a proper development strategic plan ((U.S. National Science and Technology Council, 2016). The purpose is to ensure the cost-effective utilization of AI technology. The impact on the utilization of AI technology hence has to be explored further in the future research. Impact is a multi-dimensional concept. Some definitions focus on very precise understandings of impact, while others cast a much broader net. How impact is defined and used has a significant effect on the design, management and evaluation of development programmes in the utilization of these AI technology. The development programmes in the utilization of these AI technology should hold explicit conversations with different stakeholders about how impact is used and understood, in order to come to a shared understanding. The six dimensions of impact and pose guiding questions to help stakeholders clarify their interpretation and come to a shared understanding for the implementation of these programmes in the utilization of these AI technology which include the Application, Scope of use, Subject and level of change caused by the application, the Degrees of impact, Immediacy, rate and durability of change and lastly Homogeneity of benefits (Cameron, Mishra, & Brown, 2015). Each of these six dimensions has specific implications for what, when and how frequently change is measured and to determine if the impact of use worth the efforts.

Introducing other free online AI technology-based system such as cleverbot (https://www.cleverbot.com/?say=hi) and commercial AI technology-based product such as Tmall Genie R (天猫精灵方糖R). The aim is to allow students to expose to other alternatives for personal speaking skill development. They also have the opportunities to try and compare different systems, applications and products. Thus, this also opens up future research opportunities and direction by comparing the effectiveness on the use of those AI technology-based application for the improvement of speaking skill, at the same time opens up commercial AI-based supporting educational tools (Zhai, 2019).

This looks like a timely recognition that the earlier approaches taken in AI technology systems have limitations that need to be transcended, and an excellent opportunity to revisit how some of the ideas developed in earlier dialog systems research might influence practical developments (Dale, 2016). If we want to have better conversations with machines, we stand to benefit from having better studies pertaining to the practical utilization of AI technology for language classroom. For future more in-depth study, qualitative research design, such as interview can be employed (Pereira & Díaz, 2018a, b). This is to ensure the broadening of the scope in open innovation in the use of AI in supporting language instruction. In this manner, we will be able to understand how to get full potential in the use of AI technology to assist students in enhancing their speaking skill. It is also interesting to compare the real conversations with artificial intelligence which studies on the comparison between human–human online conversations and human–chatbot conversations could be done (Hill, Ford, & Farreras, 2015). Users can decide to create and participate in events, make comments, use the chat function to chat with friends and acquire speaking skill as well. By having such studies, we are able to ensure that the human-AI technology could be done as nice as real human-human conversations and even can be better than the later mode of conversations.

As summary, research gaps and/or research priorities on the use of AI to support language learning is still called for. The need in determining research priorities is an ongoing process to enhance the use of AI in supporting language instruction.

7. CONCLUSION

However, in the great enthusiasm in applying and introducing AI technology in the language classroom, the instructors still need to keep in mind that all these AI technologies should be first tested (Gibney, 2017). AI technology should in the position of supporting the instructors but not to replace them (Yang, 2018; Wang, 2018). This is to ensure that the responses given by the AI technology-based application are in decent language and suitable for developing the speaking skill development and in accordance to the making of a smart and self-learning speaking practicing environment with the empowerment of AI technology (Marinova, Ko, Huang, Meuter, & Challagalla, 2017; Soucy, 2016).

ACKNOWLEDGMENT

The research was supported by the Research Management Unit of MARA University of Technology.

REFERENCES

Abdul-Qawy, A. S. (2015). The Internet of Things (IoT): An Overview. *Int. Journal of Engineering Research and Applications*. Accessed at www.ijera.com

Acemoglu, D., & Restrepo, P. (2017). Robots and Jobs: Evidence from US Labor Markets. *NBER Working Paper Series*. Available at http://www.nber.org/papers/w23285]

Augello, A., Gentile, M., Weideveld, L., & Dignum, F. (2016). A model of a social chatbot. In *Bankins, S. & Formosa, P. (2019). When AI meets PC: exploring the implications of workplace social robots and a human-robot psychological contract*. European Journal of Work and Organizational Psychology. doi:10.1007/978-3-319-39345-2_57

Cameron, D. B., Mishra, A., & Brown, A. N. (2015). The growth of impact evaluation for international development: How much have we learned? *Journal of Development Effectiveness*.

Castrounis, A. (2017). *Artificial Intelligence, Deep Learning, and Neural Networks, Explained*. Kdnuggets.com. Available at: http://www.kdnuggets.com/2016/10/artificial-intelligence-deep-learning-neuralnetworks-explained.html

Chen, K.Q., Sha, J.H., He, Y., & Wang, X.F. (2017). Exploring the use of AI. *Journal of Distance Education, 2017*(5).

Chung, T. S., Wedel, M., & Rust, R. T. (2016). Adaptive Personalization Using Social Networks. *Journal of the Academy of Marketing Science, 44*(1), 66–87. doi:10.100711747-015-0441-x

Colby, C. L., & Mithas, S. P. A. (2016). *Service Robots: How Ready are Consumers to Adopt and What Drives Acceptance?* The 2016 Frontiers in Service Conference, Bergen, Norway.

Corti, K., & Gillespie, A. (2016). Co-constructing intersubjectivity with artificial conversational agents: People are more likely to initiate repairs of misunderstandings with agents represented as human. Comput. *Human Behavior*, *58*, 431–442. doi:10.1016/j.chb.2015.12.039

D'Onfro, J. (2015). *Microsoft Created a Chatbot in China that has Millions of Loyal Followers who talk to it like in the Movie 'Her'*. Business Insider, UK. Accessed at http://www.businessinsider.in/Microsoft-created-a-chatbot-in-China-that-has-millions-of-loyal-followers-who-talk-to-it-like-in-the-movie-Her/articleshow/48312697.cms

Dale, R. (2016a). Industry Watch The return of the chatbots. *Natural Language Engineering*, *22*(5), 811–817. doi:10.1017/S1351324916000243

Daniel, G., Cabot, J., Deruelle, L., & Derras, M. (2019). Multi-platform Chatbot Modeling and Deployment with the Jarvis Framework. In P. Giorgini & B. Weber (Eds.), Lecture Notes in Computer Science: Vol. 11483. *Advanced Information Systems Engineering. CAiSE 2019*. Springer. doi:10.1007/978-3-030-21290-2_12

De Pietro, G., Gallo, L., Howlett, R. J., & Jain, L. C. (Eds.), *Intelligent Interactive Multimedia Systems and Services. In SIST* (Vol. 55, pp. 637–647). Springer. doi:10.1007/978-3-319-39345-2_57

Gao, G.F., & Zhang, J. (2018). AI influence in translation application. *Journal of Foreign English*, *2018*(20).

Gibney, E. (2017). Google secretly tested AI bot. *Nature*, *541*(7636), 142. doi:10.1038/nature.2017.21253 PMID:28079098

Hill, J., Ford, W. R., & Farreras, I. G. (2015). Real conversations with artificial intelligence: A comparison between human–human online conversations and human–chatbot conversations. *Computers in Human Behavior*, *49*, 245–250. doi:10.1016/j.chb.2015.02.026

Hoffman, D. L., Novak, & Thomas, P. (2016). *Consumer and Object Experience in the Internet of Things: An Assemblage Theory Approach*. Working paper, The Center for the Connected Consumer, The George Washington University School of Business.

Huang, M. H., & Rust, R. T. (2017). Technology-Driven Service Strategy. *Journal of the Academy of Marketing Science*, *45*(6), 906–924. doi:10.100711747-017-0545-6

Huang, M. H., & Rust, R. T. (2018). Artificial Intelligence in Service. *Journal of Service Research*, *21*(2), 155–172. Advance online publication. doi:10.1177/1094670517752459

Kavaler, D., Sirovica, S., Hellendoorn, V., Aranovich, R., & Filkov, V. (2017). Perceived language complexity in GitHub issue discussions and their effect on issue resolution. In *Proceedings of the 32nd ASE Conference*, (pp. 72–83). IEEE. 10.1109/ASE.2017.8115620

Klopfenstein, L. C., Delpriori, S., Malatini, S., & Bogliolo, A. (2017). The rise of bots: a survey of conversational interfaces, patterns, and paradigms. In *Proceedings of the 12th DIS Conference*, (pp. 555–565). ACM 10.1145/3064663.3064672

Lee, I., & Lee, K. (2015). The internet of things (IoT): Applications, investments, and challenges for enterprises. Business Horizons, 58(4).

Lomas, N. (2016). *Microsoft officially outs another AI chatbot, called Zo*. Accessed at https://techcrunch.com/2016/12/14/microsoft-officially-outs-another-ai-chatbot-called-zo/

Luckin, R. (2017). Towards artificial intelligence-based assessment systems. *Nature Human Behaviour, 1*(28). doi: 10. 1038/s41562-016-0028

Luger, E., & Sellen, A. (2016). "Like Having a Really bad PA": the gulf between user expectation and experience of conversational agents. *Proceedings of CHI 2016*. 10.1145/2858036.2858288

Maderer, J. (2016). *Artificial intelligence course creates AI teaching assistant*. Georgia Tech News Center. http://www.news.gatech.edu/2016/05/09/artificial-intelligence-course-creates-ai-teaching-assistant

Marinova, D., Ko, R., Huang, M. H., Meuter, M., & Challagalla, G. (2017). Getting Smart: Learning from Technology Empowered Frontline Interactions. *Journal of Service Research, 20*(1), 29–42. doi:10.1177/1094670516679273

Masche, J., & Le, N. T. (2018). A review of technologies for conversational systems. In N.-T. Le, T. Van Do, N. T. Nguyen, & H. A. L. Thi (Eds.), *ICCSAMA 2017. AISC* (Vol. 629, pp. 212–225). Springer. doi:10.1007/978-3-319-61911-8_19

Mayo, J. (2017). *Programming the Microsoft Bot Framework: A Multiplatform Approach to Building Chatbots*. Microsoft Press.

Medhi, T. I., Menon, N., Magapu, S., Subramony, M., & O'Neill, J. (2017). How Do You Want Your Chatbot? An Exploratory Wizard-of-Oz Study with Young, Urban Indians. In Human-Computer Interaction - INTERACT 2017. INTERACT 2017. Lecture Notes in Computer Science, vol 10513. Springer.

Ng, I., & Wakenshaw, S. Y. L. (2017). The Internet-of-Things: Review and Research Directions. *International Journal of Research in Marketing, 34*(1), 3–21. doi:10.1016/j.ijresmar.2016.11.003

Pereira, J., & Díaz, Ó. (2018a). A quality analysis of Facebook Messenger's most popular chatbots. In *Proceedings of the 33rd SAC Symposium,* (pp. 2144–2150). ACM 10.1145/3167132.3167362

Pereira, J., & Díaz, Ó. (2018b). Chatbot dimensions that matter: lessons from the trenches. In T. Mikkonen, R. Klamma, & J. Hernández (Eds.), *ICWE 2018. LNCS* (Vol. 10845, pp. 129–135). Springer. doi:10.1007/978-3-319-91662-0_9

Popenici, S. A. D., & Kerr, S. (2017). Exploring the impact of artificial intelligence on teaching and learning in higher education. *Research and Practice in Technology Enhanced Learning, 12*(1), 22. doi:10.118641039-017-0062-8 PMID:30595727

Przegalinska, A., Ciechanowski, L., Stroz, A., Gloor, P., & Mazurek, G. (2019, November–December). In bot we trust: A new methodology of chatbot performance measures. *Business Horizons, 62*(6), 785–797. doi:10.1016/j.bushor.2019.08.005

Radziwill, N. M., & Benton, M. C. (2017). *Evaluating quality of chatbots and intelligent conversational agents.* arXiv preprint arXiv:1704.04579

Soucy, P. (2016, July 7). Self-Learning Intelligent Search, Explained. *KM World,* p. S34.

Stuart, S. (2017). How Do You Feel? Affectiva's AI Can Tell. *PC Magazine.* Available at https://www.pcmag.com/news/349956/how-do-you-feel-affectivas-ai-can-tell

Tang, Q. & Wei, M. (2019). Exploring AI for the teaching of Chinese as a foreign language. *Journal of Wuhan Yejin Guanli Ganbu College, 2019*(1).

The Wall Street Journal. (2017). *How Artificial Intelligence Will Change Everything.* Available at https://www.wsj.com/articles/howartificialintelligencewillchangeeverything148885632

U.S. National Science and Technology Council. (2016). *National Artificial Intelligence Research and development strategic plan.* Networking and Information Technology Research and Development Subcommittee.

Wang, Y.B. (2018). The position of foreign language instructors in AI era. *Journal of Jilin Broadcasting Television University, 2018*(11).

Weber, R. H. (2015). Internet of things: Privacy issues revisited. Computer Law & Security Review, 31(5).

Xu, A., Liu, Z., Guo, Y., Sinha, V., & Akkiraju, R. (2017). A new chatbot for customer service on social media. In *Proceedings of the 35th CHI Conference*, (pp. 3506–3510). ACM. 10.1145/3025453.3025496

Xu, Y. P. (2018). Analyzing the use of AI for translation. *Journal of Cooperative Economy and Technology, 2018*(19).

Yang, Y. (2018). Foreign language teachers in the AI era. *Journal of Zhiku Shidai, 2018*(27).

Yang, Z.L. (2017). Contemplation on AI translation. *Journal of Campus English, 2017*(52).

Yu, H. & Xie, H. J. (2018). The analysis and design research of intelligent teaching system for foreign Chinese vocabulary. *Sinogram Culture, 3*.

Zhai, Y.Y. (2019). Influence and suggestion for AI translation occupation. *Journal of Modern Business Industry, 2019*(09).

Zhao, S. (2018). AI for writing instruction. *Journal of Educational Technology, 2018*(9).

KEY TERMS AND DEFINITIONS

Artificial Intelligence: (AI): The simulation of human intelligence processes by machines, especially computer systems. These processes include learning, reasoning, and self-correction. Some of the applications of AI include expert systems, speech recognition and machine vision.

Intelligent Agent (IA): It refers to an autonomous entity which acts, directing its activity towards achieving goals (i.e., it is an agent), upon an environment using observation through sensors and consequent actuators (i.e., it is intelligent).

Intelligent Computer-Assisted Language Learning (ICALL), or Intelligent Computer-Assisted Language Instruction (ICALI): It involves the application of computing technologies to the teaching and learning of second or foreign languages.

Speaking Skills: It is the ability to talk at any time and in any situation.

Speech Processing: It is the study of speech signals and the processing methods of signals. The signals are usually processed in a digital representation, so speech processing can be regarded as a special case of digital signal processing, applied to speech signals.

Speech Recognition: The process of enabling a computer to identify and respond to the sounds produced in human speech.

Wandoujia: An AI technology-based application that can be downloaded for interactive conversation.

Compilation of References

Abdul-Qawy, A. S. (2015). The Internet of Things (IoT): An Overview. *Int. Journal of Engineering Research and Applications*. Accessed at www.ijera.com

Acemoglu, D., & Restrepo, P. (2017). Robots and Jobs: Evidence from US Labor Markets. *NBER Working Paper Series*. Available at http://www.nber.org/papers/w23285]

Adetunji, A. B., Oguntoye, J. P., Fenwa, O. D., & Akande, N. O. (2018). Web Document Classification Using Naïve Bayes. *Journal of Advances in Mathematics and Computer Science*, 1-11.

Affairs, S. (2020). *Department of Economic and Social Affairs World population projected to reach 9 . 8 billion in 2050, and 11*. Academic Press.

Aghababaeyan, Khan, & Siddiqui. (2011). Forecasting the Tehran Stock Market by artificial neural network. *International Journal of Advanced Computer Science and Applications*, 13-17.

Agrawal, V., Singh, P., & Sneha, S. (2019, April). Hyperglycemia Prediction Using Machine Learning: A Probabilistic Approach. In *International Conference on Advances in Computing and Data Sciences* (pp. 304-312). Springer. 10.1007/978-981-13-9942-8_29

Al-fuqaha, A., Member, S., Guizani, M., Mohammadi, M., & Member, S. (2015). *Internet of Things : A Survey on Enabling*. Academic Press.

Alpaydin, E. (2020). *Introduction to machine learning*. MIT Press.

Androulaki, E. (2018). *Hyperledger Fabric: A Distributed Operating System for Permissioned Blockchains*. Academic Press.

An, G., Omodaka, K., Hashimoto, K., Tsuda, S., Shiga, Y., Takada, N., Kikawa, T., Yokota, H., Akiba, M., & Nakazawa, T. (2019). Glaucoma diagnosis with machine learning based on optical coherence tomography and color fundus images. *Journal of Healthcare Engineering, 2019*, 2019. doi:10.1155/2019/4061313 PMID:30911364

Augello, A., Gentile, M., Weideveld, L., & Dignum, F. (2016). A model of a social chatbot. In *Bankins, S. & Formosa, P. (2019). When AI meets PC: exploring the implications of workplace social robots and a human-robot psychological contract*. European Journal of Work and Organizational Psychology. doi:10.1007/978-3-319-39345-2_57

Compilation of References

Aven, T. (2015). *Risk Analysis. John Wiley & Sons Ltd.* doi:10.1002/9781119057819

Aven, T. (2015). Risk assessment and risk management: Review of recent advances on their foundation. *European Journal of Operational Research*, 1–13. doi:10.1016/j.ejor.2015.12.023

Ayaz, M., Ammad-Uddin, M., Baig, I., & Aggoune, E. H. M. (2018). Wireless sensor's civil applications, prototypes, and future integration possibilities: A review. *IEEE Sensors Journal*, *18*(1), 4–30. doi:10.1109/JSEN.2017.2766364

Ayaz, M., Ammad-Uddin, M., Sharif, Z., Mansour, A., & Aggoune, E. H. M. (2019). Internet-of-Things (IoT)-based smart agriculture: Toward making the fields talk. *IEEE Access: Practical Innovations, Open Solutions*, *7*, 129551–129583. doi:10.1109/ACCESS.2019.2932609

B22B-01 : Improving Nitrogen and Water Management in Crop Production on a National Scale (Invited). (2020). *December 2018*, 346794.

Bagdasaryan, E., Veit, A., Hua, Y., Estrin, D., & Shmatikov, V. (2018). *How to backdoor federated learning.* arXiv preprint arXiv:1807.00459

Baynham-Herd, Z. (2017). Enlist blockchain to boost conservation. *Nature*, *548*(7669), 523–523. doi:10.1038/548523c PMID:28858318

Benet, J. (2014). *Ipfs-content addressed, versioned, p2p file system.* arXiv preprint arXiv:1407.3561

Berg, E., & Hagersten, E. (2004, March). StatCache: a probabilistic approach to efficient and accurate data locality analysis. In *IEEE International Symposium on-ISPASS Performance Analysis of Systems and Software*, 2004 (pp. 20-27). IEEE. 10.1109/ISPASS.2004.1291352

Bhadoria, R. S., & Agasti, V. (2019). The Paradigms of Blockchain Technology: Myths, Facts & Future. *International Journal of Information Systems and Social Change*, *10*(2), 1–14. doi:10.4018/IJISSC.2019040101

Bhadoria, R. S., Arora, Y., & Gautam, K. (2020). Blockchain Hands-on for Developing Genesis Block. In S. Kim & G. Deka (Eds.), *Advanced Applications of Blockchain Technology. Studies in Big Data.* doi:10.1007/978-981-13-8775-3_13

Bhadoria, R. S., Nimbalkar, A., & Saxena, N. (2020). On the Role of Blockchain Technology in the Internet of Things. In S. Kim & G. Deka (Eds.), *Advanced Applications of Blockchain Technology. Studies in Big Data.* doi:10.1007/978-981-13-8775-3_6

Bhatia, R. (2018). Regression Algorithms Used In Analytics & Data Mining. *Analytics India Magazine.*

Blockchain, H., & Safety, F. (2020). *How Blockchain and IoT Tech will Guarantee Food Safety.* Academic Press.

Boeckl, K., Fagan, M., Fisher, W., Lefkovitz, N., Megas, K. N., Nadeau, E., & Piccarreta, B. (2018). *Draft NIST Internal Report 8228: Considerations for Managing Internet of Things (IoT) Cybersecurity and Privacy Risks*. Applied Cybersecurity Division, Information Technology Laboratory. doi:10.6028/NIST.IR.8228-draft

Bonawitz, K., Eichner, H., Grieskamp, W., Huba, D., Ingerman, A., Ivanov, V., . . . Van Overveldt, T. (2019). *Towards federated learning at scale: System design*. arXiv preprint arXiv:1902.01046

Bonawitz, K., Ivanov, V., Kreuter, B., Marcedone, A., McMahan, H. B., Patel, S., ... Seth, K. (2017, October). Practical secure aggregation for privacy-preserving machine learning. In *Proceedings of the 2017 ACM SIGSAC Conference on Computer and Communications Security* (pp. 1175-1191). 10.1145/3133956.3133982

Brambilla, M., Ferrante, E., Birattari, M., & Dorigo, M. (2013). Swarm robotics: A review from the swarm engineering perspective. *Swarm Intelligence, 7*(1), 1–41. doi:10.100711721-012-0075-2

Broder, J. F., & Tucker, E. (2012). Risk analysis and security Survey (4th ed.). Butterworth-Heinemann. doi:10.1016/C2009-0-63855-1

Bruinsma, J. (2017). World agriculture: Towards 2015/2030: An FAO Study. *World Agriculture: Towards 2015/2030: An FAO Study*. doi:10.4324/9781315083858

Buterin, V. (2014). Ethereum white paper: a next-generation smart contract & decentralized application platform. *First version, 53*.

Buterin, V. (n.d.). *A next-generation smart contract and decentralized application platform*. https://github.com/ethereum/wiki/wiki/White-Paper

Cambra, C., Sendra, S., Lloret, J., & Garcia, L. (2017). An IoT service-oriented system for agriculture monitoring. *IEEE International Conference on Communications, May*. 10.1109/ICC.2017.7996640

Cameron, D. B., Mishra, A., & Brown, A. N. (2015). The growth of impact evaluation for international development: How much have we learned? *Journal of Development Effectiveness*.

Campbell, D. (2018). *Combining AI and Blockchain to Push Frontiers in Healthcare*. Available: https://www.macadamian.com/2018/03/16/combining-ai-and-blockchain-in-healthcare

Castrounis, A. (2017). *Artificial Intelligence, Deep Learning, and Neural Networks, Explained*. Kdnuggets.com. Available at: http://www.kdnuggets.com/2016/10/artificial-intelligence-deep-learning-neuralnetworks-explained.html

Chauhan, S., & Panda, N. K. (2015). *In Hacking Web Intelligence*. https://www.sciencedirect.com/topics/computer-science/weak-password

Chen, J., & Jenkins, W. K. (2017, August). Facial recognition with PCA and machine learning methods. In *2017 IEEE 60th International Midwest Symposium on Circuits and Systems (MWSCAS)* (pp. 973-976). IEEE. 10.1109/MWSCAS.2017.8053088

Chen, K.Q., Sha, J.H., He, Y., & Wang, X.F. (2017). Exploring the use of AI. *Journal of Distance Education, 2017*(5).

Chen, X., Shi, Q., Yang, L., & Xu, J. (2018). ThriftyEdge: Resource-Efficient Edge Computing for Intelligent IoT Applications. *IEEE Network, 32*(1), 61–65. doi:10.1109/MNET.2018.1700145

Chern, C. C., Chen, Y. J., & Hsiao, B. (2019). Decision tree–based classifier in providing telehealth service. *BMC Medical Informatics and Decision Making, 19*(1), 104. doi:10.118612911-019-0825-9 PMID:31146749

Cheruvu, S., Kumar, A., Smith, N., & Wheeler, D. (2019). Demystifying Internet of Things Security: Successful IoT Device/Edge and Platform Security Deployment. Apress.

Chung, T. S., Wedel, M., & Rust, R. T. (2016). Adaptive Personalization Using Social Networks. *Journal of the Academy of Marketing Science, 44*(1), 66–87. doi:10.100711747-015-0441-x

COGECA. C. (2018). EU Code of conduct on agricultural data sharing by contractual agreement. *Copa Cogeca*, 1–11. https://cema-agri.org/sites/default/files/publications/EU_Code_2018_web_version.pdf

Colby, C. L., & Mithas, S. P. A. (2016). *Service Robots: How Ready are Consumers to Adopt and What Drives Acceptance?* The 2016 Frontiers in Service Conference, Bergen, Norway.

Composer, H. (2019). *Welcome to hyperledger composer*. https://hyperledger.github.io/composer/latest/introduction/introduction.html

Corti, K., & Gillespie, A. (2016). Co-constructing intersubjectivity with artificial conversational agents: People are more likely to initiate repairs of misunderstandings with agents represented as human. Comput. *Human Behavior, 58*, 431–442. doi:10.1016/j.chb.2015.12.039

Crosby, M., Pattanayak, P., Verma, S., & Kalyanaraman, V. (2016). Blockchain technology: Beyond bitcoin. *Applied Innovation, 2*(6-10), 71.

D'Onfro, J. (2015). *Microsoft Created a Chatbot in China that has Millions of Loyal Followers who talk to it like in the Movie 'Her'*. Business Insider, UK. Accessed at http://www.businessinsider.in/Microsoft-created-a-chatbot-in-China-that-has-millions-of-loyal-followers-who-talk-to-it-like-in-the-movie-Her/articleshow/48312697.cms

Dale, R. (2016a). Industry Watch The return of the chatbots. *Natural Language Engineering, 22*(5), 811–817. doi:10.1017/S1351324916000243

Daniel, G., Cabot, J., Deruelle, L., & Derras, M. (2019). Multi-platform Chatbot Modeling and Deployment with the Jarvis Framework. In P. Giorgini & B. Weber (Eds.), Lecture Notes in Computer Science: Vol. 11483. *Advanced Information Systems Engineering. CAiSE 2019*. Springer. doi:10.1007/978-3-030-21290-2_12

De Clercq, M., Vats, A., & Biel, A. (2018). Agriculture 4.0: The Future of Farming Technology. *Proceedings of the World Government Summit*, 11-13.

Decision tree. (2003, May 23). *Wikipedia, the free encyclopedia*. Retrieved May 30, 2020, https://en.wikipedia.org/wiki/Decision_tree

Deisenroth, M. P., Faisal, A. A., & Ong, C. S. (2020). *Mathematics for machine learning*. Cambridge University Press. doi:10.1017/9781108679930

Difference between quantitative and qualitative risk analysis. (2020, May 23). *Projectcubicle*. https://www.projectcubicle.com/difference-between-quantitative-and-qualitative-risk-analysis/

Dinh, T. N., & Thai, M. T. (2018). Ai and blockchain: A disruptive integration. *Computer*, *51*(9), 48–53. doi:10.1109/MC.2018.3620971

Dolci, R. (2017). IoT Solutions for Precision Farming and Food Manufacturing: Artificial Intelligence Applications in Digital Food. *Proceedings - International Computer Software and Applications Conference, 2*, 384–385. 10.1109/COMPSAC.2017.157

Dubey, S., Singh, M. K., Singh, P., & Aggarwal, S. (2020). Waste Management of Residential Society using Machine Learning and IoT Approach. *2020 International Conference on Emerging Smart Computing and Informatics (ESCI)*, 293-297, 10.1109/ESCI48226.2020.9167526

Dubey, S., Singh, P., Yadav, P., & Singh, K. K. (2020). Household Waste Management System Using IoT and Machine Learning. *Procedia Computer Science, 167*, 1950–1959. doi:10.1016/j.procs.2020.03.222

Elijah, O., Rahman, T. A., Orikumhi, I., Leow, C. Y., & Hindia, M. N. (2018). An Overview of Internet of Things (IoT) and Data Analytics in Agriculture: Benefits and Challenges. *IEEE Internet of Things Journal, 5*(5), 3758–3773. doi:10.1109/JIOT.2018.2844296

Estimation techniques - Three point. (n.d.). *RxJS, ggplot2, Python Data Persistence, Caffe2, PyBrain, Python Data Access, H2O, Colab, Theano, Flutter, KNime, Mean.js, Weka, Solidity*. https://www.tutorialspoint.com/estimation_techniques/estimation_techniques_three_point.htm

Ezenkwu, C. P., Ozuomba, S., & Kalu, C. (2015). *Application of K-Means algorithm for efficient customer segmentation: a strategy for targeted customer services*. Academic Press.

Fabric, H. (2019). *Business network cards*. https://hyperledger.github.io/composer/v0.16/playground/id-cards-playground

Fahimi, F. (2009). Autonomous robots. *Modeling, Path Planning and Control*.

Fayjie, A. R., Hossain, S., Oualid, D., & Lee, D. J. (2018, June). Driverless car: Autonomous driving using deep reinforcement learning in urban environment. In *2018 15th International Conference on Ubiquitous Robots (UR)* (pp. 896-901). IEEE.

Feng, X., Yan, F., & Liu, X. (2019). Study of Wireless Communication Technologies on Internet of Things for Precision Agriculture. *Wireless Personal Communications, 108*(3), 1785–1802. doi:10.100711277-019-06496-7

Ferrer, E. C. (2016). *The blockchain: A new framework for robotic swarm systems.* Available: https://arxiv.org/abs/1608.00695

Gallier, J., & Quaintance, J. (2019). *Linear A lgebra for Computer Vision.* Robotics, and Machine Learning.

Gao, G.F., & Zhang, J. (2018). AI influence in translation application. *Journal of Foreign English, 2018*(20).

Gatsis, K., & Pappas, G. J. (2017). Poster abstract: Wireless control for the IoT: Power, spectrum, and security challenges. *Proceedings - 2017 IEEE/ACM 2nd International Conference on Internet-of-Things Design and Implementation, IoTDI 2017 (Part of CPS Week), 1,* 341–342. 10.1145/3054977.3057313

Geyer, R. C., Klein, T., & Nabi, M. (2017). *Differentially private federated learning: A client level perspective.* arXiv preprint arXiv:1712.07557

Giacomo, R., & David, G. (2017). Unmanned Aerial Systems (UAS) in Agriculture: Regulations and Good Practices. In E-Agriculture in Action: Drones for Agriculture. Academic Press.

Gibney, E. (2017). Google secretly tested AI bot. *Nature, 541*(7636), 142. doi:10.1038/nature.2017.21253 PMID:28079098

Goodrich, B. (n.d.). *Qualitative Risk Analysis vs Quantitative Risk Analysis.* PMP Concepts Learning Series.

Green, H. (2016). Introducing the DAO: The organisation that will kill corporations. City AM, 3.

Greenwald, H. S., & Oertel, C. K. (2017). Future directions in machine learning. *Frontiers in Robotics and AI, 3,* 79. doi:10.3389/frobt.2016.00079

Grofit, S. (2020). *Climate monitoring device Add to Cart.* Academic Press.

Gupta, O., & Raskar, R. (2018). Distributed learning of deep neural network over multiple agents. *Journal of Network and Computer Applications, 116,* 1–8. doi:10.1016/j.jnca.2018.05.003

Gupta, S. C., & Kapoor, V. K. (2001). *Fundamental of Mathematical Statistics.* Sultan Chand & Sons.

Hajdarbegovic, N. (2014). *Bitcoin Miners Ditch Ghash. io Pool Over Fears of 51% Attack.* Academic Press.

Hamid, N. A., & Sjarif, N. N. A. (2017). *Handwritten recognition using SVM, KNN and neural network.* arXiv preprint arXiv:1702.00723

Han, J., Pei, J., & Kamber, M. (2011). *Data mining: concepts and techniques.* Elsevier.

Hasan, A., Moin, S., Karim, A., & Shamshirband, S. (2018). Machine learning-based sentiment analysis for twitter accounts. *Mathematical and Computational Applications, 23*(1), 11. doi:10.3390/mca23010011

Hill, J., Ford, W. R., & Farreras, I. G. (2015). Real conversations with artificial intelligence: A comparison between human–human online conversations and human–chatbot conversations. *Computers in Human Behavior, 49*, 245–250. doi:10.1016/j.chb.2015.02.026

Hoffman, D. L., Novak, & Thomas, P. (2016). *Consumer and Object Experience in the Internet of Things: An Assemblage Theory Approach.* Working paper, The Center for the Connected Consumer, The George Washington University School of Business.

How to perform a qualitative risk analysis. (2020, March 9). *TechRepublic.* https://www.techrepublic.com/article/how-to-perform-a-qualitative-risk-analysis/

How to recover files recently deleted from a computer? (n.d.). *Best Windows Data Recovery Software 2020 Free Download.* https://hetmanrecovery.com/recovery_news/how-to-recover-files-recently-deleted-from-a-computer.htm

Huang, M. H., & Rust, R. T. (2017). Technology-Driven Service Strategy. *Journal of the Academy of Marketing Science, 45*(6), 906–924. doi:10.100711747-017-0545-6

Huang, M. H., & Rust, R. T. (2018). Artificial Intelligence in Service. *Journal of Service Research, 21*(2), 155–172. Advance online publication. doi:10.1177/1094670517752459

I.E.S. (2016). *Agricultural produce market committee (APMC).* http://www.arthapedia.in/index.php%3Ftitle%3DAgricultural_Produce_Market_Committee_(APMC)

Ibrahim, H., Mostafa, N., Halawa, H., Elsalamouny, M., Daoud, R., Amer, H., Adel, Y., Shaarawi, A., Khattab, A., & ElSayed, H. (2019). A layered IoT architecture for greenhouse monitoring and remote control. *SN Applied Sciences, 1*(3), 1–12. doi:10.100742452-019-0227-8

Internet of Things (IoT). (2020, April 6). *Mobio Solutions.* https://mobiosolutions.com/internet-of-things-iot/

IO. E. (2017). *EOS. IO technical white paper.* EOS. IO (accessed 18 December 2017) https://github. com/EOSIO/Documentation

Janson, S., Merkle, D., & Middendorf, M. (2008). A decentralization approach for swarm intelligence algorithms in networks applied to multi swarm PSO. *International Journal of Intelligent Computing and Cybernetics.*

Jose, J. T., Zachariah, U., Lijo, V. P., Gnanasigamani, L. J., & Mathew, J. (2017). Case Study on Enhanced K-Means Algorithm for Bioinformatics Data Clustering. *International Journal of Applied Engineering Research, 12*(24), 15147–15151.

Juels, A., Kosba, A., & Shi, E. (2016, October). The ring of gyges: Investigating the future of criminal smart contracts. In *Proceedings of the 2016 ACM SIGSAC Conference on Computer and Communications Security* (pp. 283-295). 10.1145/2976749.2978362

Jung, A. (2018). *Machine learning: Basic principles.* arXiv preprint arXiv:1805.05052

Kaewmard, N., & Saiyod, S. (2014). Sensor data collection and irrigation control on vegetable crop using smart phone and wireless sensor networks for smart farm. *ICWiSe 2014 - 2014 IEEE Conference on Wireless Sensors*, 106–112. 10.1109/ICWISE.2014.7042670

Kahneman, D. (2011). *Thinking, fast and slow*. Macmillan.

Kaku, M. (2015). *The future of the mind: The scientific quest to understand, enhance, and empower the mind*. Anchor Books.

Kamiński, B., Jakubczyk, M., & Szufel, P. (2017). A framework for sensitivity analysis of decision trees". *Central European Journal of Operations Research*, 26(1), 135–159. doi:10.100710100-017-0479-6 PMID:29375266

Kavaler, D., Sirovica, S., Hellendoorn, V., Aranovich, R., & Filkov, V. (2017). Perceived language complexity in GitHub issue discussions and their effect on issue resolution. In *Proceedings of the 32nd ASE Conference*, (pp. 72–83). IEEE. 10.1109/ASE.2017.8115620

Kepuska, V., & Bohouta, G. (2018, January). Next-generation of virtual personal assistants (microsoft cortana, apple siri, amazon alexa and google home). In *2018 IEEE 8th Annual Computing and Communication Workshop and Conference (CCWC)* (pp. 99-103). IEEE.

Khan, R. S., Zardar, A. A., & Bhatti, Z. (2018). *Artificial Intelligence based Smart Doctor using Decision Tree Algorithm*. arXiv preprint arXiv:1808.01884

Khanna, A., & Kaur, S. (2019). Evolution of Internet of Things (IoT) and its significant impact in the field of Precision Agriculture. *Computers and Electronics in Agriculture*, 157(January), 218–231. doi:10.1016/j.compag.2018.12.039

Khurana, R. (2014). *Operating System*. Vikas Publishing House Pvt Ltd.

Kim, H., Park, J., Bennis, M., & Kim, S. L. (2018). *On-device federated learning via blockchain and its latency analysis*. arXiv preprint arXiv:1808.03949

King, T., Cole, M., Farber, J. M., Eisenbrand, G., Zabaras, D., Fox, E. M., & Hill, J. P. (2017). Food safety for food security: Relationship between global megatrends and developments in food safety. *Trends in Food Science & Technology*, 68, 160–175. doi:10.1016/j.tifs.2017.08.014

Klopfenstein, L. C., Delpriori, S., Malatini, S., & Bogliolo, A. (2017). The rise of bots: a survey of conversational interfaces, patterns, and paradigms. In *Proceedings of the 12th DIS Conference*, (pp. 555–565). ACM 10.1145/3064663.3064672

Konečný, J., McMahan, H. B., Yu, F. X., Richtárik, P., Suresh, A. T., & Bacon, D. (2016). *Federated learning: Strategies for improving communication efficiency*. arXiv preprint arXiv:1610.05492

Kononenko, I., Bratko, I., & Kukar, M. (1997). Application of machine learning to medical diagnosis. *Machine Learning and Data Mining: Methods and Applications*, 389, 408.

Koshy, S. S., Sunnam, V. S., Rajgarhia, P., Chinnusamy, K., Ravulapalli, D. P., & Chunduri, S. (2018). Application of the internet of things (IoT) for smart farming: A case study on groundnut and castor pest and disease forewarning. *CSI Transactions on ICT, 6*(3–4), 311–318. doi:10.100740012-018-0213-0

Kulshrestha, A. K. (2003). Teaching of mathematics. R. Lall Book Dept.

Kumar, N., Kharkwal, N., Kohli, R., & Choudhary, S. (2016, February). Ethical aspects and future of artificial intelligence. In *2016 International Conference on Innovation and Challenges in Cyber Security (ICICCS-INBUSH)* (pp. 111-114). IEEE. 10.1109/ICICCS.2016.7542339

Lasi, H., Fettke, P., Kemper, H. G., Feld, T., & Hoffmann, M. (2014). Industry 4.0. *Business & Information Systems Engineering, 6*(4), 239–242. doi:10.100712599-014-0334-4

Leahy, R. M., Clackdoyle, R., & Noo, F. (2009). Computed tomography. In *The Essential Guide to Image Processing* (pp. 741–776). Academic Press. doi:10.1016/B978-0-12-374457-9.00026-3

LeCun, Y., Bengio, Y., & Hinton, G. (2015). Deep learning. *Nature, 521*(7553), 436-444.

Lee, I., & Lee, K. (2015). The internet of things (IoT): Applications, investments, and challenges for enterprises. Business Horizons, 58(4).

Lee, I., & Lee, K. (2015). The Internet of Things (IoT): Applications, investments, and challenges for enterprises. *Business Horizons, 58*(4), 431–440. doi:10.1016/j.bushor.2015.03.008

Lin, C., He, D., Huang, X., Choo, K. K. R., & Vasilakos, A. V. (2018). BSeIn: A blockchain-based secure mutual authentication with fine-grained access control system for industry 4.0. *Journal of Network and Computer Applications, 116*, 42–52. doi:10.1016/j.jnca.2018.05.005

Lin, I. C., & Liao, T. C. (2017). A survey of blockchain security issues and challenges. *International Journal of Network Security, 19*(5), 653–659.

Lin, J., Yu, W., Zhang, N., Yang, X., Zhang, H., & Zhao, W. (2017). A Survey on Internet of Things: Architecture, Enabling Technologies, Security and Privacy, and Applications. *IEEE Internet of Things Journal, 4*(5), 1125–1142. doi:10.1109/JIOT.2017.2683200

Li, S., Simonian, A., & Chin, B. A. (2010). Sensors for agriculture and the food industry. *The Electrochemical Society Interface, 19*(4), 41–46. doi:10.1149/2.F05104if

Liu, H., & Setiono, R. (1997). Feature selection via discretization. *IEEE Transactions on Knowledge and Data Engineering, 9*(4), 642–645. doi:10.1109/69.617056

Liu, W., Li, Y., Tao, D., & Wang, Y. (2015). A general framework for co-training and its applications. *Neurocomputing, 167*, 112–121. doi:10.1016/j.neucom.2015.04.087

Li, X., Zhong, Z., Wu, J., Yang, Y., Lin, Z., & Liu, H. (2019). Expectation-maximization attention networks for semantic segmentation. In *Proceedings of the IEEE International Conference on Computer Vision* (pp. 9167-9176). IEEE.

Li, Z., & Ren, X. (2016). Analysis of the impact of blockchain on the Internet finance and its prospects. *Technical Economics and Management Studies, 10*, 75–78.

Lomas, N. (2016). *Microsoft officially outs another AI chatbot, called Zo.* Accessed at https://techcrunch.com/2016/12/14/microsoft-officially-outs-another-ai-chatbot-called-zo/

Luckin, R. (2017). Towards artificial intelligence-based assessment systems. *Nature Human Behaviour, 1*(28). doi: 10. 1038/s41562-016-0028

Luger, E., & Sellen, A. (2016). "Like Having a Really bad PA": the gulf between user expectation and experience of conversational agents. *Proceedings of CHI 2016.* 10.1145/2858036.2858288

Lundervold, A. S., & Lundervold, A. (2019). An overview of deep learning in medical imaging focusing on MRI. *Zeitschrift fur Medizinische Physik, 29*(2), 102–127. doi:10.1016/j.zemedi.2018.11.002 PMID:30553609

Luu, L., Chu, D. H., Olickel, H., Saxena, P., & Hobor, A. (2016, October). Making smart contracts smarter. In *Proceedings of the 2016 ACM SIGSAC conference on computer and communications security* (pp. 254-269). 10.1145/2976749.2978309

Madakam, S., Ramaswamy, R., & Tripathi, S. (2015). Internet of Things (IoT): A Literature Review. *Journal of Computer and Communications, 03*(05), 164–173. doi:10.4236/jcc.2015.35021

Maderer, J. (2016). *Artificial intelligence course creates AI teaching assistant.* Georgia Tech News Center. http://www.news.gatech.edu/2016/05/09/artificial-intelligence-course-creates-ai-teaching-assistant

Magazzeni, D., McBurney, P., & Nash, W. (2017). Validation and verification of smart contracts: A research agenda. *Computer, 50*(9), 50–57. doi:10.1109/MC.2017.3571045

Malik, S., Dedeoglu, V., Kanhere, S. S., & Jurdak, R. (2019). TrustChain: Trust Management in Blockchain and IoT Supported Supply Chains. *2019 IEEE International Conference on Blockchain (Blockchain)*, 184-193. 10.1109/Blockchain.2019.00032

Mamoshina, P., Ojomoko, L., Yanovich, Y., Ostrovski, A., Botezatu, A., Prikhodko, P., ... Ogu, I. O. (2018). Converging blockchain and next-generation artificial intelligence technologies to decentralize and accelerate biomedical research and healthcare. *Oncotarget, 9*(5), 5665–5690. doi:10.18632/oncotarget.22345 PMID:29464026

Marinova, D., Ko, R., Huang, M. H., Meuter, M., & Challagalla, G. (2017). Getting Smart: Learning from Technology Empowered Frontline Interactions. *Journal of Service Research, 20*(1), 29–42. doi:10.1177/1094670516679273

Marr, B. (2018). Artificial intelligence and blockchain: 3 major benefits of combining these two mega-trends. *Forbes*.

Masche, J., & Le, N. T. (2018). A review of technologies for conversational systems. In N.-T. Le, T. Van Do, N. T. Nguyen, & H. A. L. Thi (Eds.), *ICCSAMA 2017. AISC* (Vol. 629, pp. 212–225). Springer. doi:10.1007/978-3-319-61911-8_19

Mathews, S., Golden, S., Demski, R., Pronovost, P., & Ishii, L. (2017). Advancing health care quality and safety through action learning. *Leadership in Health Services*, *30*(2), 148–158. doi:10.1108/LHS-10-2016-0051 PMID:28514917

Maxmen, A. (2018). AI researchers embrace Bitcoin technology to share medical data. *Nature*, *555*(7696), 293–294. doi:10.1038/d41586-018-02641-7

Mayo, J. (2017). *Programming the Microsoft Bot Framework: A Multiplatform Approach to Building Chatbots*. Microsoft Press.

Medhi, T. I., Menon, N., Magapu, S., Subramony, M., & O'Neill, J. (2017). How Do You Want Your Chatbot? An Exploratory Wizard-of-Oz Study with Young, Urban Indians. In Human-Computer Interaction - INTERACT 2017. INTERACT 2017. Lecture Notes in Computer Science, vol 10513. Springer.

Meidan, Y., Bohadana, M., Shabtai, A., Guarnizo, J. D., Ochoa, M., Tippenhauer, N. O., & Elovici, Y. (2017, April). ProfilIoT: a machine learning approach for IoT device identification based on network traffic analysis. In *Proceedings of the symposium on applied computing* (pp. 506-509). 10.1145/3019612.3019878

Miljković, D. (2017, May). Brief review of self-organizing maps. In *2017 40th International Convention on Information and Communication Technology, Electronics and Microelectronics (MIPRO)* (pp. 1061-1066). IEEE. 10.23919/MIPRO.2017.7973581

Mohammeda, Z. K. A., & Ahmedb, E. S. A. (2017). Internet of Things Applications, Challenges and Related Future Technologies. *World Scientific News, 67*(2), 126-148.

Monitor, D. T. (2017). *Agriculture : Focus on IoT aspects Agriculture : Focus on IoT aspects*. Academic Press.

Monte Carlo simulation. (n.d.). *RxJS, ggplot2, Python Data Persistence, Caffe2, PyBrain, Python Data Access, H2O, Colab, Theano, Flutter, KNime, Mean.js, Weka, Solidity*. https://www.tutorialspoint.com/modelling_and_simulation/modelling_and_simulation_monte_carlo_simulation.htm

Morris, D. (2014). Bitcoin is Not Just Digital Currency. It's Napster for Finance. *Fortune, 21*.

Morris, D. Z. (2016). Leaderless, blockchain-based venture capital fund raises $100 million, and counting. *Fortune*, 5-23.

Myers, D. S., Bazinet, A. L., & Cummings, M. P. (2008). Expanding the reach of Grid computing: combining Globus-and BOINC-based systems. *Grids for Bioinformatics and Computational Biology*, 71-85.

Nadir, R. M. (2019). Comparative study of permissioned blockchain solutions for enterprises. *2019 International Conference on Innovative Computing (ICIC)*, 1-6. 10.1109/ICIC48496.2019.8966735

Nagpal, D. P. (2014). Data Communications and Networking. S. Chand & Company Pvt. Ltd.

Nakamoto, S. (n.d.). *Bitcoin: A peer-to-peer electronic cash system*. https://bitcoin.org/bitcoin.pdf

Nakamoto, S. (2019). *Bitcoin: A peer-to-peer electronic cash system*. Manubot.

Nandyala, C. S., & Kim, H. K. (2016). Green IoT Agriculture and Healthcare Application (GAHA). *International Journal of Smart Home, 10*(4), 289–300. doi:10.14257/ijsh.2016.10.4.26

Nasr, M., Shokri, R., & Houmansadr, A. (2018). *Comprehensive privacy analysis of deep learning: Stand-alone and federated learning under passive and active white-box inference attacks*. arXiv preprint arXiv:1812.00910

Natoli, C., & Gramoli, V. (2016, October). The blockchain anomaly. In *2016 IEEE 15th International Symposium on Network Computing and Applications (NCA)* (pp. 310-317). IEEE. 10.1109/NCA.2016.7778635

Navulur, S., Sastry, A. S. C. S., & Prasad, M. N. G. (2017). *Agricultural Management through Wireless Sensors and Internet of Things*. doi:10.11591/ijece.v7i6.pp3492-3499

Ng, I., & Wakenshaw, S. Y. L. (2017). The Internet-of-Things: Review and Research Directions. *International Journal of Research in Marketing, 34*(1), 3–21. doi:10.1016/j.ijresmar.2016.11.003

Palisade. (n.d.). *What is Monte Carlo Simulation? Monte Carlo simulation: What is It and How does It work?-Palisade*. https://www.palisade.com/risk/monte_carlo_simulation.asp

Panarello, A., Tapas, N., Merlino, G., Longo, F., & Puliafito, A. (2018). Blockchain and iot integration: A systematic survey. *Sensors (Basel), 18*(8), 2575. doi:10.339018082575 PMID:30082633

Parr, T., & Howard, J. (2018). *The matrix calculus you need for deep learning*. arXiv preprint arXiv:1802.01528

Pavón-Pulido, N., López-Riquelme, J. A., Torres, R., Morais, R., & Pastor, J. A. (2017). New trends in precision agriculture: A novel cloud-based system for enabling data storage and agricultural task planning and automation. *Precision Agriculture, 18*(6), 1038–1068. doi:10.100711119-017-9532-7

Pearl, L., & Steyvers, M. (2012). Detecting authorship deception: A supervised machine learning approach using author writeprints. *Literary and Linguistic Computing, 27*(2), 183–196. doi:10.1093/llc/fqs003

Pedregosa, F., Varoquaux, G., Gramfort, A., Michel, V., Thirion, B., Grisel, O., ... Vanderplas, J. (2011). Scikit-learn: Machine learning in Python. *The Journal of Machine Learning Research, 12*, 2825-2830.

Pereira, T., & Santos, H. (2014). Challenges in Information Security Protection. In *Conference: 13th European Conference on Cyber Warfare and Security (ECCWS-2014)*. The University of Piraeus.

Pereira, J., & Díaz, Ó. (2018a). A quality analysis of Facebook Messenger's most popular chatbots. In *Proceedings of the 33rd SAC Symposium*, (pp. 2144–2150). ACM 10.1145/3167132.3167362

Pereira, J., & Díaz, Ó. (2018b). Chatbot dimensions that matter: lessons from the trenches. In T. Mikkonen, R. Klamma, & J. Hernández (Eds.), *ICWE 2018. LNCS* (Vol. 10845, pp. 129–135). Springer. doi:10.1007/978-3-319-91662-0_9

Popenici, S. A. D., & Kerr, S. (2017). Exploring the impact of artificial intelligence on teaching and learning in higher education. *Research and Practice in Technology Enhanced Learning, 12*(1), 22. doi:10.118641039-017-0062-8 PMID:30595727

Pourmajidi, W., & Miranskyy, A. V. (n.d.). *Logchain: Blockchain-assisted log storage.* Available: https://arxiv.org/abs/1805.08868

Prakash, R. M., & Kumari, R. S. S. (2018). *Modified Expectation Maximization Method for Automatic Segmentation of MR Brain Images.* Conference: MRBRAINS13, Japan.

Prasatha, V. S., Alfeilate, H. A. A., Hassanate, A. B., Lasassmehe, O., Tarawnehf, A. S., Alhasanatg, M. B., & Salmane, H. S. E. (2017). *Effects of Distance Measure Choice on KNN Classifier Performance-A Review.* arXiv preprint arXiv:1708.04321

Premsankar, G., Di Francesco, M., & Taleb, T. (2018). Edge Computing for the Internet of Things: A Case Study. *IEEE Internet of Things Journal, 5*(2), 1275–1284. doi:10.1109/JIOT.2018.2805263

Priambodo, B., Rahayu, S., Naf'an, E., Handriani, I., Putra, Z. P., Nseaf, A. K., ... Jumaryadi, Y. (2019, December). Predicting GDP of Indonesia Using K-Nearest Neighbour Regression. *Journal of Physics: Conference Series, 1339*(1), 012040. doi:10.1088/1742-6596/1339/1/012040

Private vs Public Blockchain in a nutshell. (n.d.). https://medium.com/coinmonks/public-vs-private-blockchain-in-a-nutshell-c9fe284fa39f#:~:text=Public%20blockchains%20are%20 decentralised%2C%20no,Blockchain%20is%20a%20permissioned%20blockchain

Production, F. (2019). *Blockchain in Agriculture – Improving Agricultural Techniques.* Academic Press.

Przegalinska, A., Ciechanowski, L., Stroz, A., Gloor, P., & Mazurek, G. (2019, November–December). In bot we trust: A new methodology of chatbot performance measures. *Business Horizons, 62*(6), 785–797. doi:10.1016/j.bushor.2019.08.005

Radziwill, N. M., & Benton, M. C. (2017). *Evaluating quality of chatbots and intelligent conversational agents.* arXiv preprint arXiv:1704.04579

Reshi, Y. S., & Khan, R. A. (2014). Creating business intelligence through machine learning: An Effective business decision making tool. In Information and Knowledge Management (Vol. 4, No. 1, pp. 65-75). Academic Press.

Reuven, Rubinstein, & Kroese. (2016). Simulation and the Monte Carlo Method. Doi:10.1002/9781118631980

Risk management: 7 steps of risk management process. (2019, October 3). *iEduNote.com.* https://www.iedunote.com/risk-management

RMstudy-Risk Management Certification Courses. (n.d.). http://www.rmstudy.com/rmdocs / Identify%20Risks.pdf

Roman, Najera, & Lopez. (2011). Securing the Internet of Things. *IEEE Computer, 44*, 51-58.

Ross, S. (2010). *A first course in Probability Theory.* Pearson Publication.

Rothblatt, M. (2014). *Virtually Human: The Promise---and the Peril---of Digital Immortality.* Macmillan.

Rouse, M. (2020). *What is Risk analysis.* https://searchsecurity.techtarget.com/ definition/risk-analysis

Rusland, N. F., Wahid, N., Kasim, S., & Hafit, H. (2017, August). Analysis of Naïve Bayes algorithm for email spam filtering across multiple datasets. *IOP Conference Series. Materials Science and Engineering, 226*(1), 012091. doi:10.1088/1757-899X/226/1/012091

Rustam, Z., & Kintandani, P. (2019). Application of Support Vector Regression in Indonesian Stock Price Prediction with Feature Selection Using Particle Swarm Optimisation. *Modelling and Simulation in Engineering, 2019,* 2019. doi:10.1155/2019/8962717

Saadatfar, H., Khosravi, S., Joloudari, J. H., Mosavi, A., & Shamshirband, S. (2020). A New K-Nearest Neighbors Classifier for Big Data Based on Efficient Data Pruning. *Mathematics, 8*(2), 286. doi:10.3390/math8020286

Salah, K., Alfalasi, A., & Alfalasi, M. (2019, April). A Blockchain-based System for Online Consumer Reviews. In *IEEE INFOCOM 2019-IEEE Conference on Computer Communications Workshops (INFOCOM WKSHPS)* (pp. 853-858). IEEE. 10.1109/INFCOMW.2019.8845186

Sensitivity analysis. (2003, November 26). *Investopedia.* https://www.investopedia.com/terms/s/sensitivityanalysis.asp

Sfar, A. R., Chtourou, Z., & Challal, Y. (2017). A systemic and cognitive vision for IoT security: A case study of military live simulation and security challenges. *2017 International Conference on Smart, Monitored and Controlled Cities, SM2C 2017,* 101–105. 10.1109/SM2C.2017.8071828

Shah, V. (2019). *9 Main Security Challenges for the Future of the Internet Of Things (IoT).* https://readwrite.com/2019/09/05/9-main-security-challenges-for-the-future-of-the-internet-of-things-iot/

Shah, V. (2019). *AgriChain: Supply-Chain Management for Agri Foods using Block-chain Technology* (Master Thesis). DA-IICT, Gandhinagar.

Shahid, N., Rappon, T., & Berta, W. (2019). Applications of artificial neural networks in health care organizational decision-making: A scoping review. *PLoS One, 14*(2), e0212356. doi:10.1371/journal.pone.0212356 PMID:30779785

Shi, X., An, X., Zhao, Q., Liu, H., Xia, L., Sun, X., & Guo, Y. (2019). State-of-the-art internet of things in protected agriculture. *Sensors (Switzerland), 19*(8), 1833. Advance online publication. doi:10.339019081833 PMID:30999637

Sidey-Gibbons, J. A., & Sidey-Gibbons, C. J. (2019). Machine learning in medicine: A practical introduction. *BMC Medical Research Methodology, 19*(1), 64. doi:10.118612874-019-0681-4 PMID:30890124

Singh, D., Singh, N., & Sharma, D. (n.d.). *NCERT Solutions books Model Test Papers Question Pdf.* https://ncerthelp.com/

Singh, L. K., & Garg, H. P. (2020b). Automated Glaucoma Type Identification Using Machine Learning or Deep Learning Techniques. In Advancement of Machine Intelligence in Interactive Medical Image Analysis (pp. 241-263). Springer.

Singh, P., & Singh, N. (2020). Blockchain with IoT & AI: A Review of Agriculture and Healthcare. International Journal of Applied Evolutionary Computation, 11(4).

Singh, L. K., Khanna, M., & Garg, H. (2020c). Multimodal Biometric Based on Fusion of Ridge Features with Minutiae Features and Face Features. *International Journal of Information System Modeling and Design, 11*(1), 37–57. doi:10.4018/IJISMD.2020010103

Singh, L. K., Pooja, & Garg, H. (2020a). Detection of Glaucoma in Retinal Images Based on Multiobjective Approach. *International Journal of Applied Evolutionary Computation, 11*(2), 15–27. doi:10.4018/IJAEC.2020040102

Singh, N., Singh, P., Singh, K. K., & Singh, A. (2020a). (in press). Diagnosing of Disease using Machine Learning, accepted for Machine Learning & Internet of medical things in healthcare. *Elsevier Publications.*

Singh, P., & Agrawal, R. (2018). A customer centric best connected channel model for heterogeneous and IoT networks. *Journal of Organizational and End User Computing, 30*(4), 32–50. doi:10.4018/JOEUC.2018100103

Singh, P., & Agrawal, R. (2018). Prospects of Open Source Software for Maximizing the User Expectations in Heterogeneous Network. *International Journal of Open Source Software and Processes, 9*(3), 1–14. doi:10.4018/IJOSSP.2018070101

Singh, P., & Agrawal, V. (2019). A Collaborative Model for Customer Retention on User Service Experience. In *Advances in Computer Communication and Computational Sciences* (pp. 55–64). Springer. doi:10.1007/978-981-13-6861-5_5

Singh, P., & Singh, N. (2020). (in press). Role of Data Mining Techniques in Bioinformatics. *International Journal of Applied Research in Bioinformatics, 11*(6).

Sisinni, E., Saifullah, A., Han, S., Jennehag, U., & Gidlund, M. (2018). Industrial internet of things: Challenges, opportunities, and directions. *IEEE Transactions on Industrial Informatics, 14*(11), 4724–4734. doi:10.1109/TII.2018.2852491

Smola, A., & Vishwanathan, S. V. N. (2008). Introduction to machine learning. Cambridge University.

Soucy, P. (2016, July 7). Self-Learning Intelligent Search, Explained. *KM World*, p. S34.

Srivastava, A., Bhattacharya, P., Singh, A., & Mathur, A. (2018). *A Systematic Review on Evolution of Blockchain Generations.* Academic Press.

Stallings, W. (2013). *Cryptography and Network Security: Principles and Practice* (6th ed.). Prentice Hall Press.

Stephens, M. (2007). Mortgage market deregulation and its consequences. *Housing Studies*, 22(2), 201–220. doi:10.1080/02673030601132797

Stokes, P. (2018). IoT applications in agriculture: the potential of smart farming on the current stage. *Data Driven Investor*, 1–8. https://medium.com/datadriveninvestor/iot-applications-in-agriculture-the-potential-of-smart-farming-on-the-current-stage-275066f946d8

Strobel, V., Castelló Ferrer, E., & Dorigo, M. (2018, July). Managing byzantine robots via blockchain technology in a swarm robotics collective decision making scenario. In *Proceedings of the 17th International Conference on Autonomous Agents and MultiAgent Systems* (pp. 541-549). International Foundation for Autonomous Agents and Multiagent Systems.

Stuart, S. (2017). How Do You Feel? Affectiva's AI Can Tell. *PC Magazine.* Available at https://www.pcmag.com/news/349956/how-do-you-feel-affectivas-ai-can-tell

Study, C. (n.d.). *Spirent IoT.* https://www.spirent.com/blogs/wireless/2016/june/cutting-costs-with-iot-connected-avocados

Sun, S., Cao, Z., Zhu, H., & Zhao, J. (2019). A Survey of Optimization Methods from a Machine Learning Perspective. *IEEE Transactions on Cybernetics.* Advance online publication. doi:10.1109/TCYB.2019.2950779 PMID:31751262

Surasak, T., Wattanavichean, N., Preuksakarn, C., & Huang, S. C. H. Thai Agriculture Products Traceability System using Blockchain and Internet of Things. *System, 14*, 15.

Sutton, R. (1998). *S. and Barto, Andrew G. Reinforcement Learning: An Introduction.* MIT.

Sutton, R. S., & Barto, A. G. (1998). *Introduction to reinforcement learning* (Vol. 135). MIT Press.

Swan, M. (2014). *Blockchain AI: Consensus as the mechanism to foster 'friendly' AI.* Institute for Ethics and Emerging Technologies.

Swan, M. (2015). Blockchain thinking: The brain as a decentralized autonomous corporation [commentary]. *IEEE Technology and Society Magazine, 34*(4), 41–52. doi:10.1109/MTS.2015.2494358

Swan, M. (2015). *Blockchain: Blueprint for a new economy.* O'Reilly Media, Inc.

Talavera, J. M., Tobón, L. E., Gómez, J. A., Culman, M. A., Aranda, J. M., Parra, D. T., Quiroz, L. A., Hoyos, A., & Garreta, L. E. (2017). Review of IoT applications in agro-industrial and environmental fields. *Computers and Electronics in Agriculture, 142*(September), 283–297. doi:10.1016/j.compag.2017.09.015

Tang, Q. & Wei, M. (2019). Exploring AI for the teaching of Chinese as a foreign language. *Journal of Wuhan Yejin Guanli Ganbu College, 2019*(1).

Tasatanattakool, P., & Techapanupreeda, C. (2018, January). Blockchain: Challenges and applications. In *2018 International Conference on Information Networking (ICOIN)* (pp. 473-475). IEEE. 10.1109/ICOIN.2018.8343163

Team, N. A. (2018). *NEBULA AI (NBAI)—Decentralized Ai Blockchain Whitepaper*. Academic Press.

Technology illuminates the future - when blockchain technology and adaptive security technology enter social management and economic life. (n.d.). Retrieved October 02, 2019, from http://blog.sina.com.cn/s/blog_67804b9a0102z2gn.html

The fusion of artificial intelligence and blockchain technology represents the future of the digital economy. (n.d.). Retrieved May 14, 2019, from http://www.sohu.com/a/313838766_99985608?qq-pf-to=pcqq.c2c

The Wall Street Journal. (2017). *How Artificial Intelligence Will Change Everything*. Available at https://www.wsj.com/articles/howartificialintelligencewillchangeeverything148885632

Torrado, R. R., Bontrager, P., Togelius, J., Liu, J., & Perez-Liebana, D. (2018, August). Deep reinforcement learning for general video game ai. In *2018 IEEE Conference on Computational Intelligence and Games (CIG)* (pp. 1-8). IEEE. 10.1109/CIG.2018.8490422

Truex, S., Baracaldo, N., Anwar, A., Steinke, T., Ludwig, H., Zhang, R., & Zhou, Y. (2019, November). A hybrid approach to privacy-preserving federated learning. In *Proceedings of the 12th ACM Workshop on Artificial Intelligence and Security* (pp. 1-11). 10.1145/3338501.3357370

U.S. National Science and Technology Council. (2016). *National Artificial Intelligence Research and development strategic plan*. Networking and Information Technology Research and Development Subcommittee.

Un. (2009). Food Production Must Double By 2050 To Meet Demand From World'S Growing Population, Innovative Strategies Needed To Combat Hunger, Experts Tell Second Committee. *Second Committee, Panel Discussion (AM) GA/EF/3242, 64,* 2–5. https://www.un.org/News/Press/docs/2009/gaef3242.doc.htm

Usama, M., Qadir, J., Raza, A., Arif, H., Yau, K. L. A., Elkhatib, Y., Hussain, A., & Al-Fuqaha, A. (2019). Unsupervised machine learning for networking: Techniques, applications and research challenges. *IEEE Access: Practical Innovations, Open Solutions, 7,* 65579–65615. doi:10.1109/ACCESS.2019.2916648

Vaidya, S., Ambad, P., & Bhosle, S. (2018). Industry 4.0–a glimpse. *Procedia Manufacturing, 20,* 233–238. doi:10.1016/j.promfg.2018.02.034

Vepakomma, P., Gupta, O., Swedish, T., & Raskar, R. (2018). *Split learning for health: Distributed deep learning without sharing raw patient data.* arXiv preprint arXiv:1812.00564

Vitelli, M., & Nayebi, A. (2016). Carma: A deep reinforcement learning approach to autonomous driving. Tech. rep. Stanford University.

Wang, Y.B. (2018). The position of foreign language instructors in AI era. *Journal of Jilin Broadcasting Television University, 2018*(11).

Weber, R. H. (2015). Internet of things: Privacy issues revisited. Computer Law & Security Review, 31(5).

Wehbe, Y., Al Zaabi, M., & Svetinovic, D. (2018, November). Blockchain ai framework for healthcare records management: Constrained goal model. In *2018 26th Telecommunications Forum (TELFOR)* (pp. 420-425). IEEE.

Wenbin, U. (2015). Principles, models and proposals of banking trading blockchain. *Hebei University Journal, 6,* 159–160.

Weng, J., Weng, J., Zhang, J., Li, M., Zhang, Y., & Luo, W. (2019). Deepchain: Auditable and privacy-preserving deep learning with blockchain-based incentive. *IEEE Transactions on Dependable and Secure Computing,* 1. doi:10.1109/TDSC.2019.2952332

What are the 5 risk management process steps? (2018, June 26). *Continuing Professional Development.* https://continuingprofessionaldevelopment.org/risk-management-steps-in-risk-management-process/

What is the Internet of things? I IoT technology. (n.d.). *SAP.* https://www.sap.com/india/trends/internet-of-things.html

Wintrode, J., Bui, N., Stepinski, J., & Reed, C. (2017, June). Online Expectation Maximization for Language Characterization of Streaming Text. In *International Conference on Web Engineering* (pp. 200-208). Springer.

Wood, G. (2014). Ethereum: A secure decentralised generalised transaction ledger. *Ethereum project yellow paper, 151*(2014), 1-32.

Xu, A., Liu, Z., Guo, Y., Sinha, V., & Akkiraju, R. (2017). A new chatbot for customer service on social media. In *Proceedings of the 35th CHI Conference,* (pp. 3506–3510). ACM. 10.1145/3025453.3025496

Xu, Y. P. (2018). Analyzing the use of AI for translation. *Journal of Cooperative Economy and Technology, 2018*(19).

Xu, Y., Yao, H., & Lin, K. (2018). An overview of neural networks for drug discovery and the inputs used. *Expert Opinion on Drug Discovery, 13*(12), 1091–1102. doi:10.1080/17460441.2 018.1547278 PMID:30449189

Yan-E, D. (2011). Design of intelligent agriculture management information system based on IoT. *Proceedings - 4th International Conference on Intelligent Computation Technology and Automation, ICICTA 2011, 1*, 1045–1049. 10.1109/ICICTA.2011.262

Yang, Q., Liu, Y., Chen, T., & Tong, Y. (2019). Federated machine learning: Concept and applications. *ACM Transactions on Intelligent Systems and Technology, 10*(2), 1–19. doi:10.1145/3298981

Yang, X., Chen, Y., & Chen, X. (2019). Effective Scheme against 51% Attack on Proof-of-Work Blockchain with History Weighted Information. *2019 IEEE International Conference on Blockchain (Blockchain)*, 261-265. 10.1109/Blockchain.2019.00041

Yang, Y. (2018). Foreign language teachers in the AI era. *Journal of Zhiku Shidai, 2018*(27).

Yang, Z.L. (2017). Contemplation on AI translation. *Journal of Campus English, 2017*(52).

Yin, B., Balvert, M., van der Spek, R. A., Dutilh, B. E., Bohte, S., Veldink, J., & Schönhuth, A. (2019). Using the structure of genome data in the design of deep neural networks for predicting amyotrophic lateral sclerosis from genotype. *Bioinformatics (Oxford, England), 35*(14), i538–i547. doi:10.1093/bioinformatics/btz369 PMID:31510706

Yoon, H. J. (2019). Blockchain technology and healthcare. *Healthcare Informatics Research, 25*(2), 59. doi:10.4258/hir.2019.25.2.59 PMID:31131139

Yu, H. & Xie, H. J. (2018). The analysis and design research of intelligent teaching system for foreign Chinese vocabulary. *Sinogram Culture, 3*.

Zhai, Y.Y. (2019). Influence and suggestion for AI translation occupation. *Journal of Modern Business Industry, 2019*(09).

Zhang, G., Li, T., Li, Y., Hui, P., & Jin, D. (2018). Blockchain-based data sharing system for ai-powered network operations. *Journal of Communications and Information Networks, 3*(3), 1–8. doi:10.100741650-018-0024-3

Zhang, Y., Chen, Q., Liu, G., Shen, W., & Wang, G. (2016). Environment Parameters Control Based on Wireless Sensor Network in Livestock Buildings. *International Journal of Distributed Sensor Networks, 2016*(5), 9079748. Advance online publication. doi:10.1155/2016/9079748

Zhao, S. (2018). AI for writing instruction. *Journal of Educational Technology, 2018*(9).

Zhao, Z., & Liu, H. (2007, June). Spectral feature selection for supervised and unsupervised learning. In *Proceedings of the 24th international conference on Machine learning* (pp. 1151-1157). 10.1145/1273496.1273641

Compilation of References

Zheng, Z., Xie, S., Dai, H. N., Chen, X., & Wang, H. (2018). Blockchain challenges and opportunities: A survey. *International Journal of Web and Grid Services*, *14*(4), 352–375. doi:10.1504/IJWGS.2018.095647

Zhu, X. (2007, June). Semi-supervised learning tutorial. In *International Conference on Machine Learning (ICML)* (pp. 1-135). Academic Press.

Zhu, X., Li, H., & Yu, Y. (2018, December). Blockchain-based privacy preserving deep learning. In *International Conference on Information Security and Cryptology* (pp. 370-383). Springer.

About the Contributors

Ganesh Chandra Deka is Deputy Director, DGT, Ministry of Skill Development and Entrepreneurship, Govt of India. His Research interests include Bigdata Analytics,NoSQL Databases and Blockchain Technology. As on date he has Edited 19 books on his area of interest. He has published 4 Journal Special Issue (International Journal of Applied Evolutionary Computation (IJAEC), IGI Global. USA (Volume 8, Issue 1 Special Issue on: Emerging Research Trend in Computing and Communication Technologies), Journal of Organizational and End User Computing (JOEUC), Volume 29, Issue 4(Special Issue: Bigdata Analytics in Business, Healthcare, and Governance), Volume 30, Issue 4,(Special Issue on Internet of Things: Issues, Challenges and Opportunities).

* * *

Jyotshana Bagwari received the Bachelor of Technology degree (with Honors) and Master of Technology degree in Computer Science & Engineering from Uttarakhand Technical University, Dehradun. She has published several research papers in various reputed international SCI/ISI indexed journals and conferences including IEEE international conferences as well.

Ankit Barai joined Reliance Jio, Centre of excellence in AI/ML in 2020 as an Intern. He is pursuing Bachelor of Technology in Computer Science engineering from Indian Institute of Information Technology, Nagpur, India. He is active contributor in research community and published his works in conferences like High Performance computing, Soft Computing: Theories and Applications and various journals like Eurasian Journal of Medicine and Oncology. His research interests include AI/ML, Deep learning, Blockchain and Internet of Things. He is also ACM student member and holds past research attachments with Indian Institute of Science, Bangalore and Indian Institute of Technology Kharagpur.

Robin Bhadoria has obtained his Ph.D. degree in the month of January 2018 from Discipline of Computer Science & Engineering at Indian Institute of Technology (IIT) Indore, Madhya Pradesh, India. He also finished his Master of Technology (M.Tech) and Bachelor of Engineering (B. Eng.) in CSE from Rajiv Gandhi Technological University (RGTU) of Madhya Pradesh, India in 2011 and 2008 respectively. He received Gold Medal at M.Tech. His current area of Interests are Big Data Analytics, Service-Oriented Architecture, Internet of Things and Wireless Sensor Network. He has published more than 50 articles in IEEE, Elsevier, and Springer that also includes the book chapters. Presently, a professional member for - IEEE (USA), IAENG (Hong-Kong), Internet Society, Virginia (USA), IACSIT (Singapore).

Manish Dixit is working as Professor in Dept. of Computer Science & Engineering at MITS, Gwalior, India. He has rich experience of more than 24 years into academic as well as research in the field of Image processing, Data Mining, Wireless Sensor Network, Web Technologies and many more. He has published more than 80 articles at national and international level in conference & journals.

Amit Dua has been actively working in the field of security and blockchain technology. He has proposed various architectures and mechanisms for secure real-life solutions including smart grids, electronic-waste, transportation systems, health care, etc. As part of his institute project, he has developed controller and efficient data structures for power saving through Software Defined Networking. He has worked on the project to enhance the mobility and data dissemination in Vehicular ad hoc networks. His works have been published in various IEEE Transactions and other high impact journals. Amit Dua is actively serving as a reviewer of various IEEE Transactions, Elsevier, and Springer journals. He has been awarded International travel grants from SERB and DST. He is the recipient of an excellent presentation award at IEEE ICCC at Chengdu, China in Dec. 2017.

Hitendra Garg did his Ph.D. (CSE) from Motilal Nehru National Institute of Technology, Allahabad and Masters (Software Systems) from BITS-Pilani. He is presently working as an Associate Professor in the Department of Computer Engineering & Application, GLA University, Mathura-Indi. He has a total experience of more than 18 years in the field of academics/research. He has more than 30 research papers in the international journals/conference of repute. His research areas are Image Processing, Cryptography, 3D data processing, etc.

Somasena Reddy K is currently working as an Assistant Professor (Ad Hoc) at Department of CSE, JNTUACEA, Ananthapuramu. He obtained his M. Tech. degree in Computer Science from JNTUCEA, JNTUA, Ananthapuram. He has more than

10 years of teaching experience which includes sound administrative experience. He attended several FDPs and workshops. He guided many UG and PG projects. His research interests include, Blockchain, Internet of Things, Software Defined Networks, Artificial Intelligence, and Machine Learning. He recently authored a book chapter on "Internet of Things (IoT) in Agriculture" for the "Handbook of Research on Blockchain Technology in AI and IoT Applications" for IGI Global Publications.

Munish Khanna is presently an Associate Professor and Head of the Department of Computer Science & Engineering, Hindustan College of Science & Technology, Mathura, India. He has a teaching experience of more than 17 years and he has successfully completed his Ph.D. from YMCA University of Science & Technology, Faridabad, India. He has published many papers in SCI, ESCI and Scopus indexed journals. He is a member of professional technical societies like CSI and IEEE. His research interest includes Algorithms, Software Testing, Automata Theory, Artificial Intelligence, Applications of soft computing techniques in Computer Science.

Muralidhar Kurni is an Independent Consultant for Pedagogy Refinement, EduRefine, India. He is currently a Research Scholar at JNTUA, Ananthapuramu, India. Previously he worked as Assistant Professor in Department of Computer Science & Engineering at Anantha Lakshmi Institute of Technology & Sciences, Anantapuramu, Andhra Pradesh, India, Head, Department of Computer Applications, Sri Sai College of Technology & Management, Kadapa, Andhra Pradesh, India. Mr. Muralidhar Kurni has received his M.Sc. in Computer Science from S. K. University and M.Tech. in Computer Science & Engineering from JNTUA, Ananthapuram, Andhra Pradesh, India. He has more than 19 years of teaching experience. He is an IUCEE & IGIP certified International Engineering Educator & researcher. He has several scholarly publications to his credit. He presented about 30 papers at various national and international conferences and journals. Four of his papers received the best paper awards. Two of them are the IEEE Conference Best Paper awards. He has been a reviewer for various International Conferences & Journals including SCIE & Scopus indexed Journals. He served as a Guest Editor for the Special Issue on "Security, Privacy, and Trust in IoT" of IJWNBT Journal, IGI Global, Volume 8, Issue 2, July-December 2019, ISSN: 2155-6261, eISSN: 2155-627X, doi:10.4018/IJWNBT.20190701. His research interests include Blockchain, Digital Pedagogy, Design Thinking, Pedagogy refinement & Engineering Education Research. Recently he signed a contract with Springer for publishing an authored book entitled "A Beginner's Guide to Learning Analytics."

Vardan Mkrttchian graduated from State Engineering University of Armenia, the Faculty of Cybernetics as an Electronics Engineer & received his Doctorate of Sciences (Engineering) in Control Systems from Lomonosov Moscow State University (former USSR). Dr. Vardan Mkrttchian taught for undergraduate and graduate student's courses of control system, information sciences and technology, at the Astrakhan State University (Russian Federation), where he was is the Professor of the Information Systems (www.aspu.ru) six years. Now he is full professor CAD & Economy departments of Penza State University (www.pnzgu.ru). He is currently chief executive of HHH University, Australia and team leader of the international academics (www.hhhuniversity.com). He also serves as executive director of the HHH Technology Incorporation. Professor Vardan Mkrttchian has authored over 400 refereed publications. He is the author of over twenty books published of IGI Global, included ten books indexed of SCOPUS in IT, Control System, Digital Economy, and Education Technology, and 41 works in SCOPUS and 17 in WoS. He also is Editor-in-Chief of International Journal of Applied Research in Bioinformatics (IJARB).

Ivan Perl is a PhD in Computer Science. For more than ten years has been working in software development industry in Motorola and later in Oracle. Recent four years of engineering career were dedicated to design and development of high-scale enterprise solutions related to the Internet of Things (IoT). Graduated Saint-Petersburg University of Fine Mechanics and Optics, now known as ITMO University (2009 Master degree, 2012 - PhD). Focusing on research in applied mathematics and mathematic modelling. Key research projects topics are high-efficient remote Earth sensing (RES) and efficient cloud-based system dynamics modelling (sdCloud project).

Pooja is Ph.D in computer Science & Engineering from National Institute of Technology, India. She got her first patent published in 2019. She has 80+ research publications in Scopus / SCI / International Journals and conferences. She got the "Best Teacher" award from ISTE, (Pb., Chd., HP, J&K Section) in 2014. She is an experienced professional with hands-on skills on Deep Learning, Machine Learning, Image Processing, Pattern Recognition, Natural Language Processing, Genetic Algorithms and Data Mining. She has been imparting learning for 15 years to undergraduate and post-graduate students.

Viral Shah completed master's degree from DAIICT in 2019. Currently working as a Software developer in Tekion India, Banglore. Overall with 2.5 years of experience, while pursuing M.Tech in DAIICT was working in the blockchain technology for the agricultural supply chain solution.

Narendra Singh is an Assistant Professor in the area of IT and Marketing at G. L. Bajaj Institute of Management and Research, Greater Noida. He has fifteen years of teaching and research experience. He is pursuing Ph.D (Management) from Dr. A.P.J. Abdul Kalam Technical University, U.P., Lucknow. and Master in Business Administration (MBA) from Uttar Pradesh Technical University, Lucknow. His research areas include Consumer Behavior, Customer Relationship Management, Electronic Commerce, Management Information System and IoT. Mr. Singh has 14 publications of repute in his credit. His research work has appeared in various refereed international journals with publication houses like, Emerald and Inderscience. His research work has been published in International journals. He has also participated in various National Conferences, Workshops, and Faculty Development Programme held at various places like IITR and IITK, etc.

Pushpa Singh is working as Associate Professor in Computer Science & Engineering in Delhi Technical campus, Gr. Noida, India. She is having more than 16+ years exposure to teaching B.Tech and MCA students. Dr. Singh has acquired MCA, M.Tech (CSE), and Ph. D (CSE) from AKTU Lucknow in the area of Wireless Network. Her current areas of research include performance evaluation of heterogeneous networks, Machine Learning, and Cryptography. She has 29 papers in reputable international journals and conferences. She has published 4 books and contributed in book chapter. She is also a member of Computer Society of India (CSI).

Law Singh is doing Ph.D. computer science and engineering from Sharda University,Greater Noida and working as assistant professor Hindustan college of Science and Technology(Mathura).

Radha Madhu Seekar Vedula is currently pursuing his Master's in Information Security from Atal Bihari Vajpayee-Indian Institute of Information Technology and Management (ABV-IIITM), Gwalior. He is mainly interested in the fields of mathematics and computer security. He is aspiring to be a good author in the mentioned fields and hoping to contribute to the fields for further improvements when and where possible.

J. K. Verma is Assistant Professor at School of Computing Science & Engineering, Galgotias University. He received the degree of Ph.D. from Jawaharlal Nehru University (JNU), New Delhi, India in 2017, degree of M.Tech from JNU in 2013 and degree of B.Tech in Computer Science & Engineering from Kamla Nehru Institute of Technology (KNIT), Sultanpur, Uttar Pradesh, India in 2008. He carried out his research work of M.Tech and Ph.D. under the supervision of Prof. C. P. Katti (Retired). Over his short career, he has published several papers in peer-reviewed

International Journals and attended various national and international seminars and workshops. He is awardee of prestigious DAAD "A new Passage to India" Fellowship (2015-16) funded by Federal Ministry of Education and Research - BMBF, Germany, providing international research collaboration and research stay via academic exchange with JULIUS-MAXIMILIAN UNIVERSITY OF WÜRZBURG, GERMANY (mother of 14 Nobel Laureate) as a Visiting Research Scholar. His research interest includes cloud computing, Mobile cloud, Machine learning, Soft computing, Fuzzy systems.

Goh Ying Soon is a senior lecturer and he currently teaches Mandarin as the third language to non-native learners in MARA University of Technology, Malaysia. He is a member of the International Society for Chinese Language Teaching. He has experiences in teaching Mandarin at primary, secondary and tertiary level for more than 25 years. He has been actively presenting papers in national and international conferences. His research interests are on the use of educational technology in Mandarin teaching and learning, web-based instruction, translation, and etc. Updated resume: click here (dropbox). Google Scholar record. researchgate, academia.edu, cnki, scopus (Author ID: 25925392000), book publication, http://www.researcherid.com/rid/U-7238-2017, http://orcid.org/0000-0002-6654-2887, http://myrid.gov.my/2014-1221-3221.

Index

A

Adaptive Trade Systems 118
Agri-chain 46, 53, 68
Application 2, 6, 10, 13, 15, 18, 20, 22, 29, 39, 41, 68, 85, 88, 90, 92, 96, 99-100, 103-105, 107-108, 110, 112-113, 117, 122, 129, 131, 133-134, 137-138, 147, 149-153, 156, 160, 168, 174, 178, 180, 183-184, 188-190, 195-200, 202-204, 206, 209, 211, 214, 216-221, 223, 226-227
Artificial and Natural Intelligence Technologies 118-119
Artificial Intelligence 1-2, 4, 23-25, 71, 85, 87, 111, 121-125, 130-132, 138, 147, 153, 156, 176-177, 179, 205, 210-211, 220-226

B

Block chain Technology 118
Blockchain 1-25, 46-50, 52-53, 58, 60, 63-69, 71, 86, 88, 95, 104-106, 110-111, 113, 118-127, 129-135, 158-160, 167-180, 202-203, 207-208

C

Cryptocurrency 2-4, 9, 11-12, 20, 47, 49

D

Digital Economy 118-119, 123-124, 132, 135

E

EDI (Electronic Data Interchange) 135
Electronic Commerce 118-119, 136
Epochs 70, 81-83
Ethereum 4, 12-13, 20, 22, 25, 47, 68, 135

F

Federated Learning 158-162, 164-166, 171, 173-177

I

Implementation Multi chain 119
Intellectual Capital 136
Intelligent Agent (IA) 226
Intelligent Computer-Assisted Language Learning (ICALL), or Intelligent Computer-Assisted Language Instruction (ICALI) 226
Interactive 157, 209-210, 223, 227
Internet of Things 26-28, 31, 40, 42-45, 88-92, 110-113, 118, 121-124, 132, 162, 207, 210, 222-225
IoT 6, 8, 19, 24, 26-36, 38-45, 69, 88-92, 94-107, 109-117, 120-122, 124, 154-155, 157, 174, 202-204, 207, 210, 222, 224
IPFS 4, 17, 21

L

Linear Algebra 179, 182-183

Ensure Quality Research is Introduced to the Academic Community

Become an IGI Global Reviewer for Authored Book Projects

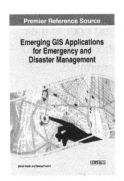
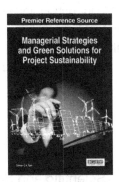
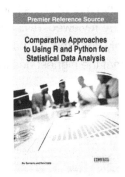

The overall success of an authored book project is dependent on quality and timely reviews.

In this competitive age of scholarly publishing, constructive and timely feedback significantly expedites the turnaround time of manuscripts from submission to acceptance, allowing the publication and discovery of forward-thinking research at a much more expeditious rate. Several IGI Global authored book projects are currently seeking highly-qualified experts in the field to fill vacancies on their respective editorial review boards:

Applications and Inquiries may be sent to:
development@igi-global.com

Applicants must have a doctorate (or an equivalent degree) as well as publishing and reviewing experience. Reviewers are asked to complete the open-ended evaluation questions with as much detail as possible in a timely, collegial, and constructive manner. All reviewers' tenures run for one-year terms on the editorial review boards and are expected to complete at least three reviews per term. Upon successful completion of this term, reviewers can be considered for an additional term.

If you have a colleague that may be interested in this opportunity, we encourage you to share this information with them.

IGI Global Proudly Partners With eContent Pro International

Receive a 25% Discount on all Editorial Services

Editorial Services

IGI Global expects all final manuscripts submitted for publication to be in their final form. This means they must be reviewed, revised, and professionally copy edited prior to their final submission. Not only does this support with accelerating the publication process, but it also ensures that the highest quality scholarly work can be disseminated.

English Language Copy Editing

Let eContent Pro International's expert copy editors perform edits on your manuscript to resolve spelling, punctuaion, grammar, syntax, flow, formatting issues and more.

Scientific and Scholarly Editing

Allow colleagues in your research area to examine the content of your manuscript and provide you with valuable feedback and suggestions before submission.

Figure, Table, Chart & Equation Conversions

Do you have poor quality figures? Do you need visual elements in your manuscript created or converted? A design expert can help!

Translation

Need your documjent translated into English? eContent Pro International's expert translators are fluent in English and more than 40 different languages.

Email: customerservice@econtentpro.com   www.igi-global.com/editorial-service-partners

IGI Global's Transformative Open Access (OA) Model:
How to Turn Your University Library's Database Acquisitions Into a Source of OA Funding

In response to the OA movement and well in advance of Plan S, IGI Global, early last year, unveiled their OA Fee Waiver (Read & Publish) Initiative.

Under this initiative, librarians who invest in IGI Global's InfoSci-Books (5,300+ reference books) and/or InfoSci-Journals (185+ scholarly journals) databases will be able to subsidize their patron's OA article processing charges (APC) when their work is submitted and accepted (after the peer review process) into an IGI Global journal. *See website for details.

How Does it Work?

1. When a library subscribes or perpetually purchases IGI Global's InfoSci-Databases and/or their discipline/subject-focused subsets, IGI Global will match the library's investment with a fund of equal value to go toward subsidizing the OA article processing charges (APCs) for their patrons.

   Researchers: Be sure to recommend the InfoSci-Books and InfoSci-Journals to take advantage of this initiative.

2. When a student, faculty, or staff member submits a paper and it is accepted (following the peer review) into one of IGI Global's 185+ scholarly journals, the author will have the option to have their paper published under a traditional publishing model or as OA.

3. When the author chooses to have their paper published under OA, IGI Global will notify them of the OA Fee Waiver (Read & Publish) Initiative. If the author decides they would like to take advantage of this initiative, IGI Global will deduct the US$ 2,000 APC from the created fund.

4. This fund will be offered on an annual basis and will renew as the subscription is renewed for each year thereafter. IGI Global will manage the fund and award the APC waivers unless the librarian has a preference as to how the funds should be managed.

Hear From the Experts on This Initiative:

"I'm very happy to have been able to make one of my recent research contributions, "Visualizing the Social Media Conversations of a National Information Technology Professional Association" featured in the *International Journal of Human Capital and Information Technology Professionals*, freely available along with having access to the valuable resources found within IGI Global's InfoSci-Journals database."

– **Prof. Stuart Palmer,**
Deakin University, Australia

Printed in the United States
By Bookmasters